KT-227-368

E-COMMERCE
A MANAGER'S GUIDE
TO APPLICATIONS AND IMPACT

REX PEREIRA

Chandos Publishing
Oxford · England

Chandos Publishing (Oxford) Limited
Chandos House
5 & 6 Steadys Lane
Stanton Harcourt
Oxford OX8 1RL
England
Tel: +44 (0) 1865 882727 Fax: +44 (0) 1865 884448
Email: sales@chandospublishing.com
www.chandospublishing.com

••

First published in Great Britain in 2001

ISBN 1 902375 75 0

© R. Pereira, 2001

All rights reserved. No part of this publication may be reproduced, stored in or introduced into a retrieval system, or transmitted, in any form, or by any means (electronic, mechanical, photocopying, recording or otherwise) without the prior written permission of the Publishers. This publication may not be lent, resold, hired out or otherwise disposed of by way of trade in any form of binding or cover other than that in which it is published without the prior consent of the Publishers. Any person who does any unauthorised act in relation to this publication may be liable to criminal prosecution and civil claims for damages.

The Publishers make no representation, express or implied, with regard to the accuracy of the information contained in this publication and cannot accept any legal responsibility or liability for any errors or omissions.

The material contained in this publication constitutes general guidelines only and does not represent to be advice on any particular matter. No reader or purchaser should act on the basis of material contained in this publication without first taking professional advice appropriate to their particular circumstances. Readers of this publication should be aware that only Acts of Parliament and Statutory Instruments have the force of law and that only courts can authoritatively interpret the law.

Printed by Biddles, Guildford, UK

Contents

Preface

E-commerce: A Manager's Guide to Applications and Impact, is written for managers who desire an overview of contemporary electronic commerce (EC) management. It explains the relevant issues of effective management of electronic commerce activities and highlights the areas of greatest potential application of the technology. No assumptions are made concerning the reader's experience with electronic commerce, but it is assumed that the reader has had some course work or work experience in business management.

The purpose of the book is to provide perspective on the management implications of the explosion of electronic commerce. Huge leaps in the growth of scientific knowledge have stimulated a dramatic increase in the number of new products and services based on the exploding presence of the Internet. These products and services have influenced the very heart of a corporation's strategy and operations, and they will continue to do so. In many cases, the firm's competitiveness and its very survival are at stake. The radical changes in electronic commerce are coupled with the increasingly global nature of business; this puts an enormous burden on individual managers to keep abreast of events and to make intelligent decisions and plans. The broad objective of this book is to help managers harness the power of the Internet to enable them to make better decisions and more effectively manage their firms, thereby enabling them to compete more effectively.

Electronic commerce continues to evolve dramatically. This book examines the subject by emphasizing issues related to the development of an electronic-commerce-enabled strategy that permits a firm to simultaneously achieve the scale, scope and efficiency that come from being large and the flexibility, speed and responsiveness of being small. This book highlights the special challenges related to electronic commerce within and between organizations and pays particular attention to the key enabling technologies required to implement the electronic commerce infrastructure for the 21st century. It will help present and future managers identify, implement and deliver effective electronic commerce services.

E-commerce: A Manager's Guide to Applications and Impact, is organized around a management audit of the electronic commerce activity. This management audit details the questions that should be asked in identifying whether a firm is appropriately using and managing the electronic commerce resource. The book's text, examples, tables and figures convey and illustrate key conceptual frameworks. Chapter 1 presents an overview of key questions to ask in assessing the effectiveness of an electronic commerce activity. Subsequent chapters show how electronic commerce can best be applied and how the electronic commerce activities can best be organized, planned and managed.

The material in this book is the outgrowth of directed, field-based research I have conducted since the early 1990s. I am indebted to the many firms and government organizations that provided me with so much time and insight during the course of my research. All of the examples and concepts in this book are based on observation of actual practice. Without the cooperation of these organizations, it would have been impossible to prepare this book.

Rex Eugene Pereira

Chapter 1

Foundations of Electronic Commerce

The growth of the Internet and the World Wide Web has been extraordinary. Although to-date it is disproportionately concentrated among English speakers in the United States, it is likely that with advances in communications technology and lower computer prices, Web use will be dispersed across developed and less-developed countries. The impact of the Web will be far reaching as people will be able to communicate at very low cost across geographic boundaries and many real-world activities will be performed virtually through the Web. Markets that were previously beyond geographic reach will be accessible electronically, and existing markets will be serviced with a greater degree of refinement.

The Web's share of commercial transactions is likely to increase in the next few years as the use of computers grows more widespread, and as consumers gain more confidence in the safety of Web transactions through security improvements and governmental regulation of electronic commerce. Companies need a strategy for marketing on the Web as an integral part of marketing strategy.

In the six years from 1994 to 2000, advertising spending on the World Wide Web grew from zero to almost $8 billion. Though still barely 3% of all U.S. advertising on print, television and radio, it seems fair to conclude that a new advertising medium has been born. But the Web is more than an advertising medium. It is a medium for direct marketing, for retailing and distribution, for the delivery of service and information products, for marketing research, and even for posting and testing prices. The Web is a comprehensive marketing environment.

EVOLUTION OF THE WORLD WIDE WEB

A user who surfs the Web is drawing on a chain of technology advances that began in the 1970s and shows no signs of slowing down.

First came the *Internet*, a network of computers that spans the globe. It grew out of experiments to link together the main computers of the US Department of Defense in the early 1970s, but many date its birth from 1983 when the US Department of Defense imposed rules for information exchange on all users. In 1985, the Internet began to grow explosively after the National Science Foundation connected six supercomputer centers with a high-speed backbone that gave scientists the ability to move files across the system. The number of host computers that make up the Internet has doubled every year since 1985 and may well continue to double annually for some time.

Second came the *World Wide Web in 1989.* The Web is no more than a set of rules governing a library of files (text, pictures, sound or video) stored on the computers that make up the Internet. It is termed a Web because any one file can contain pathways to many other files. Tim Berners-Lee developed the Web at the University of Geneva, Switzerland.

Third came *Mosaic* in 1993, which a year later became Netscape. These software products are called browsers because they let personal computer users browse easily from one file on the Web to another. Only after the browsers became widely available in 1994 did the Web begin to be noticed for its commercial potential. Suddenly, the Internet was not seen as a way to run computers from a distance, but rather as a highway that could carry things as disparate as telephony, television, radio and mail, and combine their functions into a whole more effective than any of its parts.

Fourth came *broadband access*. Early traffic on the Internet tended to travel on telephone wires. Consequently the early Web experience was excruciatingly slow, leading some to call it the World Wide Wait. In the late 1990s, telephone and television companies began to build new transmission capacity, designed expressly to transmit data in large quantities. Its rollout was slow, and by the end of 1999 fewer than 2% of U.S. homes could access the Web on these transmission lines. For these consumers, however, the experience was transformed. The full flowering of the Web as a commercial medium with mass-market reach could now be seen to depend on the rate at which broadband access would roll out.

An industry is taking shape to support commerce on the Internet that is a relatively complex structure of collaborators and competitors. Figure 1-1 illustrates the main functions that the industry performs and identifies some of the firms that compete to do the work. The allocation of firms to functions is fluid at this stage in the evolution of the industry, and there is a vigorous rate of vertical integration by firms who attempt to anticipate the future structure of the industry. Thus AOL has acquired Netscape, and Microsoft and Yahoo! have acquired a number of small suppliers of electronic commerce services.

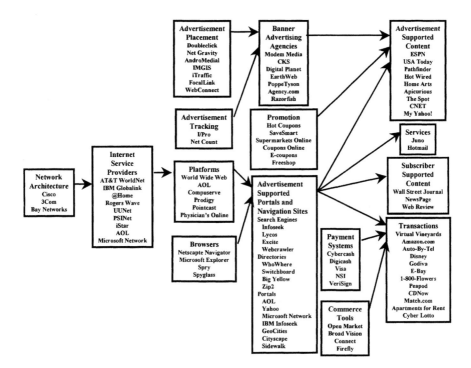

Figure 1-1: Structure of the industry-supporting electronic commerce

Demographics Of Web Users

In 2000, half of the approximately 150 million people who use the Web with some frequency live in the U.S., where the computer penetration level in households is also high.

Category	Households (in thousands)
U.S. Households	99,500
Households with PC	48,550
Households with PC and Modem	31,000
Households Online	24,200
Online Service Subscriptions	35,400

Table 1-1: Personal Computer, Modem and Online Penetration in the USA,   April 2000

Demographic Characteristic	April 2000	US Average
Male/Female (%)	52/48	49/51
Median Age	35.1	33
Education (% with college degree or higher)	50	22
Median Household Income	$52,500	$31,000
Occupation (% in professional or management positions)	22	27

Table 1-2: Demographics of Web and Online Users

BENEFITS OF ELECTRONIC COMMERCE

From no audience to speak of in 1994, the Web is now in a third of American homes. No previous medium, not radio or television, has built an audience for itself so fast. Such rapid growth suggests remarkable user appeal, and perhaps the power to effect a revolution in the practice of marketing.

The Internet combines addressability with responsiveness: it is an interactive medium. It can reach out to an audience, collect a response and reach out again with a second message whose content takes account of that response. Such interactivity can be achieved with direct mail, telemarketing and personal selling. However, the Web facilitates much shorter and less expensive cycles of send and response, eliminating paper and mailing costs from the interaction. The result is a very low cost medium with the potential to be as subtle, flexible, pertinent and persuasive as good conversation, with a better memory than the most diligent salesperson, and no distaste for repetitive tasks.

The Web has other attractive properties:

Selectivity of the Audience

Broadcast media such as radio and television communicate with broad segments of a market. The Web, at least in principle, can communicate with individuals. Merchants can tailor marketing communications to individuals based on previous site visits, psychographics and preferences. Artificial intelligence can analyze digital responses to digital inquiries in order to diagnose the likely characteristics of a customer. Amazon.com, for example, uses a procedure known as collaborative filtering to infer the tastes of book readers from the similarity of their purchases to those of other customers.

Direct Marketing

The Web can connect customers with producers directly, thus potentially reducing the importance of intermediaries. In so doing, the producer can increase profits by dealing directly with the customer and saving on distributor margins. However, the producer now has to assume some functions which were previously performed by

4

distributors including communications, warehousing, bulk breaking, providing assortment, physical delivery, financing and after-sales service. At issue is whether the producer can be more efficient than its distributors in carrying out functions previously performed by them.

Distributors, however, can circumvent the threat of disintermediation if they take on new roles. For example, they can add value to the channel system by serving as a nexus for information between the buyer and the seller. Faced with the potential of information overload, buyers and sellers may find it more efficient to deal through an information consolidator who will collect, collate, interpret, and disseminate vast amounts of information. A good example of a "cybermediary" is FastParts.com[1] which links buyers and sellers of surplus electronic parts.

Greater Ability to Search

With the Web, customers are accorded greater ability to search across vendors to find offerings that possess the set of attributes that they desire. Thus, although having a Web presence will increase a vendor's probability of being considered, it may also intensify price competition, as the vendor's offering will be considered along with others. The Web's consequences for the retailer's profits will depend on its ability to reap cost savings through greater efficiencies by marketing on the Web, and also on the ability to harness the discriminating power of information to differentiate the offering and its quality. By doing the latter, the retailer will be able to price products or services at a premium.

Improving Customer Service

Electronic commerce offers the opportunity for improving the service that merchants provide to customers, while simultaneously reducing the costs of providing this service. In addition to streamlining the supply chain, electronic commerce via the Internet offers the potential for streamlining the demand chain as well. Components of the demand chain include: the marketing and promotion of products and services; the acceptance of orders for these products and services; the process of paying for these orders; the actual delivery of the products and services; and the support for the products and services.

In terms of marketing and promotion, the Web offers a dynamic environment in which to interact with customers. Marketing material can include graphics, animation, video and audio to create a compelling multimedia presentation. Moreover, for many customers, the Web offers superior convenience compared to conventional media. Marketing via the Internet provides immediate access to a world-wide market of potential consumers. The potential customer base is not limited by the number of catalogs or brochures that are printed and mailed. Internet-based catalogs can be updated immediately to reflect changes in pricing or product availability. This results in more economically efficient outcomes and improved service for customers. Online catalogs can also provide more thorough information than conventional catalogs. Online merchants are not constrained by the size of their catalog, so can provide considerably

---

[1] http://www.fastparts.com

more detail where appropriate or necessary. The costs of printing and mailing catalogs and brochures can also be avoided. Thus, e-commerce offers the potential for reducing the costs of marketing to customers.

The transaction costs of serving customers and taking orders can be reduced, sometimes dramatically, by conducting transactions over the Internet. Table 1-3 illustrates the magnitude of this effect in the commercial banking industry. The expansion of the electronic payment infrastructure will create more efficient ties between consumers, merchants and banks. The emergence of electronic cash will put competitive pressure on credit card providers, and will likely lead to reduced costs for merchants.

Transaction Type	Average Cost of Transaction
Teller	$1.07
Check	$0.68
Phone	$0.35
ATM	$0.27
Internet	$0.01

Table 1-3: The Average Cost of Retail Banking Transactions

The Internet can be an ideal channel for the actual delivery of digital products, such as publications, pictures, graphics, software, audio, video, etc. This eliminates most manufacturing, packaging and distribution costs, and is thus considerably less costly than conventional distribution approaches. International Data Corporation has estimated that the value of software distributed electronically will be $4.6 billion in the year 2000.

The Internet provides the potential to offer support for many products and services. Online support services can enhance the capabilities of telephone support centers. Static information describing the product or service can be made available from a Web page with text and graphics. Search tools and "frequently asked questions" sections can improve the usefulness of this information. Artificial intelligence on the Web server could be used to serve information dynamically. E-mail can be used for asynchronous communications and Q&A sessions between the customer and the customer service representative. Online chat sessions would make these communications dynamic and synchronous. Eventually, it will be feasible to provide the live streaming of audio and video, via the Internet, between the customer and the customer service representative.

LIMITATIONS OF ELECTRONIC COMMERCE

For all its strengths, the Web as it exists today has some very unattractive properties when compared to its rival commercial media such as television, radio, and print. Its ability to command share of mind is poor. Where the average American watches four hours of television each day, the minority of Americans who have access to the Web from home log on for only 36 minutes. The Web may be a useful medium, but it is not as addictive as television. It is, at least today, a tool, and not a diversion or entertainment. The Web is best viewed as a marketing medium not better or worse than existing media, but different.

6

The primary obstacles to the widespread acceptance and growth of electronic commerce on the Internet include: inadequate security, lack of standards, limited penetration of Internet access, limited bandwidth, and existing distribution channels that create channel conflict for some incumbents.

Security is widely considered to be the greatest factor limiting electronic commerce on the Internet. The Internet was designed as an open, public network without serious regard for either the security or support of commercial transactions. Technologies such as firewalls, encryption, digital signatures and smart cards have emerged to address these security issues. The Secure Electronic Transaction (SET) protocol is a non-proprietary encryption standard for allowing secure credit card payments via the Internet. The SET protocol was developed by Visa and MasterCard, with technical input from IBM and Microsoft. The SET specifications have received widespread industry support.

Additional limitations of using the Internet for electronic commerce include the somewhat limited penetration of Internet access and the congestion and bandwidth problems that can slow Internet communication. Morgan Stanley projects that Internet users will represent about 50 % of the total U.S. population by 2010 and that the world-wide penetration of Web access will be about 7% in 2010. Obviously this so-called worldwide consumer marketplace is still limited in terms of its penetration.

CATEGORIES OF ELECTRONIC COMMERCE

Electronic commerce seems destined to become a substantial part of the economy. According to ActivMedia Inc.,[2] it will grow to $1.2 trillion in 2002. While profits are already being made, there is still some skepticism. Naysayers point to the relatively small volume of transactions, the limited selection of products sold on the Web, and the fact that many of the companies selling on the Web still get most of their revenues from other channels, such as catalogs or retail stores.

Business	1999 revenues
Financial Services	$3 billion
Apparel & footwear	$314 million
PC hardware and software	$2.1 billion
Ticket event sales	$900 million
Entertainment	$1.2 billion
Travel	$3.4 billion
Books and music	$556 million
Business-to-Business sales	$98 billion

Table 1-4: Revenues of Web business sectors in 1999

The Web has created a rare opportunity for organizations to access global markets – from the smallest retailer to the largest manufacturer. It allows for mass customization, the building of stronger business relationships, a greater degree of channel coordination, heightened communication with various publics, and enhanced customer service.

---

[2] http://www.activmedia.com

However, before implementing this new technology as part of corporate strategy, management must address it within the strategic scope of the organization.

The Web challenges managers to develop a more thorough understanding of the multifaceted implications of this new technology. To develop long-term competitive strategies, areas of strategic interest must be explored fully. The decision on how the Web will influence a company entails assessing how it fits into the firm's long-range plans, as well as its influence on the firm's competitive environment.

The growth of Web-based commerce has generated a number of approaches to creating a model of how it influences business. Using a business-oriented perspective to define the key boundaries of the Web, Figure 1-2 presents the framework for strategic planning. Such a critical boundary approach suggests multiple interactions from a single company perspective: business-to-business, business-to-consumer, and the marketspace in which business, partner and consumer connect. Each of these areas has a set of strategic activities and issues. Opportunities for creating value exist at each of the boundaries. The importance of each boundary to an organization may differ, but the need to include each within the strategic development process is critical for maintaining a long-term competitive position.

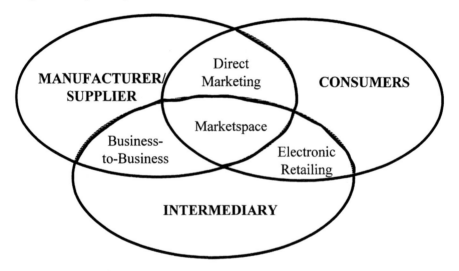

Figure 1-2: Electronic Commerce Model with Key Relationships

The Web-based commerce model referred to in Figure 1-2 is a depiction of business. Its four boundary concerns set the parameters of a firm's operations. Each depicts a mosaic of strategic issues that must be considered by management when positioning the firm competitively in the virtual marketplace. Although the model is compelling from an applied business perspective, its inherent importance becomes clear when industry leaders are examined. Instances of firms capitalizing on various boundary parameters can offer insights into achieving competitive advantages in their own markets. Table 1-5 summarizes the activities and provides examples of specific firms or industries currently leading in certain boundaries. Table 1-6 suggests the underlying technology benefits and costs.

	Electronic Retailing	Business-to-Business	Marketspace	Direct Marketing
Issue 1	Leveraging your firm's logistical system (Dell)	Establishing business-to-business relationships to sell competitively to consumers (Corporate Express)	Selling in a virtual world (Microsoft)	Eliminating Intermediaries (American Airlines)
Issue 2	Pricing and managing online transactions (Spiegel)	Strengthening the value chain (Godiva)	Staying real or becoming virtual (Egghead)	Establishing your place in the value chain (Ameritrade)
Issue 3	Optimizing communication to key consumer markets (Target)	Providing value through communication (Boeing / McDonell Douglas)	Communicating with a community (Johnson & Johnson)	Comparative information in a virtual world (Internet Travel Network)
Issue 4	Achieving excellence through service (Nordstrom's)	Optimizing business-to-business service (Roadway)	Value-added services in the marketspace (Yahoo)	Optimizing the service offering across partner firms (Sun)

Table 1-5: Examples of Specific Electronic Commerce Strategies

	Electronic Retailing	Business-to-Business	Marketspace	Direct Marketing
Technology Applications	Product description and specification; order entry system	Electronic Data Interchange (EDI); Electronic Funds Transfer (EFT); product replenishment	Product development and configuration; order entry	Direct customer ordering system
Benefits	Wider search capability for consumer; consumer convenience	Rapid exchange of information; lower lead times	Rapid information sharing; greater information coordination	Rapid delivery; lower costs
Costs	Staffing 24-hour store front; security	Translation; security	Possible direct marketing opportunity	Reduced service; lack of producer access to channels

Table 1-6: A Comparison of Key Electronic Commerce Relationships

Business-to-Business Electronic Commerce

The business-to-business space includes the myriad upstream and downstream transactions that can enhance channel coordination and customer relationships. Forrester[3] estimates that by the year 2002, Internet-based business-to-business transactions will total almost $350 billion. Electronic Data Interchange (EDI) is the exchange of business data in digital form between a company and its suppliers, customers and collaborators. It makes efficient supply-chain management possible and has been a key factor in the success of many large firms. Among small firms, it is tempting to think that the Web will make possible "EDI in a box", or low cost, off-the-shelf tools that firms of every size can use to capture the logistical efficiencies. There are obstacles to this utopian future, however. Legacy computer systems, the absence of universal standards, and large firms' disincentives to co-operate are some impediments. In the near future, the benefits of the Web will tend to be captured by large corporations. They build extranets, or limited-access networks accessible only to their suppliers, and intranets, or networks that improve communication within and among divisions of the corporation.

Electronic Retailing

The business-to-consumer space encompasses all interactions between the consumer and the firm: product ordering, sharing product information, creating display space, defining consumer information, co-developing products, and providing customer service. International Data Corporation estimates that online consumer purchases in the

---

[3] http://www.forrester.com

year 2000 within the U.S. alone will be $16 billion. For consumers the main problem in buying from the Web has been safety concerns in transmitting credit card numbers and other payment data. Lack of sales assistance and limited selection of products have also been problems with start-up online stores. These are offset by convenience: 24-hour availability, time-savings, etc. The safety concerns are being gradually overcome, both due to an improved perception of Web merchants and due to industry efforts. Traditionally quite wary of Internet transactions, credit card giants Visa and MasterCard have co-sponsored the Secure Electronic Transaction (SET) protocol, which should increase consumer confidence levels.

The Marketspace

The marketspace involves the company, its partners and its customers, and provides the opportunity for developing communication interactions, including customer-to-manufacturer surveys and information exchanges on such things as product, warranty and service capabilities. Manufacturers, suppliers, intermediaries and end consumers can identify and coordinate data transfers with each other.

Direct Marketing

The area of opportunity is the direct marketing strategy that connects manufacturers and suppliers directly with their end consumers. Connections that sell directly to the customer or buy direct from the manufacturer are a potential risk, especially as the marketspace makes customer-manufacturer contact easier and more likely.

Consumer-to-Consumer Electronic Commerce

In addition to companies, individuals are active in electronic commerce. A number of sites provide room for classified ads, and collector and hobby sites are active in connecting parties. Unfortunately, the volume of this sector of e-commerce is hard to track or estimate. A managed form of consumer-to-consumer selling is auction sites, which either act as middlemen in the transaction or enable it by providing a virtual marketplace, and get their revenue from fees and commissions. For example, eBay[4], an auction site for individuals, facilitated $800 million in sales in 1999, generating $42 million in revenue for the company.

OPPORTUNITIES PROVIDED BY ELECTRONIC COMMERCE

The Internet is fast becoming an important new channel for commerce in a wide variety of businesses. Determining how to take advantage of the opportunities this new channel is creating will not be easy for most executives, especially those in large, well-established companies. The Internet poses a difficult challenge for established businesses. The opportunities presented by the Internet seem to be readily apparent: by allowing for direct, ubiquitous links to anyone, anywhere, the Internet lets companies build interactive

---

[4] http://www.ebay.com

11

relationships with customers and suppliers, and deliver new products and services at very low cost. But the companies that have taken greatest advantage of these opportunities are start-ups such as Yahoo! and Amazon.com. Established businesses that have built brands and physical distribution relationships risk damaging all they have created when they pursue commerce in cyberspace. Electronic commerce is such a new phenomenon that it is difficult for executives at most companies to decide the best way to use the new channel. And it is even more difficult for them to accurately estimate the returns on any Internet investment they may make.

Nevertheless, managers cannot afford to avoid thinking about the impact of electronic commerce on their businesses. At the very least, they need to understand the opportunities available to them and recognize how their companies may be vulnerable if rivals seize those opportunities first. To determine what opportunities and threats the Internet poses, managers should focus in a systematic way on what the Internet can allow their organization to do.

The Internet presents four distinct types of opportunities. First, through the Internet, companies can establish a direct link to customers, suppliers and distributors to complete transactions or trade information more easily. Second, the technology allows companies to bypass others in the value chain. Third, companies can use the Internet to develop and deliver new products and services for new customers. Fourth, a company could conceivably use the Internet to become the dominant player in the electronic channel of a specific industry or segment, controlling access to customers and setting new business rules.

By exploring the opportunities and threats they face in each of these four domains, executives can realistically assess what, if any, investments they should begin to make in electronic commerce and determine what risks they will need to plan for. A sound electronic commerce strategy begins by articulating what is possible.

Establishing The Internet Channel

To deliver new services to customers, or to bypass intermediaries in the value chain, companies first need to build direct connections to customers. Companies can build momentum in their digital channels by using Internet technology to deliver three forms of service to customers. First, they can give customers the same level of service through the Internet that they can currently deliver through a salesperson. Second, companies can use new Internet technologies to personalize interactions with their customers and build customer loyalty. One way is to tailor the information and options customers see at a site to provide customers exactly what they want. Third, companies can provide valuable new services inexpensively. For example, a company could draw on data from its entire customer database to make available knowledge on some topics. If a customer has a problem with a product, he or she might consult a site's directory of frequently asked questions to see how others have solved the problem. Or the customer might benefit from knowing how others have used a particular product. The combination of these three levels of service could make the Internet channel very compelling for customers.

The opportunity for those companies that move first to establish electronic channels is a threat to those that do not. The average customer, once he or she has established a relationship with one electronic seller, will be reluctant to invest the time and effort to evaluate other suppliers. The reluctance to abandon what works is a formidable obstacle to companies that do not move aggressively enough. Followers in this new channel risk being stuck with the unenviable task of getting customers to abandon investments they have already made in a competitor. This will be a barrier that increases over time as the relationship between customer and supplier deepens. Companies that currently do not want to participate in electronic commerce may be forced to do so by competitors or customers.

As pioneering companies in an industry begin to build electronic channels, rivals will need to re-examine their value chains. New companies have no existing value chains to protect, and so can set up their businesses in ways that take full advantage of the Internet. But companies that deal through others to reach end customers (such as Compaq and IBM in the computer industry) will need to weigh the importance of protecting existing relationships with their distributors and partners that account for most of their current revenue against the advantages of establishing future strategic positions and revenue streams. This is one of the most difficult issues that large established companies face in making decisions about engaging in electronic commerce.

The Virtual Value Chain

Companies may find they have little choice but to risk damaging relationships in their physical chains to compete in the electronic channel. The ubiquity of the Internet makes it possible for a participant in the value chain to usurp the role of any other participant.   Once companies establish an electronic channel, they choose to become pirates in the value chain, capturing margins from other participants up and down the chain. Pirates will probably emerge from the ranks of those innovative companies that can recognize where the core value will be most effectively delivered to customers over a network. Value chain pirates are in a position to define new business rules and introduce new business models. But pirates will also need to develop new capabilities. Those companies that stand to lose margins to pirates currently provide very real value to customers such as merchandising skills, logistics expertise and information management. To succeed, pirates must be able to provide that value, either by building the skills in-house or by allying with others.

Digital Value Creation

Companies that establish Internet channels can choose to introduce new products and services. The Internet is a platform for innovation. It is a way to produce and distribute new combinations of digital information – or to create new transaction models and services – without incurring the traditional costs of complexity that exist in the physical world. The Internet presents three opportunities for creating new value. First, a company can use its direct access to customers. Each time a customer visits a company's Web site is an opportunity to deliver additional services or provide a path for other businesses that want to reach that customer. Second, a company can mine its own digital assets to serve new customer segments. Third, a company can take advantage of its ability to conduct transactions over the Internet to take away value from others. For example, a major bank that has traditionally provided check-clearing services is using the Internet to offer complete bill payment services for universities and order management services for retailers. The new, targeted services help strengthen the bank's core transaction-processing business, and it eats away at the business of companies that currently provide these services, such as those that furnish electronic data interchange (EDI) services. In all three cases, each addition of digital value by one company weakens the business proposition of another company in a small way. Ultimately, the risk for established businesses is not from digital tornadoes but from digital termites.

Creating A Customer Magnet

Companies that can establish direct links to their customers, pirate their industry's value chain, and take away bits of value digitally from other companies may put themselves in a position to become powerful new forces in electronic commerce. There are economies of scale inherent in concentration on the Internet. Traditional reasons for having numerous suppliers in an industry are not valid on the Internet. First, the Internet makes physical distance between consumers and suppliers largely irrelevant. Any store is equally accessible to any customer. Second, stores that establish a strong position or dominant brand on the Internet can grow rapidly, relatively unhampered by the costs and delays common when expanding in the physical world. Third, single stores can differentiate services for many customer segments, customizing offerings and tailoring the way visitors enter and move around the site to address regional or individual differences. As a result, a small number of companies can meet the diverse needs of large segments of the global market.

More importantly, if customers are not willing to learn how to navigate hundreds of different sites, each with its own unique layout, then the Web will turn out to be a naturally concentrating medium. People feel comfortable returning to the stores they know, virtual or physical, because they can easily navigate the familiar aisles and find what they are looking for. They will gravitate toward sites that can meet all their needs in specific categories. Customers will head for the places many other customers frequent if they can interact with one another and derive some value from the interaction.

It is conceivable that some companies will attempt to control the electronic channel by becoming the site that can provide customers with everything they could want. Customer magnets could organize themselves around a specific type of product or service, a particular segment of customers, an entire industry, or a unique business model. Being few in number, they will have a tremendous influence on the shape of their industry. They could control access to suppliers and subtly sway customers' choices by promoting or ignoring individual brands. Over time, a customer magnet could become the electronic gateway to an entire industry.

Clearly, few companies can justify the investment that will be needed to become a customer magnet. Managers can't yet quantify the financial rewards from such an initiative, and the risks are daunting. It is difficult and expensive for companies to integrate their existing business applications with the Internet technologies they will need to conduct commerce online. It will also be difficult to integrate electronic processes for commerce with existing physical processes that often involve numerous functions and many business units within an organization. And companies that create customer magnets will likely need to work with competitors – and their systems and processes – to offer customers everything they could want.

But if companies decide that electronic commerce is too important to ignore, it may be possible for them to adopt less risky approaches to protect their positions in the electronic channel. For example, more than ten of the nation's largest banks, including Banc One, Citicorp and First Union, have formed a joint venture with IBM to create a common industry interface for retail banking over the Internet. The banks recognize that owning direct access to the customer is critical. They do not want to cede that access to an industry outsider, such as a home-banking software provider like Intuit or Microsoft, or to a single enterprising bank. Instead, the partners in the joint venture are sharing the costs of building a technological base for electronic banking, and in the process they are attempting to protect their industry's existing relationships with its customers.

Established companies might also stake out competitive positions in the electronic channel by allying with others to create cascading value chains. That is, companies that furnish complementary services to a common customer base could band together to establish an exclusive bundle of services in the electronic channel. For example, hotels, travel agents, guidebook publishers and car rental agencies could create an exclusive network that would provide customers with everything they need when traveling.

Finally, established companies could find ways to embed their products or services in customer magnets. For example, Amazon.com has become a book provider to Yahoo's customers.

For managers in established businesses, the Internet is a tough nut to crack. It is very simple to set up a Web presence but quite difficult to create a Web-based business model. One thing is certain: the changes made possible by the Internet are strategic and fundamental. However these changes play out in individual industries, they will unquestionably affect every company's relationship with its customers and the value propositions for many companies in the foreseeable future.

APPLICATIONS OF ELECTRONIC COMMERCE

Online Publishing

The Web was designed for sharing information in a network. Text-based documents are easily and efficiently digitized for convenient transmission via computer networks. Thus, it is natural that among the first commercial uses for the Web was for it to serve as a distribution channel for published material. There are at least three different strategies that are currently being employed by online publishers. Some online publishers receive all of their revenue from advertisements (for example, CNN Interactive). Some charge subscription fees for access to any information (for example, Wall Street Journal), and others use a hybrid approach whereby they offer some information freely, charge for other information, and earn advertisement revenue as well (for example, ESPN Sportszone). The high costs and relatively long lead times of conventional print publishing make Internet distribution an attractive alternative relative to conventional print publishing.

Internet Advertising

Given the difficulty that many Web-based content providers will encounter in attempting to charge for content, advertising revenue will be an important component of the business models for many Internet-based businesses. Dataquest predicts that Internet advertising will amount to $923 million in the year 2000. Still, Internet advertising will represent less than 2 percent of the total advertising revenue from traditional media.

There are many aspects of Internet advertising that marketers find appealing, including the attractive demographics of Web users and the potential for delivering targeted advertisements to these individuals. Internet users tend to be relatively young, affluent and well-educated. Thus, they are among the most attractive of consumers. In contrast to traditional advertising where advertisements are broadcast to a wide audience, Internet advertising offers the potential to tailor advertisements to individual tastes. The demographics and Web-surfing activity of specific individuals can be monitored and analyzed to develop detailed profiles of these individuals. With these profiles, marketers can deliver advertisements that closely match the interests of potential consumers. And these advertisements can be delivered based on the precise psychographics of the individual, rather than the general demographics of a group. Instead of being an inconvenience or annoyance, such advertisements offer the potential to actually provide value to the customer.

Business-to-Consumer Retailing

Another of the first commercial uses of the Web was for companies to place marketing material and product information on their public Web sites. Security and competitive concerns caused many companies to hesitate before publishing pricing or delivery information, much less accept orders online. However, the many potential benefits of electronic commerce soon attracted a plethora of online merchants.

Today, consumers can order an amazing variety of products via the Internet. 1-800-Flowers accepts orders for flowers. Amazon.com sells books. CDNet sells compact disks. Dell Computer sells computers. There are hundreds of Internet-based shopping malls, one being the Internet Shopping Network, which offers over 35,000 products from over 1,000 manufacturers on their Web site. Even traditional stores such as Macy's and Wal-Mart accept orders through their Web sites.

In order to provide automated delivery information and automated order entry via their Web sites, online merchants must usually integrate their Web server directly with their information technology infrastructure and corporate databases. This creates even more serious and challenging security concerns. As security solutions that address these problems become pervasive, the potential for Web-based business-to-consumer transactions becomes more promising.

Home Banking

For many years, banks have used private networks for electronic fund transfers (EFT's). A multitude of banks have begun to offer Internet-based services for their retail consumers. Home banking can be viewed as a subset of the business-to-consumer

16

segment of electronic commerce. Like the other electronic commerce applications, home banking is driven both by the opportunity to provide more effective services to customers and the opportunity to dramatically reduce the costs of providing these services. The incumbents in the banking industry are already being challenged by the new entrants who are eager to exploit these opportunities. Security First Network Bank (SFNB) was the first completely virtual bank (i.e., they have no branches). Many established banks began moving to offer Internet services for their customers. Wells Fargo Bank and Bank of America were among the most aggressive incumbents, offering Web-based capabilities to access account statements, to transfer funds between accounts, and to make online bill payments.

Business-to-Business Wholesaling

Electronic Data Interchange (EDI) has become a common approach for large companies to conduct transactions electronically. With the emergence of the Internet as a viable alternative for commercial applications, EDI providers have begun to offer EDI services over the Internet. Aggregators have emerged that offer a wide variety of complementary products via the Internet, often in targeted vertical markets. Some businesses have developed or purchased customized Web commerce applications for selling directly to their customers and trading partners.

The Internet presents an attractive alternative to the proprietary Value Added Networks (VANs) at a potentially much lower cost. Internet Service Providers (ISPs) offer flat monthly fees, rather than basing charges on either the volume or the time-of-day of transactions. For a company performing between 10,000 and 30,000 transactions per month, the cost of using an ISP runs about $400 per month, while the cost for a VAN runs between $1,865 and $3,775 per month. The Web also provides great flexibility in terms of adding and subtracting suppliers and customers because they are not tied to the proprietary VAN network. This allows companies to potentially establish a world-wide network with their trading partners.

In addition to using private networks, VAN providers have begun to offer Internet connections to their customers. They have developed Web-enabled EDI software. Migrating EDI to the public Internet creates security challenges, and the standards for achieving Web-based EDI are still being developed. However, in spite of these challenges, the potential for Web-based EDI appears promising. An alternative to EDI for business-to-business transactions is to utilize customized Web commerce applications.

MANAGERIAL ISSUES FOR SUCCESS IN ELECTRONIC COMMERCE

Given the mainstream hype afforded electronic commerce, managers often feel they must start a project first, to keep from falling behind everyone else, but without adequate planning for the project's success. Although it is definitely important to get on board quickly with the Internet, the relative expense and long-lasting repercussions of a poorly executed project cannot be understated. Table 1-7 provides a framework of critical success factors designed to aid managers in planning for new projects, identifying stumbling blocks, and finding potential solutions to the problems likely to be encountered.

17

Type of Issue	Relevant Questions
Technical	• How will security be implemented? • What protocols will be the standards of future electronic commerce? • What are the future technologies used to "wire" people and households?
Societal	• How will the privacy of individuals be protected? • How will consumer data be used, and will it be misused? • How do user perceptions of issues reflect reality?
Economic	• How will electronic and physical markets differ? • Will economic theories succeed as instantaneous access to information emerges? • What will be the price of information?
Legal	• Should governments continue to subsidize the Internet? • How will real-world laws apply to the legality of virtual sites? • Who is liable for information accuracy?
Behavioral	• How satisfied will users be with virtual experiences compared to the real world? • How will a sense of community and social needs be represented through electronic commerce? • What are the characteristics of Internet users?
Organizational /Managerial	• What are the differences between managing an electronic commerce business and a more tangible one? • How will the organization of the firm change as electronic commerce becomes more prevalent? • What products lend themselves to success with electronic commerce?

Table 1-7: A Framework of Critical Success Factors in Electronic Commerce

Technical Issues

The proliferation of electronic commerce is not possible without the infrastructure to support it. The creation and modification of electronic commerce on the public Internet leads to several important questions that should be addressed.

Development of Security Features

A stumbling block to the widespread acceptance of electronic commerce is the perceived lack of security on public networks. Encryption algorithms can be used to code and decode messages as they travel from sender to receiver. Unfortunately, there will probably never be truly foolproof ways of conducting secure electronic trade. We can only take advantage of the best products technology currently offers and stay within our budgets. Virtual Private Networks (VPNs) are one of the most popular ways to solve the problem of conducting secure, private business over open, public networks. VPNs use a tunneling protocol to encrypt data between the sender and the receiver over public Internet lines, such that someone using a common packet sniffer program would receive nothing but garbage. Secure hypertext transport protocol is another way of conducting secure business over the Internet. Web browsers and servers establish a coded conversation that can only be understood by each other completely transparent to the user.

Infrastructure Development

The Internet is becoming increasingly frustrating to use because of the heavy network traffic. When the amount of traffic exceeds the bandwidth of the network carrying it, the network slows as the messages queue up to be delivered through the network lines. The waiting and delays can frustrate potential users, who may refuse to use a system perceived as annoying. Newer technologies, such as streaming video, require large amounts of bandwidth – more than is readily available commercially – and thus cannot proliferate. When you negotiate contracts with Internet Service Providers or Web hosting services, the amount of bandwidth available to your server is crucial. T-1 (1.544 megabits per second) is probably the minimum bandwidth any server should have to conduct serious electronic commerce. Many will find that this slows down with medium usage and will want to have several T-1 lines feeding the server, or perhaps even a T-3 (44.1 megabits per second) connection.

Future Platforms for Electronic Trade

While the World Wide Web is based on open technologies that suit electronic commerce well, the technologies have inherent limitations. Hypertext Markup Language (HTML) is good for displaying static text, pictures and some animation, but the modifications necessary for complex database access and data retrieval tend to be slow. As the technology in this arena changes rapidly, we can expect a replacement for HTML in delivering content to users. As with all things computerized, there will be format changes as researchers discover better platforms for facilitating electronic commerce, including security and speed as major factors.

Societal Issues

The emergence of electronic commerce has not only changed the world technologically, but also socially. Many societal aspects are involved in using the computer and in doing business traditionally. Electronic commerce could disturb the balance in both of these areas.

Privacy

People have always had a need to maintain some level of privacy or anonymity. In commerce, this is made possible through the cash transaction at the retail outlet. But most forms of electronic commerce have no equivalent counterpart. Moreover, consumers may have data gathered about them inconspicuously by certain organizations. A cookie is a text file placed on a user's hard drive by a Web server to track the identity of the user's computer. As new Web pages are loaded on that computer, the server checks for the presence of a cookie and, upon finding it, identifies the user loading the page. Organizations can thereby track the movements of people via the Web site and, with other confirming information, may even be able to positively identify them. This can be greatly disturbing to users who wish their online pursuits to remain anonymous. Corporations should be careful about the information they gather on their potential customers, collecting only what is truly necessary and making sure the users know these data are being collected about them. This will help companies be seen as responsible Internet marketers.

Social Benefits and Losses

Many people shop together in pairs or in groups, deriving a hedonic value from interaction with others during a shopping excursion. However, the direct marketing model proposed by electronic commerce is solitary. Users are not likely to congregate in front of the computer as they do at the shopping mall. Some electronic providers have offered an alternative to social shopping by creating virtual communities.

Economic Issues

Electronic markets have created a way for buyers and sellers to connect with each other instantaneously and compare prices for the same goods, services or commodities.

Legal and Regulatory Issues

Each introduction of new technology usually raises new legal questions that have to be addressed by the courts. Computing and electronic commerce have been advancing so rapidly that the laws cannot keep up with the technology. Many areas for concern are noted below. It is not difficult to imagine any of these scenarios in many organizations, each producing an unwanted side effect from embracing electronic commerce. Policies need to be established to deal with any of these possibilities.

Publicly Subsidized Networks

The government has embraced the Internet, and has provided masses of public information on the World Wide Web. This might create a dichotomous spread of information between those who can afford Internet access and those who cannot. If the government is using the Internet as a means to spread information to all citizens, one cannot help but ask if it then has a responsibility to provide access to the Internet for all citizens.

Responsibility for Information Accuracy

Electronic commerce requires a vendor to store a large amount of information about its consumers. This includes not only traditional information, such as that required on invoices and billing statements, but also electronic information about the terminals used and digital signatures to authenticate a user's existence. Who will be responsible when this information is wrong?

Enforcing Local Standards

The openness of the Internet ignores both state and national boundaries. In cyberspace, it does not matter where you are physically located. This facilitates international electronic commerce. However, it also makes the enforcement of local standards and laws virtually impossible.

Down Time

When a computer housing a company's electronic commerce presence goes down, it is equivalent to the front door being locked and the business being closed. With electronic commerce, it is not always clear why a computer is unreachable. It could be a problem with the computer, or with the network that connects it to other computers. If the external network is the problem, is the company's ISP or other service provider liable for lost profits and transactions? What recourse does the electronic vendor have against this entity that has effectively locked the door on his site? Or is it the firm's responsibility to have backup connections ready in case the primary connection goes down, making the network fault tolerant? Will the laws of telephone communications apply as they might to mail-order catalog companies? Or will laws relating to more traditional forms of denial of entry apply?

Behavioral Issues

The creation of virtual worlds and electronic shopping creates many more opportunities for managers and marketers to study the behavioral patterns of their customers.

Social Benefits of Shopping

Why don't people take advantage of the home shopping through the computer? Perhaps there is some social benefit derived from shopping that is not fulfilled by sitting alone in front of a keyboard and wielding a mouse. Electronic commerce providers should think of ways to create a sense of community surrounding their sites.

Characteristics of Internet Users

Several surveys that have been published in the popular press indicate that the most prevalent Internet user is 25-40 years old, college educated, with some disposable income. This picture offers some insight into the characteristics of Internet users, but certainly not in complete detail. To increase the likelihood of success for electronic commerce projects, particularly with firms that already have traditional means of ordering, it is important to know the type of person who is likely to use electronic means to purchase goods and services and who is the target market.

End-User Satisfaction

User satisfaction is a typical measure of the success of an information system. Electronic commerce is no different, for consumers must be satisfied if they are to use the system and ultimately make a purchase. Testing your Web site before releasing it to the general public is a good way to get feedback before making your worldwide debut. Internal testing should also be carried out, using the system in the same way a consumer might. What loads quickly and looks flashy on a local hard drive may take so long over a modem that consumers won't even bother and will try somewhere else. Often sites can provide a graphical version and a text-only version to give users a choice based on the bandwidth available to them.

Organizational/Managerial Issues

Just as important to the success of the electronic commerce process is the successful adaptation of current organizational and managerial processes.

Managing the Paperless Organization

Electronic commerce processes further enhance the possibility of virtual organizations. These companies consist of many workers remotely located and often isolated from other workers. It is difficult to apply traditional managerial and motivational strategies to deal with these employees. What techniques can managers use to optimize their remotely located workers? Will videoconferences and e-mail be acceptable substitutes for face-to-face management? How might workers respond to electronic monitoring over distances as opposed to knowing that the boss is in the building? Your organization should be aware of these issues as you embark on electronic projects. Written policies for video conferencing versus travel and telecommuting should be established as early as possible to avoid confusion. Be sure employees are aware of these policies and understand them. It is also a good idea to establish an Acceptable Use Policy (AUP) so that employees know how they can and cannot use company Internet resources, the methods used to enforce these policies, and what the penalties are for violating them. A company might establish a policy that allows employees to use travel sites such as Travelocity[5] for company-related travel but restricts its use for personal

---

[5] http://www.travelocity.com

travel. Such policies have to be enforced to be effective. There are technological means available to do this, including such software tools as Little Brother, SurfWatch and NetNanny, which restricts employees' access to certain Web sites.

Working in the Paperless Office

As with managing, being a worker in the paperless office is also different from traditional office work. What is interesting is the skill set needed to thrive in a wired world, particularly one that exists without the benefits of frequent face-to-face meetings. Study your employees to gain an understanding of the skills and personality traits required for a remote worker to succeed on the job.

Marketing

Many firms place the marketing department in charge of their electronic commerce systems. The non-stop availability of product information and ordering often requires a very different marketing plan. As electronic commerce and sales grab a larger portion of the firm's total sales, how does the overall marketing plan change? How much is it limited by technology? Does the successful electronic marketing plan complement or replace the traditional one? All these questions demand planning by companies as they use information systems even more strategically in their sales plans.

Pricing

All the networks, hardware and software used to support electronic commerce are not free. Someone must pay for their development and maintenance. Some sites are still experimenting with charging the end user, while most are now completely paid for by the company as part of overhead, like the rent on the virtual storefront. Whereas this second model may seem more in line with traditional thought, consumers are saving money and time by not having to go to the storefront, purchase items, and transport them home.

Product/Service Offered

Obviously, some goods and services just do not lend themselves well to being provided through electronic commerce. The key to success with these services and products is in repositioning the product to maximize the effectiveness of the electronic commerce channel. Knowing your product and your industry is vital to the success of your project. Visit your competitor's Web sites and see what they are doing electronically. A report can then be created, listing potential ways in which electronic commerce can be deployed at various places in the firm's value chain to benefit the firm.

THE EMERGENCE OF ELECTRONIC BUSINESS COMMUNITIES

The World Wide Web has accomplished wonders for consumers around the globe by supplying them with large quantities of information on every product or service imaginable. It has become a viable marketing channel for most companies selling goods, from financial services to hot sauce. A growing number of companies are doing an excellent job at creating new value for their customers and profits for themselves through creative marketing on the Web. This process has seen the transformation of certain supply chains by connecting buyers globally with sources of supply, thereby satisfying the requirements of consumers more efficiently.

Despite the popular attention given to marketing consumer goods on the Internet, the market for business-to-business commerce via the Web is potentially huge and is estimated to be worth about ten times as much as Internet sales of consumer goods. Just as interested individuals have been grouped into loosely knit communities based on common preferences and hobbies, electronic business communities are beginning to link entire industry supply chains. The electronic business community model is not a one-dimensional interfirm linkage between buyers and sellers, nor is it limited to electronic commerce. Rather, these communities leverage information technology to forge closer relationships among competitors, suppliers, buyers and sellers. The result is a new business community that applies electronic network channels to lower the long-standing barriers between the different participants. Although the concept of online business communities is not new, their application to business is gaining momentum. Entire industry supply chains are moving toward a transaction-based business model.

If we consider global trade, specifically the market for Electronic Data Interchange (EDI), we start to see the dramatic effect electronic business communities may have on customer interactions. EDI is the process of electronically conducting all forms of business between entities in order to achieve the organization's objective. This process involves connecting two or more parties through the means of an electronic network or Value Added Network (VAN) and transferring standard formatted information and messages.

The worldwide EDI market is estimated to be $2 billion in the year 2000. Traditional EDI requires huge initial technology investments and costs – VAN connection fees, messaging fees, hardware, systems integration costs, translation software, and so on – to link a finite number of buyers and sellers. Moreover, it has been generally perceived as being inaccessible for most firms because of the complexity and cost-intensive investment associated with it. EDI networks typically have been limited to large firms – only 2 percent of America's six million companies use EDI, and then only with their most frequent trading partners. Adding more participants onto a network often proves costly, not to mention technically challenging. There is a substantial cost difference between adding a participant to an EDI network and adding someone to an electronic business community. Costs of up to $20,000 in software, hardware and services are normal when dealing with modifications or additions to traditional EDI supply chains.

In contrast, the costs of connecting different participants to a Web browser are virtually zero. Companies of all sizes are shifting away from expensive, proprietary EDI networks to relatively inexpensive, more flexible Internet technologies. One such business-to-business exchange is an extranet, defined as a network built on Internet protocols and operated over the public Internet for private business-to-business communication. As extranet opens up cost, flexibility and deployment opportunities typically unfeasible with traditional EDI, Electronic communities are able to target many more and smaller firms, extending benefits to those for whom the complexity and entry costs of EDI may otherwise have been prohibitive. This strategy of expanding services out to many more and smaller firms is precisely what is fueling the growth of electronic business communities.

Some may argue that such developments are nothing more than the automation of existing business processes and the subsequent Internet-enablement of EDI. However, this is not entirely accurate. Although technology has enabled the automation of certain core processes and the elimination of other superfluous ones, the underlying advantage to business is the integral consideration. Business-to-business commerce is actually in the midst of a unique situation in which the buying values of the individual firms that comprise various electronic business communities are being satisfied by the mere existence of the communities they populate. In other words, these communities can target and integrate different businesses that traditionally would have been deterred by competition, cost and investment barriers. Electronic business communities can target new markets by offering low entry costs, relatively minimal complexity with more flexibility, and a convenient pathway to transacting business.

This is not to say that falling costs, simplicity and convenience are the only factors driving the adoption of this new business model. The trend toward outsourcing and forming widespread strategic alliances in most industries provides an added impetus to support the sharing of supplier, customer and corporate information that was once proprietary, with competitors and other cross-industry players. Businesses today are finding themselves in an environment in which unprecedented information sharing among all participants is driving fundamental changes in the interactions, business practices and operations of everyone involved.

Although electronic business communities are evolving on a day-to-day basis, some barriers must still be overcome before they can fully realize their potential. First and foremost are concerns over security and privacy. This may be the biggest inhibitor to the progression of electronic business communities. Certain legal and regulatory issues, such as protecting intellectual property, continue to challenge the developing communities. Moreover, the issues of reliability, scalability, and performance are a constraint that one hopes will dissipate as technology continues to evolve and spawn new public and private communities of interest. At the same time, resistance to technology and lack of knowledge are major obstacles to the growth of electronic business communities.

This effect of the growing influence of technology on business is more a factor of management resistance based primarily on a market strategy that emphasizes current industry paradigms, not future or shifting ones. Managers often downplay the potential benefits of modifying their interactions with customers in favor of a reluctance or refusal to abandon old processes or technology investments. Competitive market pressure and the continued squeeze on margins and profitability should force these managers to adopt new operating methods.

Another constraint on the widespread acceptance of electronic business communities is the difficulty of collectively bringing together many disparate industry competitors, non-industry players and other parties, educating them, and ensuring a common level of knowledge, understanding and commitment. One traditional stumbling block has been a general fear and ambiguity about who controls or holds the power within the group. Such fears typically inhibit many otherwise enthusiastic participants from embracing these communities. Again, this is a consequence of business seeing the future from the mindset of the past and present.

A fundamental consideration when evaluating the future of electronic business communities is the ability of firms to approach traditional situations in more creative and progressive ways. Much more is involved than simply choosing the right technology or connecting participants through electronic channels. These communities can help businesses retain, capture and create additional value, draw closer to suppliers and buyers of products and services, and influence global markets.

Electronic business communities require cooperation and an open exchange of information among all participants. Continuing advancements and cost reductions in the necessary technology are bringing down many barriers to adopting this new model for competition. However, it will ultimately be a shift in the attitudes of management that prompts the decision to adopt such communities. In the end, their future depends on management's ability to view traditional business differently and adapt new market strategies accordingly.

Chapter 2

Retailing in Electronic Commerce

ENHANCING THE CUSTOMER'S SHOPPING EXPERIENCE

Consumers weigh five factors in determining whether they will patronize a particular store. The factors are:

- the breadth and depth of product assortment,
- the price of the goods sold,
- service,
- the convenience of the shopping experience (opening hours, travel time and parking)
- ambience.

If a consumer perceives that any given retailer's performance is superior for at least one of those factors – assuming all other factors are roughly equal – then that retailer is ahead of the game. If the consumer perceives the retailer's delivery of several factors is superior (again assuming that the others are relatively equal), there is no contest. And if the consumer thinks that a retailer cannot deliver satisfactorily on one dimension but excels on another, that retailer may win out as well. That holds true whether the competitor is physical or virtual. E-commerce has not changed the fundamental way retailers should be thinking about their priorities.

Consider that no physical store can beat Amazon.com for the breadth and depth of its assortment. Certainly, the customer loses something of the experience of shopping in a bookstore, but the convenience of being able to determine from home whether a certain book is in stock is a key point of superiority. And while traditional bookstores would contend that Amazon.com's ambience can't hold a candle to theirs – in truth Amazon does offer a sufficient substitute. The company's referral service, the fact that it offers recommendations and reviews, cancels out the inability to browse.

Too many retailers still downplay the potential impact of e-commerce. The fact is, naysayers' reactions to the Internet are similar to those we heard 20 years ago when direct mail catalogs started becoming more prominent. One common preconception about direct mail was that it would work only with certain products. Another was that it was unreliable, that buying through the mail was too risky for consumers. Still another assumption was that if a retailer engaged in direct mail, catalog sales would cannibalize store sales. All three proved to be myths, and – as they relate to e-commerce – all three will again, given time.

Many people, for example, said clothing could not be sold successfully through the mail. And while it seemed at first that direct mail could succeed only if it offered a combination of low-risk branded products and inexpensive trinkets, it was not too long before L.L. Bean, Lands' End, and other clothiers really began to take off. We just don't know yet what can and will be sold over the Internet. As consumers become increasingly familiar with and confident in the medium, the five factors will determine that – not some preconceived notion of what is suited to online sales and what isn't.

As for consumer risk, credit card companies have a great, vested interest in ensuring the confidentiality of transactions. This early problem is well on the way to being solved. And far from cannibalizing a retailer's physical-store sales, Web sites that offer shopping will serve as an advertising mechanism. Direct mail proved to *increase* store sales, in addition to generating its own revenue. Online shopping sites will do the same.

But for those who believe that the Internet will never account for a significant percentage of overall sales, consider the following. Even if the overall percentage of retail sales on the Internet averages just 5% across all categories, that shift will still create tremendous pressure on physical retailers, particularly in the United States. The United States has more square meters of retail space per capita than any other developed country in the world, even adjusting for purchasing power. Essentially, the United States is "overstored". Space is more readily available there, so stores tend to be larger. Increased and sustained use of online shopping will spawn more intense competition among physical retailers, and some stores will close.

Of course, the impact of e-commerce will be felt differently, and at different times, by different retailers. Right now, the Internet is more of a transactional-sales medium than a relationship-building medium. And so retailers that market their own, very premium branded goods – that is, retailers that sell a lifestyle concept along with their particular products or services – might not be feeling the competitive pinch just yet. Personal contact with highly trained and motivated salespeople – the service factor and in part the ambience factor – is still the critical differentiator for such businesses, and online experiences have yet to match that or offer a suitable counter value.

But for retailers that offer convenience goods, the Internet is a more immediate concern. Some retailers have fallen back on the in-store experience as a point of differentiation both from other retailers and from e-commerce competitors. It might be more prudent for them to concentrate instead on improving their value propositions - the performance of their product or service assortment relative to its price - because apart from the look of a store, it is very difficult to deliver a consistent in-store shopping experience. In a physical store, you are employing full-time and part-time workers, some of whom may have no personal interest at all in the product they are selling. For all sorts of reasons, the customer's experience is unpredictable. It is routinely easier to offer a consistent experience online.

Finally, for supermarkets, wholesale clubs and retailers that offer a great assortment of merchandise, the Internet may pose a threat that is presently unformed but may someday be formidable. Manufacturers that today reach consumers through retailers and wholesalers may soon find it necessary to sell directly to end users. Supermarkets may think they are immune, but we know from the experiences of Peapod and Streamline that at least a small percentage of consumers are now willing to pay a premium to buy over the Internet. What if Colgate-Palmolive or Proctor & Gamble began offering monthly "care packages" to consumers over the Internet? There might be incremental shipping costs, but those costs might be offset by the convenience.

In addition, manufacturers might find e-commerce a good way to lock in customers to their product portfolios over time. They might launch their own frequent-buyer or reward programs. Smaller manufacturers could engage in strategic alliances to do the same. Two-income households that are time sensitive and price insensitive have the greatest purchasing power.

Given the current state of e-commerce, physical retailers should concentrate on the five factors – and e-commerce, both as competition and as opportunity. Many retailers are highly predictable in the way they face the dilemma of how much to bet their futures on e-commerce and how much to concentrate on traditional retailing, and therefore they are thinking defensively. They believe they must have a Web site to avoid being thought of as behind the times, but they don't really know if they need to go the whole hog into the online world. And they are not sure how their physical stores must be to excel in the long term.

The best advice is to not enter e-commerce half-heartedly. If you decide to enter e-commerce, skip the brochure site and move directly into sales. But don't even try to go online unless you are confident that you are thinking clearly and correctly about the five factors and about how they work for and against the consumers whom you consider to be your target market.

ESTABLISHING THE INTERNET BUSINESS STRATEGY

The bright line that once distinguished the dot-com from the incumbent is rapidly fading. Companies are recognizing that success in the new economy will go to those who can execute clicks-and-mortar strategies that bridge the physical and the virtual worlds. But in forging such strategies, executives face a decision that is as difficult as it is crucial: should we integrate our Internet business with our traditional business or should we keep the two separate? Despite the obvious benefits that integration offers – cross-promotion, shared information, purchasing leverage, distribution economies, and the like – many executives now assume that Internet businesses need to be separate to thrive. They believe that the very nature of a traditional business – its protectiveness of current customers, its fear of cannibalization, its general myopia – will smother any Internet initiative.

Barnes & Noble is one company that embraced such thinking. To compete with Amazon.com, it established a completely separate division – BarnesandNoble.com – which it ultimately spun off as a stand-alone company. By breaking free of the existing organization, the online outfit gained many advantages. It was able to speed up its decision making, maintain a high degree of flexibility, create an entrepreneurial culture, attract quality management, and tap into the vast pool of capital available to Internet start-ups. But despite those benefits, BarnesandNoble.com has struggled. By divorcing its online business from its established stores, Barnes & Noble may have actually sacrificed more than it gained. For example, the company forfeited tremendous marketing opportunities by not promoting BarnesandNoble.com in its stores.

The benefits of integration are almost always too great to abandon entirely. Instead of focusing on an either-or choice – 'Should we develop our Internet channel in-house or launch a spin-off?' – executives should be asking, 'What degree of integration makes sense for our company?'

Office Depot has found success by tightly integrating its Web site and its physical stores to form a single seamless network. The company has two very good reasons to integrate the online business rather than spin it off. First, its existing catalog sales operation provided it with much of the service infrastructure needed to support an Internet store. Second, years earlier it had developed a sophisticated information system containing complete product, vendor, customer and order information as well as real-time inventory data for each of the company's 1,825 stores and 30 warehouses. That system made it easy to coordinate Office Depot's online store and its physical outlets. By providing information about store locations and inventory levels online, Office Depot's Web site has actually increased the traffic at its physical outlets. At the same time, the company uses its stores to promote its site. Rather than cannibalize each other, the two channels promote each other, creating a virtuous circle.

Office Depot's experience shows that in some cases, the benefits of integration overwhelm the advantages of separation. If OfficeDepot had set up its Web operation as a stand-alone business, it may have achieved greater organizational focus and flexibility, but it would have sacrificed the customer benefits and the strategic advantages that come from integration, such as cross-selling, brand recognition and purchasing leverage. As a separate operation, OfficeDepot.com would have been just another e-retailer struggling to attract customers while fighting endless price wars.

Other retailing sectors are less amenable to a tight integration between bricks and clicks. Take toys, for example. Big toy retailers don't have much expertise with catalog retailing; they tend to focus exclusively on their physical stores. So launching a Web store would require creating a whole new direct-marketing infrastructure and developing a new set of management skills. Also, toy shoppers tend to be highly price-sensitive – in stark contrast to business supplies buyers, who place a high value on a retailer's flexibility and responsiveness. If your customers want flexibility, creating a new channel provides added value to them. If all they care about is getting the lowest price, a new channel merely creates more competition for your existing outlets.

Rather than create its own Web store from scratch, KB Toys joined forces with BrainPlay.com, an e-retailer of children's products, to create KBkids.com. By joining with an existing e-retailer, KB Toys has been able to capitalize on the advantages of both integration and separation. Organizationally, KBkids keeps its distance from KB Toys. It is run largely by the management team and technical staff that launched BrainPlay. These people are used to moving at Internet speed and dealing with the unique challenges of e-commerce, and they have been able to maintain the fast-paced and free-wheeling culture of a dot-com start-up. Although they appear to be completely separate, the two companies are actually tightly integrated in certain respects. Most obvious is the shared brand. The physical stores heavily promote the Web site through in-store advertising and displays.

Another area of integration lies in customer service. Anything bought online at KBkids can be returned at any of the more than 1,300 bricks-and-mortar KB Toys stores. That provides an enormous convenience to Web shoppers – another advantage that pure-play e-retailers cannot match. At the same time, it helps the physical stores by getting more customers to walk through the door. A third integration advantage lies at the opposite end of the business – in the purchasing function, where KBkids has been able to fully leverage KB Toys' relationships with suppliers. Lacking this kind of purchasing leverage, the pure-play e-retailers are hard pressed to match KBkids' prices without falling ever farther into the red. The integrated companies have the clout to negotiate exclusives with suppliers.

The drugstore industry has seen the rise of a variety of clicks-and-mortar strategies. Walgreens.com, for example, is fully owned and operated by its bricks-and-mortar parent. Drugstore giant Rite Aid took a different approach, one centered on partnership rather than ownership. Rite Aid opted to import Internet expertise from Drugstore.com. Yet, Rite Aid and Drugstore.com are separately owned and managed, and although both brands are promoted in both channels, they remain distinct. Keeping separate names while promoting the partnership accomplishes two things. It protects the trust and recognition associated with the Rite Aid name and at the same time establishes a clean brand that fits online expectations. Rite Aid and Drugstore.com have also integrated many of their business functions including fulfillment. The Rite Aid – Drugstore.com partnership fits consumers as well as the two businesses. Customers can elect to pick up their Drugstore.com prescriptions at their local Rite Aid rather than wait for them to be shipped – a huge advantage, since 30% of all prescriptions are needed immediately. Rite Aid also enjoys increased store traffic. Ultimately, the partnership between Rite Aid and Drugstore.com lets each company take advantage of the other's expertise without sacrificing flexibility.

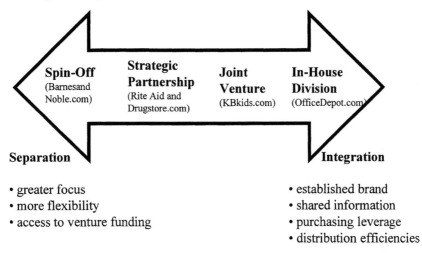

Figure 2-1: Spectrum of Click-and-Mortar Strategies

As the divergent strategies of Office Depot, KB Toys, and Rite Aid reveal, the integration-separation decision is not a binary choice. There are infinite permutations along the integration spectrum. By thinking carefully about which aspects of a business to integrate and which to keep distinct, companies can tailor their clicks-and-mortar strategies to their own particular market and competitive situation, dramatically increasing the odds of e-business success. In order to determine the optimal level of integration of the physical business and the online business, it is useful to examine four business dimensions – brand, management, operations and equity – and determine the degree of integration that makes sense along each.

Brand. The choice to integrate brands or keep them separate is largely a choice between trust and flexibility. Extending a company's current brand to the Internet gives instant credibility to a Web site (assuming, of course, that the brand is both recognized and respected). The company's current Internet-savvy customers will provide nearly immediate traffic and revenue, new consumers will know that the site is legitimate, and fewer buyers will fear credit card fraud – a frequent inhibitor of online transactions. Brand integration can result in a virtuous circle, sending online customers to the physical stores and brick-and-mortar store customers online, all the while continuing to build the brand. But in integrating a brand, a company often loses flexibility. An online store may be forced to offer the same products and prices as its physical counterparts – or risk leaving customers confused and distrustful. With a shared brand, it also becomes more difficult to use the Internet to target a different customer segment. A little creativity can pay huge dividends in the Internet space.

Management. Whether a firm should integrate or separate its management teams is a subtler question whose answer hinges both on management attitudes and on the company's business model. An integrated team can better align strategic objectives, find and exploit synergies, and share knowledge. Separate teams can focus more sharply, innovate more freely, and avoid contaminating one business model with another. Even here, companies don't have to make an all-or-nothing decision – they can integrate certain functions and leave other separate.

Operations. Decisions about integrating operations should be based on the strength of a company's existing distribution and information systems and their transferability to the Internet. Integration can provide significant cost savings, a more compelling and informative site, and a competitive advantage over pure-play competitors. Separation lets a company build state-of-the-art, customized systems without the flaws of older systems and develop sophisticated Internet-specific distribution capabilities that could provide a superior customer experience.

Equity. Integration allows the parent to capture the entire value of its Internet business. Separation can help attract and retain talented managers and provide access to outside capital. Separate ownership can also offer greater flexibility in partnering with other companies. Finally, by maintaining an equity stake in a separate Internet company, a bricks-and-mortar company could reap a windfall in the stock market.

Clicks-and-mortar businesses are here to stay. The question is, Which models will win? The answer will, to a large extent, be determined by a company's ability to manage the trade-offs between separation and integration. By avoiding an either-or choice and considering each aspect of its business on its own merits, a company can strike the right balance between the freedom, flexibility and creativity that come with separation and the operating, marketing, and information economies that come with integration.

The following factors would tend to favor greater integration between the online and the physical stores:

- The brand extends naturally to the Internet.
- Current executives have the skills and experience needed to pursue the Internet channel.

- Current managers are willing to judge the Internet initiatives by a different set of performance criteria.
- Current distribution systems translate well to the Internet.
- Current information systems provide a solid foundation on which to build.
- Either the current distribution system or the current information constitutes a significant competitive advantage.

The following factors would tend to favor greater separation between the online and the physical stores:

- The online store either targets a different customer segment or offers a different product mix than the physical stores.
- In order to stay competitive, the online stores will need to price differently than the physical stores.
- There will be major channel conflict between the online stores and the physical stores.
- The Internet fundamentally threatens the current business model.
- The Internet division is having trouble attracting and maintaining talented executives.
- Outside capital will be needed to fund the Internet venture.
- A certain supplier, distributor or other partner is key to the success of the online venture.

STRATEGIC ISSUES IN ELECTRONIC RETAILING

Issue 1: Leveraging your firm's logistical system

Direct merchants, such as catalogers, have been quick to incorporate this new technology into their marketing mix. Lands End[1], L.L. Bean[2] and Sharper Image[3] were all early adopters of the Web as an additional channel for sales. They have been able to strategically leverage their existing logistical systems for fulfilling orders generated from the Web. In Dell's case, the Web is a critical channel, extending the firm's capabilities to customize products for users and supporting daily sales of more than $7 million through Web orders. The ability to update prices and product descriptions instantaneously and reduce catalog production costs is making the Web an attractive alternative for catalog retailers.

For traditional retailers selling online, such as Wal-Mart[4], outbound logistical distribution is at issue. Although no one will question the logistics expertise of Wal-mart, the establishment of its Web site has created an electronic catalog, necessitating different types of logistical support. Many retailers have the expertise to handle such operations, but management must decide whether this area of operation fits the corporate mission and can increase shareholder value. Thus, managers should move beyond the simple make-or-buy decision, in terms of logistical support, and focus on the larger issues of the company's long-term competitive positioning.

---

[1] http://www.landsend.com
[2] http://www.llbean.com
[3] http://www.sharperimage.com
[4] http://www.wal-mart.com

Hard goods manufacturers moving into the virtual marketplace face the additional challenge of logistical support in efforts never before undertaken. Such a move not only necessitates developing an outbound logistical infrastructure, but also nurturing the existing channel relationships upon which the firm would be commencing a direct marketing strategy. Could a company like Goodyear Tire & Rubber sell directly to the customer through the Web without upsetting its current channel relationships?

Issue 2: Pricing and managing online transactions

Online pricing is a strategic issue a company must address. First, management must determine whether corporate strategic interest is served by providing pricing information online, making it easily available to consumers and competitors alike. Next, if the company decides to price on the Web, it must consider its Web-based pricing strategy in relationship to its existing pricing structure. The simplest path is to maintain a standardized pricing policy throughout all markets, even though it may be inconsistent with current strategy, such as locational pricing, segmentation, etc. Effective strategies might include using a ship-to, national pricing policy similar to that used by catalog retailers. A firm can establish a single price for each product and allocate relevant shipping costs based on shipping destination. However, management must be careful of differences between Web-based prices and prices currently charged in its traditional channels. Differences across channels could create instances of price arbitrage.

Sales necessitate a financial exchange. Spiegel[5], L.L.Bean, OfficeMax[6], and Wal-Mart all provide for online purchasing. These companies are at the cutting edge of direct Web marketing technology. Online sales, however, are still restricted by financial transaction limitations. Many customers are unwilling to provide credit card information online because of the perceived security risks.

Management should also consider how to integrate new and innovative methods of payment, such as cyber-credit or cyber-cash, into their Web site. Cyber-credit, through the use of systems such as Secure Electronic Transactions (SET), uses advanced encryption technology to safeguard credit card account numbers while minimizing chargebacks. Alternatively, cyber-cash uses Internet banking intermediaries that operate as debit accounts. Funds are transferred electronically from a customer's debit account to the financial institution of the merchant. The companies that are first to overcome today's financial challenges may be able to achieve greater online market share in their respective industries.

Issue 3: Optimizing communication to key consumer markets

The communication elements of advertising, sales promotion, and public relations are all strategic options when communicating with various publics. The Web provides a means for integrating the marketing communications mix. This gives companies a relatively low-cost method of increasing shareholder value and enhancing their image by offering customers a variety of highly specialized information.

---

[5] http://www.spiegel.com
[6] http://www.officemax.com

Issue 4: Achieving excellence through service

The Web creates a vehicle by which companies can enhance their customers' service experiences. Some firms have continued to expand customer service through the Web, increasing their overall service offering and creating a higher standard in the industry.

STRATEGIC ISSUES IN MARKETSPACE ELECTRONIC COMMERCE

Issue 1: Selling in a virtual world

Marketspace sales are derived from the interaction of consumer, intermediary, and supplier in a virtual information-based transaction environment. The selling space offers the potential of interconnecting all parties to the transaction. This new environment allows for full dispersion of information across parties, paving the way for more effective production and inventory scheduling. Further, the marketspace gives manufacturers direct access to their final consumers.

Issue 2: Staying real or becoming virtual

Another issue concerning the marketspace revolves around whether the firm should maintain its traditional establishments – brick-and-mortar or catalog – or move to the virtual commercial marketspace.

Issue 3: Communicating with a community

Industry-related sites are generating communities of interest in which manufacturers, retailers and consumers discuss the appropriate development of new products and services. This growth of electronic communities aiding the development of new initiatives has been reflected in several Web sites. Some firms welcome the establishment of these communities and support the discussion of key issues. Major pharmaceutical manufacturers, such as Johnson & Johnson[7] provide online support and advice to consumers and the research community regarding diseases, prescriptions, treatments, and current research. Similar electronic communities have evolved in the marketspace to discuss products and provide feedback from consumers to both the product manufacturer and the intermediary sales agent. Through the development of these communities, companies can take an active stance in the market, monitoring input from all sources to develop their strategies.

Issue 4: Value-added services in the marketspace

Some of the biggest success stories on the Web have leveraged service. Yahoo, Excite and the Internet Yellow Pages are just a few of them. Playing the role of value-added intermediaries, these search engines and directory sites help sellers and buyers find each other, facilitating electronic exchange while considerably reducing search time.

---

[7] http://www.johnsonandjohnson.com

Moreover, they provide the services to build the infrastructure for information retrieval and dissemination across the marketspace. Identifying and leveraging strategic value-enhancing opportunities in the Web-based marketspace will be a driving force of tomorrow's leading businesses.

STRATEGIC ISSUES IN DIRECT MARKETING IN ELECTRONIC COMMERCE

Issue 1: Eliminating intermediaries

Organizations must consider the impact a Web site will have on any pre-existing channel structure. Over the past 20 years, companies have worked hard to establish strong channel partnerships. The establishment of Web sites for direct sales has influenced current distribution structures and channel relationships. For a manufacturer, using the Web can mean creating a new channel. The use of a direct-marketing strategy must be factored into the company's channel policy. Firms considering a direct marketing strategy must carefully weigh the costs and benefits and the value of their current channel relationships to their market offering.

Issue 2: Establishing your place in the value chain

The new model of the value chain that has evolved from these new technologies is referred to as a virtual value chain. It is formed when the traditional value chain is altered to bypass the intermediaries and allow consumers to reach producers directly. Many large and small investors have begun using online trading companies, such as Ameritrade[8], rather than full-service brokerage firms. Online brokerage firms offer customers large financial savings, thus enhancing the value brought to the marketplace for investors interested solely in executing transactions. Intermediaries finding themselves being removed from the channel such as full-service brokerage firms, need to redefine or specialize the nature of the services they offer in order to provide more value to customers. They must secure their place in the market as they face competition from increasing Web site sales.

Issue 3: Comparative information in a virtual world

Information clearing houses are new institutions on the electronic landscape. In some cases, they have created direct marketing situations for suppliers by circumventing their pre-existing channel network and providing information directly to consumers. In the travel industry, Web sites such as Internet Travel Network[9], Travelcity[10], and Travel Web[11] offer consumers a wide array of comparative data regarding the market offerings of selected firms (travel destinations, agencies, airlines). Not only do these Web sites

---

[8] http://www.ameritrade.com

[9] http://www.itn.com

[10] http://www.travelcity.com

[11] http://www.travelweb.com

provide objective information concerning issues such as prices, they often provide subjective information about overall market offerings.

As these online businesses continue to grow, so will their influence. This leads to a number of strategic questions that suppliers (such as travel destinations) may wish to consider in attempting to leverage these new institutions: What aspects of your market offering do consumers use to evaluate your products? How can you best strategically position your offering in this highly competitive environment? How will you ensure that the information provided on these Web sites is accurate and positive?

Issue 4: Optimizing the service offering across partner firms

Few companies are actively trying to take away the service functions from their intermediary partners. However, scenarios are opening up in which the development of customer loyalty and expectations of service offerings do not include the intermediary provider. One example is in the provision of technical support for software and electronic products. In each case, consumers rarely contact the initial place of purchase for assistance, but look directly to the product developer or manufacturer. This direct connection between consumers and developers/manufacturers has led several companies to develop extensive online technical support resources, including Sun Microsystems[12], Microsoft and Sony Electronics[13]. In these cases, business partners have taken on additional responsibilities at the call of the marketplace.

INTRODUCING NEW TECHNOLOGIES INTO RETAILING

In the past, retailers connected with their customers through their stores, through their salespeople, through the brands and packages they sold, and through direct mail and advertising in the mass media. Today, there are many new ways to attract and engage customers – and none of them are more tempting than those fueled by new technologies. Indeed, even if one omits the obvious – the Web – retailers are still surrounded by technical innovations that promise to redefine the way they and manufacturers interact with customers. Examples of the new technologies include touch-screen kiosks, electronic shelf labels and signs, handheld shopping assistants, smart cards, self-scanning systems, virtual reality displays and intelligent agents.

These technologies will change the way retailers interface with customers in the future, however, not all of these technologies will be successful. Some of these technologies will succeed, but many will be disappointing failures. Senior managers in retailing today have to decide which technologies to embrace, where to spend precious resources, and when to pull the plug if success isn't measurable and immediate.

Hardware and software systems frequently require new expertise to implement, they are often incompatible with existing systems, and they quickly become obsolete. Retailers also worry that new technologies might threaten their existing businesses. For example, many conventional retailers have hesitated to embrace electronic commerce because they fear that when consumers shop online, they will make fewer impulse purchases and become more price sensitive.

---

[12] http://www.sun.com
[13] http://www.sony.com

Customers often see little or no value in new technologies. Why should they learn to use a self-checkout system if checkers are willing to do the work for them? Why would they use a product locator kiosk when they can ask a salesperson? Consumers also worry that technology is becoming too intrusive. They have concerns about the privacy of their personal information and the security of their financial transactions.

It is easy to be dazzled by new technologies and conclude that they represent the future of retailing. However, that conclusion would be wrong. Technology is just a platform for change. How the technology is used to create value for customers is what will determine the future – and that is the opportunity that must be addressed. To avoid costly failures, retailers need to be better prepared for the next generation of technologies that interact with customers. There are some lessons we can learn from past experiences.

Lesson 1: Use technology to create an immediate, tangible benefit for the consumers

If consumers don't see how technology is going to help them, they often assume that it is going to be used against them. When UPC scanners were first introduced, people reacted negatively because they believed that merchandise would no longer carry individual price tags and that shoppers might be overcharged at the register.

Lesson 2: Make technology easy to use

Most computer technology is pretty complex. Take Internet shopping, for example. Each site requires consumers to navigate slightly differently. Sites organize product categories in different ways, they provide different types of information about products, and they have different procedures for ordering and fulfillment. It takes customers an average of 20 to 30 minutes just to learn how to shop in most text-based Internet grocery-shopping systems. By contrast, it takes them only 2 to 3 minutes to learn how to shop in a 3-D virtual store modeled after a familiar bricks-and-mortar shop. The virtual store takes advantage of the shopper's prior knowledge to make virtual shopping more intuitive.

Lesson 3: Execution matters: prototype, test and refine

Many technologies are viable concepts but fail because of poor execution.

Lesson 4: Recognize that customers' response to technology varies

It is very difficult to create one customer interface that works well for everyone.

Lesson 5: Build systems that are compatible with the way customers make decisions

Many companies developing the next generation of customer interface technologies spend more time interacting with computers than with customers. As a result, the systems are often incompatible with customers' shopping habits.

Lesson 6: Study the effects of technology on what people buy and on how they shop

Researchers have found that consumers are more price sensitive when using text-based home-shopping systems that display lists of brands and prices than when using graphical systems that show realistic images of merchandise. Also brand names become less important as the amount of detailed information about a product's attributes increases. In some cases, technology has produced less of an effect on consumers' behavior than managers had feared. For example, a grocery retailer reported that impulse purchases were down by just 5% when customers shopped online. About the same amount of perishable products were purchased per order online as in the physical store.

Lesson 7: Coordinate all technologies that touch the customer

When a customer encounters a retailer, it shouldn't matter whether the encounter occurs via the Internet, through a catalog, by telephone, or in the physical store. The customer expects to find the same merchandise, offered at the same prices, with the same knowledgeable and courteous service. Unfortunately, it is often the case that a retailer's operations are not well integrated across media. As a consequence, a frequent shopper may be given first-class treatment in the physical store but receive marginal service on the telephone or via the Internet. Retailers need to tap into the same product, customers and transaction databases with all their communications media.

Lesson 8: Revisit technologies that failed in the past

Over the years, various technologies have been introduced with much media fanfare. Then, if the actual performance failed to meet expectations, people wrote them off and shifted their attention to the next innovation. Examples include multimedia kiosks, voice recognition, artificial intelligence, virtual reality and video telephones. However, technology continues to evolve. Performance improves and prices drop. Today, artificial intelligence is used in the selection of retail sites and to facilitate one-to-one marketing programs; voice recognition routes callers to specific store departments; virtual reality is used to test new store layouts and shelf displays; and videoconferencing assists online shoppers. Retailers need to revisit past technologies periodically to consider whether there are new opportunities to create value for customers.

Lesson 9: Use technology to tailor marketing programs to individual customers' requirements

Most conventional retailers design their stores, product offerings, promotions and services for the masses. They treat all shoppers alike even though customers' needs and wants differ and so do the volume and profitability of their purchases. Treating all customers alike puts retailers at a distinct disadvantage relative to those electronic retailers that adjust their marketing programs instantly to match the needs of individual shoppers.

Advances in information technology can give conventional retailers the opportunity to overcome these problems. By setting up frequent-shopper programs and by linking customer profiles to UPC scanner data, retailers can track the shopping patterns, sales volume, and profitability of their patrons. They can then mail out customer-specific fliers and promotions. When shoppers enter the store and swipe their frequent-shopper cards through a reader, a computer can print out customized shopping lists complete with recipes, coupons and suggestions for replenishment purchases. Retailers can tailor their services in any number of ways using the available technology, if they focus on how it can help them help their customers.

Lesson 10: Build systems that leverage existing competitive advantages.

For many years, people have said that a store's location was the key to its success. Now the buzz is that, in the world of electronic retailing, location does not matter. A consumer can do business with a merchant located across the country as easily as with one located across the street. In fact, the argument goes, having a physical store may prove to be a liability, burdening the conventional retailer with unnecessary overhead.

In theory, that may be true. But in practice, it is false. The constraints of time and space still exist. Consumers cannot wait for many types of products to be shipped across the country. Some products cannot be shipped at all. Customers may be reluctant to purchase online because the computer display is limited in its ability to convey important product information. They might prefer to shop at a local retailer because they know its reputation, location, store layout, product selection and return policies.

PATTERNS IN RETAILING

The entire retailing industry is in an acute state of uncertainty. Within every company, at every trade association meeting, in every product category, electronic commerce and its implications dominate the conversation. Fearful of missing an epochal opportunity, investors and executives are rushing to place huge bets on Internet retailing, at what appears to be very high odds. But despite all the talk and frenzied activity, the future of retailing remains decidedly cloudy. It would be foolish to try to predict which companies' Internet strategies will prove profitable in the end. Yet it seems clear that electronic commerce will, on a broad level, change the basis of competitive advantage in retailing.

The essential mission of retailing has always had four elements: getting the right product in the right place at the right price at the right time. The way retailers fulfill that mission has changed as a result of a series of disruptive technologies. A disruptive technology enables innovative companies to create new business models that alter the economics of their industry. In retailing, the first disruption arrived in the form of department stores. The second was the mail-order catalog. The third was the rise of discount department stores. Internet retailing marks the fourth disruption. A diverse group of Internet companies – retailers such as Amazon.com and Autobytel.com, distributors such as Chemdex, travel agencies such as Travelocity.com, and auction sites such as eBay – are poised to change the way things are bought and sold in their markets. These newcomers pose powerful threats to competitors with more conventional business models.

40

While disruptions change the economics of an industry, they don't necessarily change companies' profitability. In retailing, profitability is largely determined by two factors: the margins stores can earn and the frequency with which they can turn their inventory over. The average successful department store, for example, earned gross margins of approximately 40% and turned its inventory over about three times per year. In other words, it made 40% three times a year, a 120% annual return on capital invested in inventory. Compare that with the business model of the average successful discount department store, which earned a 23% gross margin and turned its inventory over five times annually. It achieved a similar return on inventory investment by changing the balance between margins and turnover rates. Internet retailers' profit margins haven't yet converged into a standard range. But if businesses like Amazon.com continue to turn inventory at present rates of 25 times annually, they could achieve traditional returns with margins of 5%.

The retailing disruption instituted by the Internet is now under way, and it promises to alter the retailing landscape fundamentally. Of the four dimensions of the retailer's mission – product, place, price and time – Internet retailers can deliver on the first three remarkably well. The right products? In categories ranging from books to chemicals, Web stores can offer a selection that no bricks-and-mortar outlet can match. The right price? Internet retailers enjoy unparalleled margin flexibility. To earn a 125% return on inventory investment, an Internet retailer such as Amazon.com, which can turn its inventory 25 times each year, needs to earn only 5% gross margins. And the right place? It is here – location – that the Internet is most revolutionary. The Internet negates the importance of location. Anyone, at any time, can become a global retailer by setting up a Web page.

With such advantages, it is no wonder electronic commerce is attracting so much attention. But how should we expect this revolution to evolve? There are two clear patterns in the way earlier retailing disruption unfolded. First, generalist stores and catalogs dominated retailing at the outset of the disruptions, but they were eventually supplanted by specialized retailers. The specialists emerged once the market for the new form of retailing had grown large enough to generate enough sales volume for a narrower but deeper product mix. Second, the disruptive retailers weighted their initial merchandise mix toward products that could sell themselves – simple, branded products whose key attributes could be comprehended visually and numerically. They then shifted their merchandise mix toward higher-margin, more complex products to maintain their profits in the face of intense competition at the low end of their businesses. We appear to be seeing a repeat of the early stages of both those patterns in Internet retailing.

Leading Internet retailers like Amazon.com have rapidly migrated toward the department store strategy. The logic is clear. The Web is a vast and confusing place, and it is currently very difficult to know who is selling what. Anybody with a few thousand dollars can set up a Web-based business. The best Internet search engines today can locate only a fraction of the Web sites that exist in a category. Internet department stores face no physical limits. They can, in theory, offer the depth of the specialist with the breadth of the generalist.

It is possible, therefore, that the Internet department stores will not yield market share to specialized retailers as the volume of purchases in individual categories grows. But there is a counterforce. The inevitable emergence of better search engines, together with the availability of greater bandwidth into homes, will make it increasingly easy for consumers to find specialized electronic retailers. The managerial benefits of focus and the ultimate ease of travel across Web sites will give a slight edge, eventually, to focused players. The odds will tilt toward specialists even more if cybermalls emerge that rent space to a collection of specialist retailers whose category brands are strong – akin to the way today's physical shopping malls have evolved.

As with the earlier disruptions, Internet retailing has initially focused on the simple end of the merchandise spectrum – books, CDs, publicly traded stocks, personal care products, commodity chemicals, and so on. The question is, How fast will the disruptors move upmarket into more complex products and value-added services? Already we see signs of upmarket migration. The transformation of some Internet-based retailers into "clicks and mortar" retailers – establishing warehouses and physical stores to give customers faster access to inventory and to handle returns and service issues conveniently and personally – is not an admission that the Internet retailing doesn't work. Rather, as competition in the simplest tiers heats up, good managers migrate toward higher price points and value-added services to keep their profit margins attractive.

Traditional retailers have always had to make a trade-off between the richness of information they could exchange with customers and the number of customers they could reach. Although local merchants could exchange rich information about products, the economics of providing such expertise meant that they could cater to only a narrow set of customers. To reach a mass market, department stores could not afford to employ expert staff to sell a broad range of complex products. They were forced to provide less rich information. The Internet seems capable of breaking this trade-off. It can enable retailers to communicate rich information about a broad set of complex products to a very large set of customers. That capability should help electronic retailers move upmarket quickly.

Of course, some products are less suited to electronic sale than others. While Internet retailers excel at getting the right product in the right place at the right price, they are at a disadvantage when it comes to delivering physical products at the right time. When shoppers need products immediately, they will head for their cars, not their computers. There are also certain experiences that the Internet cannot deliver. Even with a lot of bandwidth, communicating the feel of clothing and home furnishings will be difficult. And in those customer segments where the social experience of shopping is an important element of value, the home-bound nature of electronic commerce offers little appeal.

Although such constraints appear daunting, they are unlikely to slow the momentum of Internet retailing. Historically, experts have underestimated the ultimate reach of disruptive technologies. Blinded by their perception of the initial limitations of the new technology, they failed to appreciate the strength of the innovators' motivation to move from the fringes of commerce to its mainstream.

ESTIMATING THE SIZE OF THE ONLINE RETAILING MARKET

Electronic commerce has the potential to revolutionize the way individuals and organizations interact. E-commerce offers efficiencies for retailers in the form of increased market access and information, and decreased operating and procurement costs. For consumers, the benefits accrue in the form of enhanced price competition, customization of products, expanded information on goods and services, increased choice of products, and greater shopping convenience.

It is business-to-consumer activity that will potentially have an impact on physical retail. The excitement about rapidly growing electronic commerce sales should be tempered with the knowledge that the business-to-business sector constitutes the majority of the e-commerce growth. The estimate for virtual retail sales in 2003 ($108 billion) is less than 5% of the total estimated U.S. retail sales (excluding automobile sales). The estimates of e-commerce reveal five characteristics:

- Business-to-business sales represent the bulk, roughly 90% of e-commerce sales.
- Business-to-business sales overall, and as a percentage of total e-commerce sales, are expected to grow to represent more than 93% of the total online sales in 2003, exceeding $1 trillion.
- Travel and computer products make up the bulk (more than 75%) of business-to-consumer online sales.
- Four product categories (travel, computers, entertainment and food) will represent more than 81% of total e-retail sales.
- Catalog sales, transferred to the Internet, are expected to represent a significant portion of business-to-consumer electronic commerce revenues with an expected 40% of all catalog sales (approximately $42 billion or roughly 37% of the estimated e-retail revenues) to transfer online by 2003. The top 12 catalog firms all have electronic commerce operations.

The online population is beginning to more closely resemble the average United States resident in terms of age, gender, income, and education. While the demographics of the Internet are shifting, the average Internet user does not yet reflect the average U.S. citizen. A typical Web user today is a college-educated, middle-class, married male working in a computer- or education-related profession and living in a small town.

While consumers are spending more time per week (6.5 hours on average) online – signaling increased comfort with the Internet – the percentage of online shoppers is small. Compared with more than 80% of users that access the Internet to gather information, conduct research and surf, only 18% of Internet users go online to shop, spending an average of $100 per year online, according to Forrester Research. The majority of Web shoppers live in small towns. An end-of-1999 Ernst & Young study found that 51% of online shoppers live in towns with populations of 50,000 or less, compared with only 2% of Internet consumers that live in major metropolitan areas. Internet shopping enhances the convenience in areas where shopping opportunities are more limited.

Fantastic enthusiasm for the electronic retail format accompanies a robust physical retail sales environment. Physical store sales are strong, particularly within the power center and mall formats and the overall retail vacancy rate is near a 16-year low. Aggregate U.S. retail sales for 1999 increased 8% to $2.9 trillion. As further evidence of the robust physical retail sales environment, retailers in all sectors with e-commerce capability are expanding their physical presence at an above-average rate.

Catalysts To E-Retailing

Catalysts to e-retailing include lower operating cost, low cost of capital, sales tax advantage, government support, technology, efficiencies and convenience.

- *Lower Operating Cost.* Particularly for many service-oriented businesses, the Internet offers significant opportunity for operating cost reduction.
- *Lower Cost of Capital.* Three quarters of all venture capital money flowed into Internet companies in 1999.
- *Sales Tax Advantage.* In 1998, Congress enacted a three-year sales tax moratorium on goods sold over the Internet. As a result, pure play online retailers have a 5% to 10% pricing advantage over store-based retailers, which potentially offsets the cost of shipping and handling.
- *Government Support.* Information technology and business-to-business e-commerce sales are catalyzing economic growth. Information technologies contributed about one-third of the U.S. real economic growth in 1998 and electronic commerce – particularly business-to-business online transactions – is expected to significantly add to U.S. GDP in the future. As a result, the U.S. administration has been actively working to increase worldwide digital commerce.
- *Technology.* In the long term, technology will enhance the online experience, enabling easy and more rapid customization, navigation, and ordering. Site infrastructure will become more sophisticated, connection speed will increase, and encryption and payment security will become more standardized and accepted.
- *Efficiencies.* Efficiencies are realized in the form of customer information, complementary product and service offerings, ease of test marketing, and international and new market exposure.
- *Convenience.* Consumers are spending less time shopping but making more shopping trips. E-shopping will become increasingly convenient for certain commodity, staple and personal products.

Deterrents To E-Retailing

Deterrents to e-retailing include the logistics burden, cost of startup and marketing, site differentiation, disintermediation, evolving technology, loss of socialization, loss of sales tax advantage, increased operational flexibility requirements and consumer privacy.

- *Logistics burden.* The major deterrent to e-retailing is the cost of delivery, burden of coordinating receipt of the item purchased, and the cost of return – both for the consumer and for the retailer.
- *Cost of Startup and Marketing.* Large-scale virtual retail operation is expensive short-term and unproven long-term. The virtual store must contend with significant operating expense obstacles associated with startup and site construction, site maintenance, advertising and marketing, distribution, shipping and customer service.
- *Site Differentiation.* Long-term e-commerce site profitability may be questionable. Commodity-type goods, those that have been most successful to-date online, are also

the most price sensitive. Those with a well-known physical presence and brand name will have a competitive advantage over those with only a virtual presence.

- *Disintermediation*. As online pricing pressures escalate (particularly in the commodity goods sector), the online retailer may find profitability unattainable – replaced in some instances by the manufacturer, and in other instances by a more profitable physical store. However, a 1999 study by Ernst & Young suggests that the majority of manufacturers (57%) are unwilling to sell online because of the nature of their product and/or because of perceived channel conflict.
- *Evolving Technology*. The technological foundation for electronic commerce is still evolving. Failures may frustrate shoppers and postpone virtual sales growth. Security software, transaction standards, financial services and bandwidth are examples of some key areas lacking in sophistication. As Internet traffic increases, compatibility issues and decreased download speed will frustrate a number of online shoppers.
- *Loss of Socialization*. Shopping is a social experience. High-priced differentiated goods and apparel need to be physically examined prior to purchase. The act of shopping is, for many, a sort of ritualized event: shopping centers are still destinations. Purchasing through the Web may be convenient for certain product types, but it can also be isolating, unsatisfying and boring. Furthermore, Internet shopping does not satisfy the desire for immediate gratification, often at the root of impulse buying.
- *Loss of Sales Tax Advantage*. The online sales tax moratorium is questionable long term. The introduction of sales tax on Internet purchases would eliminate the 5% to 10% pricing advantage e-retailers have used to cushion the cost of shipping and bolster margins.
- *Increased Operational Flexibility Requirements*. E-retailing requires rapid and continual rethinking of business operations. Technology is quickly outdated and the business model incorporating that technology is equally easily outmoded. E-retailing requires Herculean flexibility and deep pockets.
- *Consumer Privacy*. Abuse of consumer information could deter online shoppers.

PRODUCT-TYPE ANALYSIS

Certain goods and services appear more suitable for an online sales format. In all instances, the Internet provides an opportunity for enhanced customer understanding, service and expanded market access, which may encourage existing brand loyalty. Travel, entertainment and financial services will comprise the majority of business-to-consumer electronic commerce over the next three to five years. Travel and entertainment are expected to represent at least 50% of Internet business-to-consumer sales in 2002. Online brokerage and financial services have grown dramatically. Approximately 20% of Internet-enabled households are investing online. Similarly, the insurance and banking industries are expected to benefit significantly from online exposure.

Commodity goods appear more suited to an online sales model than experience goods. Only a few product categories are expected to dominate business-to-consumer e-commerce. None of these categories is expected to siphon a significant percentage of physical market share in the next 3-5 years, on average taking less than 7% of physical sales, most noticeably in the travel and computer industries. Ultimately, books, music

CDs, video, and higher margin, cheap-to-ship, standardized goods will more effectively transfer to an electronic retail model.

Differentiated, higher-priced, and/or heavier products appear more protected from Internet competition. The online model would require dangerously discounted prices to offset the need for physical interaction with product and service staff. High-priced electronics and entertainment systems generally require a test-drive before purchase. Consumers of luxury items, like expensive jewelry, often demand personal attention, ambiance and a pampered experience to close the deal. Ultimately, heterogeneous and expensive products will be a difficult sell online.

Category	Estimated Sales in $Billions
Travel	11.700
Computer	10.534
Food	6.557
Books	2.200
Apparel	1.926
Gifts	1.381
Music	1.148

Table 2-1:Estimates for E-retail by Category of Goods in 2002

Rank	Site	Product Type
1	Amazon.com	Books, Music, Gifts
2	eBay.com	Auctions
3	eToys.com	Toys / Gifts
4	BarnesandNoble.com	Books, Music, Gifts
5	ToysRUs	Toys / Gifts
6	Buy.com	Computers, Books, Music, Games
7	CDNow.com	Music
8	eGreetings.com	Greeting Cards
9	Expedia.com	Travel
10	Travelocity.com	Travel

Table 2-2: Top 10 Shopping Sites by Reach in Fall 1999

	Books	Sporting Goods	Toys	Computers	Apparel	Electronics	Jewelry	Grocery
Tactility Less Important	Yes	Yes		Yes				
Generally Unpleasant In-store Experience		Yes	Yes	Yes		Yes		
Customization Important			Yes	Yes	Yes	Yes		
Personal Nature	Yes							Yes
High Margin	Yes	Yes	Yes		Yes		Yes	
Cheap-to-Ship	Yes	Yes	Yes	Yes	Yes		Yes	Yes
Instant Gratification Less Important	Yes	Yes		Yes				
Standard	Yes	Yes	Yes	Yes		Yes		
Price Sensitive	Yes	Yes	Yes	Yes		Yes		Yes
Gift Oriented	Yes	Yes	Yes				Yes	
Information Intense	Yes			Yes		Yes		Yes
Score (out of 10)	**9**	**8**	**7**	**8**	**3**	**5**	**3**	**4**

Table 2-3: Product Potential Matrix for E-commerce

PROPERTY-TYPE ANALYSIS

To determine risk level for specific retail property types (malls, community centers, strip centers, power centers), we can examine typical anchor tenants for each retail format in terms of product type, rank product categories in terms of potential sensitivity to Internet sales, and allocate property risk based on perceived anchor susceptibility to Internet-related sales erosion.

Convenience Stores

The convenience orientation of convenience stores will limit the potential erosion from Internet sales. Convenience store sales are at low risk of erosion from Internet sales.

Shopping Malls

Shopping malls are relatively insulated from electronic commerce sales growth. Traditional malls may be vulnerable to other factors, such as shifting consumer preferences for open-air shopping environments. Also, online malls have not been successful. This is because at-home, Internet shopping is often product focused and convenience oriented. Consumers go online with a specific (standardized) product in mind (such as computers, toys, books, sporting goods). Physical shopping malls thrive on the browsing experience and impulse purchases. Online malls and megastores lack both the instant gratification and the visual and tactile component that stimulates impulse buying. Over time, the Internet will cause a shift in tenancy at the mall as different

47

products win acceptance on the Web. Shopping malls have the opportunity to fill the gap between what the Internet offers and customers require, providing entertainment, display, showroom, try-on, tactility, pick-up, delivery, and return and service functions. Overall, shopping malls are at low to medium risk of erosion from Internet sales.

Discount Stores

The economics of the discount stores make them susceptible to online competition. From an economic vantage point, the Internet enables more cost efficient sales of discounted and fringe inventory. Increasingly, department stores are lowering prices to compete with the discount store. As traditional physical competition grows and discount store margins are compressed, the e-model emerges as a more viable sales format. Overall, the discount store is at low to medium risk to e-sales displacement.

Power Centers

Power centers are a higher risk due to electronic commerce sales displacement. The majority of power center tenants trade on price and are product/category focused. For example, book, toy and sporting goods stores are typical power center anchors. Power centers are at higher risk because most tenants will have to be particularly adaptable. Eventually, power centers may evolve into distribution/warehouse nodes. Overall, the power center is at medium to high risk to Internet sales displacement.

Lessons from the Historical Evolution of Other Retail Models

It is important to observe retailer adaptability. Shopping mall product and tenant mix has shifted dramatically over time and in response to new retail formats. Reacting to the emergence of the power center, shopping malls reduced the number of book, music and toy store tenants, replacing them with food, entertainment and fashion merchandisers. Rather than negatively affecting regional centers, the consistent materialization of new retail formats has strengthened the strong – and eliminated the weak – retailers, forcing efficiency and focus. Physical retail sales today are robust, and leasing activity for some centers is unprecedented. Just as the discounter format did not materially affect mall profitability, to date a rapidly expanding electronic commerce market has not negatively influenced brick-and-mortar expansion plans. The question remains: Can traditional retailers successfully acclimatize to the latest retail blueprint? If history were our guide, the answer would be yes.

THE POTENTIAL OF ELECTRONIC RETAIL

The Near-Term View

Near-term business-to-consumer electronic commerce will have a limited impact on both physical real estate and retail sales because of habit, low conversion rates, current technology, distribution difficulties and unprofitability. First, changing decades-old shopping habits will take more than a couple of years. Second, only a minority percentage of the online population actually purchases a good or service and a significant number of Web shoppers have been frustrated by the experience. Top physical shopping malls get one in three visitors making a purchase. Comparatively, roughly one in 200 visitors to the online malls make a purchase. Third, bandwidth constraints and the resulting slow download speed and poor site resolution offset the convenience of online shopping. Fourth, the time lag in gratification together with the cost of delivery and inconvenience of return will restrict consumer e-retail acceptance. Finally, in the near-term, e-retailers are not expected to be profitable as they trade margins for market share growth.

The Long-Term View

Long-term, electronic commerce will affect the entire retail spectrum. The Internet and e-commerce will encourage the following ten trends.
- E-retail will encourage a more purely competitive retail model, with lower prices and increased competition.
- Growth in e-retail will compress retailer margins.
- The Internet will stimulate greater emphasis on customization, both in store and out of store.
- Online sales will erode physical retail sales in over-stored sectors and among already-weak retailers.
- Pure-play e-retailers will build showroom and return centers to better market and service their product.
- E-retail will stimulate shifts in shopping centers' tenant mix, with an emphasis on entertainment, interactive experiences, theme stores, music, luxury goods, food, apparel and convenience items.
- Retailers will use improvements in technology and growth in Internet usage to leverage the benefits of the physical store, for example, shifting from mass promotion to targeted marketing efforts.
- The Internet will enable the development of a manufacturer-to-consumer sales model for certain high-speed, commodity products (for example, washing machines and computers). Retailers will emphasize their role as value-added distributors, with edited product assortments, personal service and experience.
- Retail property values will, in general, adjust downwards to compensate for the perceived risk of Internet sales erosion. The dominant retail model in the future will continue to be the physical store, albeit in an altered format.
- There will be shifts in leasing and in retail format (including a transition from big box retail to distribution/warehouse use), changes in parking/loading area requirements depending on pick-up and delivery strategies, lower improvement allowances for commodity, staple and at-risk retailers, and alternative measures of profitability used to evaluate retailers' performance.
- It is recommended that there should be an emphasis on tenants with a dual (physical/virtual) presence, financial stability, differentiated products, a high level of customer service, and business-to-business enabled e-commerce systems.

Given the revolutionary nature of technology and the speed with which it is affecting all aspects of commerce, it is difficult to accurately predict the ultimate impact of the Internet on physical real estate. The effect will be relatively small over the next three to five years. Beyond that point, real estate owners will experience losses in income and value if they have not adjusted their business strategy to take advantage of the Internet. There will be an opportunity for investors to win and lose. E-retail will affect the next evolution in retail stores and shopping centers, shave retail operating margins, impose new capital demands on retailers and shopping center owners, and require investment decisions based on the opportunity and threat of the Internet to present and prospective tenants. E-retail has the potential to increase brand awareness, direct customers to physical retail establishments, enhance the in-store retail shopping experience, and generate demand for return, delivery, showroom, and service-oriented and experience-oriented retail sites.

FINDING SUSTAINABLE PROFITABILITY IN ELECTRONIC COMMERCE

While many e-commerce retailers head toward commodity pricing, there are a few that are likely to profit on the Web. Only retailers who match market segment to correct strategy will win. How can business strategists discriminate between types of e-commerce that will likely be attractive and profitable and those that will end up in a commodity-market structure? Understanding the role of product quality, information transmission, reputation and risk in the context of industry structure and company capabilities can help us answer these nagging questions. A market segmentation analysis of the online retail trade can shed light on the industry and product characteristics that drive profitability. These findings lead to a set of segment-specific strategies that companies can employ to reach above-industry-average profits and, presumably, high and sustainable market valuations.

Products possess different attributes and different levels of the same attributes. For example, one important dimension on which goods differ is in the ability of consumers to ascertain the quality of products in cyberspace. On one end of the spectrum are commodity products, where quality can be clearly and contractually articulated and conveyed. On the other end of the continuum are products for which the perception of quality differs from consumer to consumer and product to product, such as used cars and works of art. Understanding how difficult it is for retailers to convey quality, reliability, or consistency for certain classes of products over the Web enables business people to think strategically about the likely long-term success of different types of e-commerce ventures.

Commodity Products

Paper clips, nails, and even Internet bandwidth, compose this new e-commerce market. In these commodity markets, the quality of products can easily be determined by their description. Consumers in these markets care little about the identity of the seller; they only care about the correct characterization of the products, the price and the terms of delivery.

Quasi-Commodity Products

The biggest increase in e-commerce has occurred in quasi-commodity products. Books, videos, CDs, toys and new cars all fall into this class of products. Economists consider these differentiated products. Consumers engage in a two-stage decision-making process. First, the consumer must find a book he prefers among the many different books available. After selecting the title, the consumer cares primarily about its price and the reliability of the e-commerce vendor.

Experience Goods

When it comes to cosmetics, suits, upholstered furniture or model homes, unbranded products have difficulty competing with their branded counterparts on the Web. Consumers need to actually touch, feel, try on, or see these products in person before they buy. Look-and-feel goods have a common characteristic – their quality is very difficult to assess from afar. Consumers in this segment may be reluctant to buy a product or unknown or less than fully known quality. But once a consumer has selected a product, there are likely few substitutes. The characteristics of other competing products will probably differ on many dimensions, including quality, look, feel and reliability. The experience goods segment is truly a differentiated market in all respects.

Experience Goods With Variable Quality

These are products where, even if the buyer has completed her search, knows the product, and recognizes the brand, she will need to see and perhaps touch and feel the individual product that will be delivered to her home or business. The distinguishing feature is that each and every individual product is different from every other. Original art and used cars fall into this category.

Two important subtleties of this framework need to be recognized. First, it is important to notice that as you move from commodity goods to quasi-commodity goods to experience goods to experience goods with variable quality, it is not only the intensity of the consumer experience that changes. In addition, a number of other aspects of the buying process change, such as how much more information the seller has about the product than the buyer, the need of the consumer to engage in a search for optimal goods, and the degree to which seller reputation is important. Second, the purpose of the product and the need to engage in searching might determine the segment to which it belongs.

SELECTING MARKETS AND GAINING COMPETITIVE ADVANTAGE

There is no single optimal strategy, because the sources of competitive advantage differ across product segments.

Commodity Goods Market Strategy

Industry structure in commodity markets is inherently unattractive. Companies are price takers held in check by customers willing and able to seek the lowest price on the same product from many competitors. Thus market power is difficult if not impossible to obtain; customer lock-in and customer loyalty are elusive. The only strategy available to managers in this market segment is to drive down costs in order to obtain profits.

The low-cost strategy would involve the following components:
- Take advantage of economies of scale.

- Utilize low-cost production technology.
- Achieve efficient distribution and low overhead.

Quasi-Commodity Goods Market Strategy

The purchase of quasi-commodity products is a two-stage process. In the first stage, consumers conduct a product search in a differentiated product market. In the second stage, consumers conduct a price search for the preferred product. The strategic challenge for companies in these markets is to differentiate themselves on the first dimension (search) and to insulate themselves from price competition in the second dimension. The problem for companies in these markets is that once a book – or any quasi-commodity product – is selected using their powerful search engines, the consumer may purchase it from another e-commerce vendor at a lower price. Web-based intermediaries are making it even easier to search for the lowest price. Yahoo, E-Compare, and other search engines will now search 10 or more Web bookstores for your title and return to you a list of vendors who have the book and their prices.

Given what is potentially fierce price competition in the second stage of this quasi-commodity market, how can companies carve out their own niche positions and retain market power? First movers will have some advantage in this market. Early movers have historically had the highest Web-site "stickiness". In addition, mechanisms that encourage consumers to stay on a site, such as creating virtual communities so consumers can talk to each other, or site-specific customer loyalty and reward programs, will be quite important for attracting repeat purchasers and engendering repeat visits.

Branding will be an important part of any quasi-commodity strategy. Product brands will not be a point of differentiation for the e-commerce vendor, but e-commerce brands will be key. Strong e-commerce brands can signal quality in the reliability of delivery, security of personal information, dependability of the return policy and customer service in general. Firms that wish to make above-industry-average margins in this business will have to invest in building e-commerce brands.

The differentiation strategy for the first stage would involve the following components:
- Use information technology to differentiate Web service.
- Develop search engines that match consumer preferences to products quickly and precisely.
- Employ database management tools that allow real-time data mining.
- Make Web site "sticky", i.e., include features that encourage Web shoppers to stay on the site.
- Offer one-stop shopping.
- Seek first-mover advantage.
- Establish e-commerce branding.

The low-cost and differentiation strategy for the second stage would involve the following components:
- Take advantage of economies of scale.
- Seek preferential treatment with wholesale suppliers.
- Ensure that the delivery of the product is reliable and timely.

- Offer additional customer services such as chat rooms, affinity programs, and other technologies to increase Web-site stickiness.
- Offer site-specific customer loyalty programs.

Experience Goods Market Strategy

In the consumer's quest for information about the quality and characteristics of the product, strong product brands will become the kingpins. Established brands provide a substantial amount of information about the product to the consumer. Well-branded incumbents, precisely because of their ability to differentiate their products, will be able to wield substantial market power and therefore obtain large profits in this segment of the market. Given the power of product brands in the experience goods market, it is highly unlikely that we will see entrepreneurs successfully inundating this space in quest of profits. More likely, we will see the rise of two forms of distribution, led by traditional incumbents. The first is a wholly owned vertical distribution system. Such markets will be difficult for e-commerce vendors to penetrate without a strong brand or entry position.

The experience goods market has a number of attractive features, including oligopolistic competition, high entry barriers and customer loyalty, which are likely to promote profits in the long term. Successful companies in these product classes can retain substantial market power, as price competition is mitigated through substantial product differentiation. The effective strategic alternatives for the pure e-commerce vendor in this segment of the market are not attractive: Either participate in the vertical structure of the market and make the investments in brands, where entry is difficult, or participate in the distribution of branded products, where the specter of price competition raises its head. Incumbent retailers in the experience goods segment are likely to survive the transition to an Internet-based economy in large numbers.

The full differentiation strategy for vertically integrated firms would involve the following components:
- Establish the equivalent of store brands.
- Incorporate latest technologies to convey look and feel to customers (e.g., virtual model and sizing technologies).
- Excel at online customer service with both interactive and phone customer support.
- Offer industry-leading warranties and return policies.

The additional differentiation strategy for hybrid firms would involve the following components:
- Employ creative pricing strategies (i.e., time-preference-based pricing).
- Provide showrooms to display merchandise.
- Develop bifurcated back-end logistics and delivery systems to ensure on-time delivery in the showrooms and to the customer at home.

Experience Goods With Variable Quality Market Strategy

In this category, quality is not only difficult to communicate, but it also varies by product, creating large obstacles for e-commerce. Each individual product needs to be inspected by the consumer. In the near future, survival and profitability in this segment will be difficult. Managers must exploit two instruments under their control: price and reputation. Repeat purchases allow the e-commerce vendor to build a reputation for quality by repeated provision of the product to a given consumer. Inexpensive products allow the consumer to mitigate risk. If the consumer does not perceive the products to be of high quality, the loss is relatively low and he can take his future business elsewhere. Thus, inexpensive prices give consumers the incentive to experiment and give the e-commerce vendor the opportunity to build a reputation. A good reputation coupled with low prices will allow some firms to survive in this segment.

The strategy for this market segment would involve the following components:

- Keep abreast of and use advances in Web-cam technology.
- Combine Web-search technologies with delivery logistics to deliver the precise items viewed on the Web.
- Develop build-to-order technical capabilities.
- Offer inexpensive products that lend themselves to repeat purchasing.
- Build reputation for quality and reliability.

Sustaining a Competitive Advantage

Traditional incumbents have substantial advantage in products that tend toward the experience-goods end of the spectrum and encounter difficulty in products that tend toward the commodity-goods end of the spectrum. That is not to say that traditional incumbents will not succeed in the commodity-goods end of the spectrum, but that they are likely to find the playing field more even in those markets, as their brands and brick-and-mortar stores provide little advantage. Incumbents in the commodity- and quasi-commodity segments with first-mover advantage and strong histories in information technology and serving a customer at a distance can become exceptions to this general rule. Such incumbents can reap rewards in these fiercely competitive segments. Commodity-goods markets are easy to enter, but profit margins are low. Experience-goods markets are difficult to enter, but they confer high margins.

Branding strategy will be important. In the commodity and quasi-commodity product segments, the actual e-commerce vendor brand is important to the extent that it signals reliability and customer service. In the experience-goods markets, product brands will dominate as a source of competitive advantage. And both e-commerce brands and product brands are important sources of competitive advantage in the experience-goods-with-variable-quality segment. An e-commerce start-up's brand strategy will be substantially determined by the markets it serves. The opportunity for new e-commerce brands has arisen in the commodity- and quasi-commodity segments. Hence, we see the rise of Amazon.com, Buy.com and Travelocity.com.

Chapter 3

Creating Value for Customers in Electronic Commerce

CUSTOMER RELATIONSHIP MANAGEMENT IN ELECTRONIC COMMERCE

The development of any successful marketing strategy depends on specification of a target market. The size of the target market can range from mass market to market niche. When market segmentation occurs, it has generally been based on demographic, geographic or lifestyle-related criteria.

Electronic commerce makes it possible to take market segmentation to another level, by providing an economical means by which firms can deliver individualized products and services to each and every customer, based on feedback and interaction with the customers. Relationship marketing strategies embrace this idea of treating each customer in an individualized way. A short-term focus on transactions is rejected in favor of an emphasis on the development of mutually beneficial long-term relationships with customers. Not only is the long-term approach viewed as serving the customer's best interests, but it is viewed as serving a firm's self-interest as well, since it is often more costly to attract customers than to retain them.

One way to conceptualize the traditional transaction marketing approach versus the relationship marketing approach is as two ends of a continuum, along which a variety of combined strategies that incorporate elements from both approaches can be implemented. Table 3-1 outlines some of the key differences between the two strategies.

	Transaction Marketing	**Relationship Marketing**
Focus	one-off exchanges, brand management	ongoing exchanges, customer management
Time Perspective	short-term focus	long-term focus
Primary Communication	mass communication	personal communications
Customer Feedback Mechanism	isolated market research	ongoing dialogue
Market Size	mass markets	markets-of-one
Criterion for Success	market share	"mind-share" (share of customers' minds)

Table 3-1: Transaction Marketing versus Relationship Marketing

why cRM?

[Relationship marketing strategies are not new; several factors – including increased fragmentation of markets, more intense competition, a generally high level of product quality, more demanding customers, and changing customer buying patterns – have long forced companies in certain industries to seek competitive advantage by focusing on the development of enduring relationships with customers. However, information technologies, in particular the Internet, have provided additional incentives for firms to adopt such strategies.]

Indeed, one of the defining characteristics of the Internet is the fact that it is a network. Each connection in that network creates the possibility of a relationship. Consequently, it is important to realize that network technology can not only be used to manage information, but can also be used to manage relationships.

Learning About Customers

Knowledge Acquisition

The key to any successful relationship marketing program is information. The better information that a firm has about a particular customer, the more value that firm will potentially be able to provide that customer. The information has to be relevant, timely and accurate.

On the Web, unobtrusive data collection can be detailed, recording each click of the mouse, the length of time spent viewing each page, the type of computer and operating system being used to access a page, etc. By placing "cookies" – identifying tags – on users' computers, firms are able to identify users from session to session and track their behavior over time. This type of behavioral data is then used to generate educated guesses about consumer preferences, demographics, etc. When a firm requires information that cannot be captured unobtrusively, it often becomes necessary to request that customers engage in some type of self-disclosure. This is why many online firms require registration to their sites, even though these sites are available to users free of charge.

Often a firm's strategic imperative to acquire information about its customers – whether by unobtrusive or intrusive means – comes into direct conflict with customers' concerns about privacy. These concerns will become more pronounced as new technologies – such as encrypted medical records, passport profiles, digital signatures, electronic wallets, biometric passwords, etc. – emerge. This is why a critical factor in successful knowledge acquisition strategies is trust. Trust accumulates slowly over multiple interactions, and yet can disappear in a flash. Firms that view privacy concerns as an inconvenience run the risk of sabotaging the primary goal of cultivating relationships with customers.

Customer Differentiation

While customers have different needs, they also represent different levels of value to a firm. A successful relationship marketing firm leverages its customer knowledge to determine how to allocate its resources. Typically, expected future profits are not simply derived from future transactions with the customer; they also result from reduced acquisition costs, revenue growth, cost savings, referrals and price premiums.

Acquisition costs are the costs associated with attracting new customers. These include advertising costs, commissions, sales force overhead, etc. Revenue growth refers to the fact that in most businesses, customer spending tends to increase over time. The customer who repeatedly buys computer hardware accessories from a computer products company may eventually notice that the company also sells software. Cost savings result from the fact that as customers get to know a firm, they tend to be more efficient in their transactions. Referrals occur when satisfied customers recommend the business to others. And finally, existing customers tend to pay higher prices than new customers, sometimes as a result of trial discounts available only to new customers, and sometimes because loyal customers tend to be less price sensitive.

Customization Of The Marketing Mix

Customizing Products and Services

The process of creating customized products and services for individual customers on a mass scale has been called "mass customization". Firms are often able to extrapolate customer's needs based on previous purchasing patterns, demographic information, etc. The idea is to leverage the collective knowledge of the entire customer base to anticipate the preferences of each individual customer.

Customizing Communications

Having a powerful customer knowledge base also enables a firm to plan a communications campaign that targets potential customers in a highly specific way. This can be done using banner advertisements, electronic mail, experiential marketing and viral marketing.

Banners are the regular ad strips that typically appear on the top or bottom of Web pages delivered by commercial sites. By clicking on a banner advertisement, users can link directly to the advertiser's Web site, thus providing the advertiser with the opportunity to directly interact with an interested consumer. When firms place such ads, they have two choices. One is to place ads with each Web site they would like to advertise on; the Web site administrators can then "serve" the ads directly to customers. For large advertisers planning to place ads on multiple sites, this process is inefficient and ineffective, because a single Web site can only provide information about its own activity and cannot provide consistent reporting of advertising results from multiple Web sites. A second alternative is to deliver ads via third-party ad-server companies (e.g., Double-Click[1]) which can serve ad messages simultaneously to multiple Web sites, measure results, produce consolidated reports, report on the success of the entire campaign, and analyze these results immediately, enabling advertisers to quickly assess the ongoing effectiveness of the campaign. Changes to the ad campaign can be made instantaneously and centrally by the ad-serving company, maximizing the effectiveness of the advertiser's investment. Banner ads can be targeted according to a wide range of criteria, including

---

[1] http://www.doubleclick.com

user profiles (from registered user information), area of content a user is viewing, time of day, day of the week, technical information (Internet domain type, browser type, platform, etc.) and keyword searches.

E-mail-based marketing is similar to direct-mail marketing in that a firm uses a database of addresses to send messages directly to the people in the database. There are two key differences, however. First, the cost of e-mail marketing is significantly lower than comparable postage rates. Second, the level of customization in e-mail advertisements tends to be much greater. Viral marketing refers to the technique of using the Internet to accelerate word-of-mouth, dramatically boosting the rate of adoption of a product or service. Viral marketing is a new form of customized communication in which a firm enlists its own customers to promote its products to friends. Potential customers thus receive a highly personalized endorsement – not from the company, but from someone they know and trust.

Customizing Channels

In traditional markets, dual distribution systems are not uncommon; there are numerous examples of companies using more than one channel of distribution to sell to different groups of customers. However, the process of managing multiple distribution systems can be both tricky and risky. Electronic commerce is posing new challenges in this regard. Perhaps not surprisingly, it is often the largest, most well-established firms that experience the most difficulty adapting to these technologies; they are, after all, the ones who typically stand to lose the most by sabotaging traditional sales channels. As a result, many large companies have been slow to respond to the opportunities afforded by the Web.

Customizing Price

Once a firm has customized its products and services to create the most value for its customers, the next objective is to establish pricing arrangements that allow it to extract as much of that value as possible. There are many forms of differential pricing, including personalized pricing and versioning. Personalized pricing occurs when a firm decides to sell to each user at a different price. In online auctions, prices are set based on the dynamics among the active customer base. This dynamic pricing mechanism has played a large part in the success of companies such as eBay[2] and Onsale. And in reverse markets, the customer is given complete control over the terms of the sale. Priceline.com[3], for example, allows users to set their price for airline tickets; it passes those prices on to airline companies who can then "bid" for the customers. Versioning occurs when a company decides to simply offer a product line and let customers choose the version of the product most appropriate for them. Differential pricing thus results from self-selection, as customers reveal the value they place on the product through the version they select. The idea is that by creating both low-end and high-end versions of a product, it is possible to sell the same thing to customers with significantly different levels of willingness and ability to pay.

---

[2] http://www.ebay.com
[3] http://www.priceline.com

While electronic commerce is creating new opportunities for differential pricing, it can also make such pricing strategies more difficult when it is used to provide customers with better information about their choices. Indeed, customer ignorance – about prices, features and relative product performance – has traditionally been a source of profit for companies. Today, however, online shopping agents ("bots" or "spiders") can perform automatic price and feature comparisons in a matter of seconds. Using a virtual database that seeks out information from dozens of online merchants, these intelligent agents can scan the Web to find the best deal on a particular product. Since no existing agent can search the entire Web universe, spider technology does not provide "perfect information"; however, many agents come close. MySimon[4], for example, searches about 2000 merchants. CompareNet[5] offers similar services. Other examples include Jango[6] (from Excite[7]), Junglee[8] (from Amazon.com), Yahoo! Shopping[9], and C2B[10] (from Inktomi). These agents are usually available free-of-charge to consumers, and drastically reduce the search costs associated with comparison shopping.

Establishing a Learning Relationship

The relationship marketing process involves an iterative cycle of knowledge acquisition, customer differentiation and customization of the entire marketing mix. This process is sometimes referred to as a "learning relationship". A learning relationship between a customer and an enterprise gets smarter and smarter with each individual interaction, defining in ever more detail the customer's own individual needs and tastes. Learning works in both directions. The firm ends up developing a knowledge base about each customer, based on what the customer has "taught" the firm about himself or herself. At the same time, the customer has developed a deep awareness of the irreplicability of the value offered by the firm. The result is that it is in both parties' interest to continue the relationship, and it becomes difficult for another firm to duplicate the level of personalization inherent in the products and services offered.

The Emergence of Mass Customization

Customer frustration is designed into our current business system. Companies create fixed product lines that represent their best guesses about what buyers will want, and buyers make do with what they're offered. There may be some minor customization at the point of purchase – a few optional features or add-ons – but by and large, the set of choices is fixed long before customers even begin to shop. The fixed product-line system is no joy for suppliers, either. Predictions of future demand, no matter how well grounded, are inevitably inaccurate. Frustrated retailers and manufacturers spend tens of billions of dollars in discounts every year to help dispose of merchandise that isn't moving the way they thought it would.

---

[4] http://www.mysimon.com
[5] http://www.comparenet.com
[6] http://www.jango.excite.com
[7] http://www.excite.com
[8] http://www.junglee.com
[9] http://www.shopping.yahoo.com
[10] http://www.inktomi.com

So why does a system that is bad for both customers and companies hold sway? Historically, there hasn't been an alternative. The slow, imprecise movement of information up the supply pipeline and of goods down it has meant that the manufacturing process must begin long before accurate information about demand exists. Our entire industrial sector operates on guesswork.

Thanks to the Internet, an alternative to the traditional, unhappy, model of supplier-customer interaction is finally becoming possible. In all sorts of markets, customers will soon be able to describe exactly what they want, and suppliers will be able to deliver the desired product or service without compromise or delay. The Internet is an interactive system that allows individual customers to design their own products by choosing from a menu of attributes, components, prices and delivery options. The customers' selections send signals to the supplier's manufacturing system that set in motion the wheels of procurement, assembly and delivery.

The role of the customer in this system shifts from passive recipient to active designer. That shift is just the most recent stage in the long-term evolution of the customer's role in the economy. For most of the twentieth century, customers were "product takers" and "price takers", adopting suppliers' goods at suppliers' prices. Over the past two decades, as customers became more sophisticated and gained greater power over the buying process, they stopped being price takers. Armed with more options and more information, they looked further, bargained harder, and eventually found lower prices. But customers are still product takers. Even though suppliers have tailored their offerings to finer and finer slices of the customer base, buyers are ultimately forced to settle for the best approximation of what they want. With the Internet, however, customers are no longer product takers. They are product makers. For example, customer today can design their own computers with Dell's online configurator, create their own dolls with Mattel's My Design Barbie, assemble their own investment portfolios with Schwab's mutual-fund evaluator, and even design their own golf clubs with Chipshot.com's PerfectFit system.

Three things are holding the Internet back. The first is simply its newness: many manufacturers feel uncomfortable doing business through the Internet. It would mean restructuring their entire manufacturing and sales systems. The second is the lack of highly responsive supply networks that can deliver components and services as needed. The third, and most important, is the lack of a critical mass of customers willing to make their purchases via the Internet. Some industrial markets have an abundance of Internet-ready customers, but in most markets, the Internet-ready segment is still a tiny sliver of the customer base.

But that last roadblock will be dismantled quickly. PC sales are strong; Internet awareness is spread rapidly, particularly among the young; and the expansion of broadband access is inevitable. And as soon as the customers are there, you can bet that the supporting infrastructure will be in place. By the end of this decade, the Internet will be involved in 30% or more of total U.S. commercial activity, as our economy moves from a supply-driven to a demand-driven system. The big questions isn't, 'Will the Internet dominate commerce?' It is, 'Who will control the Internet in each industry?'

Changing The Terms Of Competition

Because the Internet collects precise information about the preferences and behavior of individual buyers, it enables companies to secure customer loyalty as never before. With each transaction, a company becomes more knowledgeable about the customer and hence better able to anticipate and fulfill that customer's needs. That knowledge can be used to tailor, in real time, the design of the user interface itself, customizing the options presented to the buyer and promoting up-selling and cross-selling. Once aggregated, moreover, the customer information can be used to guide the evolution of entire product lines and to spot new growth opportunities at their earliest stages. In such an environment, it becomes very difficult for a competitor, lacking the in-depth customer information, to displace the existing provider.

First movers stand to gain enormous advantages. Successful Internet-based businesses act as customer magnets. They not only exert a strong pull over existing customers but also draw in new waves of online buyers. And with each new customer, the company's market knowledge grows stronger, propelling it even further ahead of the pack. Equally important, well-designed Web sites attract key suppliers, which are also hungry for accurate and timely information about demand.

For all these reasons, the rise of the Internet economy promises to redistribute power within industries. There will be three types of competitors vying for early control of the Internet. First is the individual manufacturer or assembler, such as a Dell or a Schwab. Second is a consortium of existing manufacturers; an example is MetalSite launched by a group of leading metals producers. Third, and most threatening to existing players, is the new intermediary. Because the Internet essentially provides design tools and a conduit of information, it needn't be controlled by the companies that produce the products.

What is abundant in most industries today is production capacity. What is scarce is the ownership of customer relationships. Because the companies that launch effective Internet businesses will also control customer relationships, they will be the ones that hold the power in an industry and reap the lion's share of the profits. Once a company controls the Internet business in an industry, it can use its store of customer information to expand into new industries. Information-rich customer relationships need not – and will not – end at the traditional boundaries within industries.

Today, the Internet is essentially a transactional device. Customer information is a by-product. Tomorrow, the Internet will be primarily an information collection device and a customer-relationship builder. Companies will use their Web sites to actively solicit from customers information about their satisfaction levels, their buying intentions, and their requirements and preferences. And, by means of sophisticated analytical techniques such as collaborative filtering, they will use the information to predict customers' needs and behavior across virtually all product and service categories. One-stop shopping will take on a whole new meaning, and commerce will take on a whole new look.

Roles A Company Can Play In Electronic Commerce

The key to making money on the Internet is to focus on customer relationships, not on technology for technology's sake. The biggest opportunity exists in the fact that companies now have unprecedented, direct access to individual customers. Web-smart companies use the Internet to build one-on-one relationships with their customers. Some of the most interesting thinking about electronic commerce goes into defining the different roles a company can take with its customers in cyberspace. Among the possible roles are the guide, the personalizer, the fellow participant in a community, and the coordinator or architect.

- *The guide*: Faced with a technology-educated and empowered consumer, the salesperson must play a new role, more that of a consultant than sales tactician. For instance, she might need to explain the limitations on manufacturing flexibility, then suggest the optimal product configuration for a particular set of needs. She might share information about the experience of others who had similar needs and who purchased the product. Finally, instead of playing a shell-game with prices and charges, she can negotiate a deal that affords her a reasonable margin, since both parties have the same information. The services provided by a purely online guide are similar.
- *The customizer*: The idea here is to carry the guide role even further, into "intelligent agent" territory. Tell us the specifications, the pitch goes – we will design a product just for you.
- *The community participant*: Anyone thinking of doing business on the Internet has to wrestle with a fundamental problem. The Internet grew up as a non-commercial medium. Many people still see its primary use as sharing information with others, and resent attempts to sell to them online. One of the more sophisticated attempts to think about how to respond to this challenge is the idea of electronic communities and the different roles that a business might play in them. Commercial success in the online arena will belong to those businesses that organize electronic communities to meet multiple social and commercial needs. The business definition you take into an online community may not be the one you end up with. You may, for instance, find you want to "own" a customer segment across the range of its needs and interests, rather than merely selling certain products to that segment. But this approach will require extra effort. The notion of electronic communities has a nice indirection to it: Don't just push your product on the Internet; appreciate that people are there for a variety of reasons.
- *The coordinator or architect*: The next wave of business challenges will consist of harmonizing the outputs of technology. A manager will have to make the work of complex teams and technologies coherent for the average consumer.

Common to all four roles is the fact that they focus on the customer, not on the technology. While any business person who wants to make money on the Internet will necessarily keep abreast of the latest electronic bells, whistles and polymorphous interfaces, he or she won't become bewitched by them. They are, after all, only tools. The real pay dirt here is the customer.

SALES STRATEGIES FOR ELECTRONIC COMMERCE

If the Internet has done anything, it has changed the environment for selling. Today, your sales strategy has to be carefully tailored to the kind of sales your company engages in. In particular, nearly every product or service must now be put squarely into one of two categories. Category # 1 is commodity sales. Products and services in this group are identical, or nearly so, and are purchased on the basis of price. Examples are simple insurance policies, or books. Buyers can go on the Internet, quickly find the vendor with the lowest price, and complete the transaction with little or no assistance. Category # 2 is consultative or "relationship" selling. This usually involves complex purchases. Buyers of high-end investment products or industrial machinery, for example, typically want and need hands-on assistance in making their decision.

These categories have always existed, of course, but the Internet has deepened the gap between them. Never before have buyers of commodities had so much information at their fingertips; never before has it been so easy for them to switch suppliers. As for buyers of consultative products, never before have they expected the seller to add so much value, both during and after the sales transaction. After all, what's to keep a customer from listening to an elaborate sales presentation, then going on the Web to buy the same product more cheaply from someone else? Most companies offer products and services in both categories. But whatever you are examining, you have to adapt your sales strategies to the Internet age.

Every seller's first job in the Internet environment is to determine the appropriate sales path for each product or service. Unless you make just one standard product, you will probable take one path with some things you sell and the other path with others. You may make your choice for purely competitive reasons. How do you choose the most advantageous route? Think of yourself as the buyer. You are busy and have limited time to consider the purchase. Would you like to meet with a sales consultant? If you know the book you want is Grisham's latest thriller, the answer is no – and transactional superstars like Amazon.com have capitalized on that fact. But if you are buying global computer networking for one of the newly merged oil giants, you would likely welcome the input of a veritable army of consultative sellers.

Sales Strategies for Commodity Products

- *Fire your sales force?* Customers already have all the product information that sales representatives used to provide and more, ranging from comparative performance figures to the price on the factory invoice. So you may no longer need a sales force – and you may no longer care to spend money on one. The person who wants to buy a commoditized item wants to get the lowest price for the least effort on each acquisition. In this environment, the sales representative may even be seen by the customer as a barrier to the purchase.
- *Forget trying to differentiate the product from its competition.* With so much information so easily available, minor differentiations between many competing items have been virtually eliminated – and if not in fact, then in the customer's mind. Customers may react negatively to differences they view as inconsequential.
- *Win the competitive battle by perfecting the "inhuman touch".* In a commoditized world, you win customers more with process than with product. The most successful sellers are those that offer ease of purchase and that use emerging technologies to bond with customers. They make it easy, even pleasurable, for customers to do electronic business with them.

- *Even in commodities, there may be room for sales warriors who love a fight.* A sales force in a commodity market can still be very important. However, these sales representatives must be much more focused and have greater specific product knowledge than the broad-based consultant.

Sales Strategies for Consultative or "Relationship" Products

- *Get everybody involved.* This path couldn't be more different from commodity selling. Where commodity sellers may jettison their sales force entirely, consultative sellers may put everyone on the selling team.
- *Sales representatives must add value, not just communicate it.* A sales representative who can rattle off product features may be giving a virtuoso performance, but customers no longer have time to feign interest in it. The sales professional today who merely communicates value rather than creating it is dead in the water. How can you tell the difference between creating value and just communicating it? Use this simple test: would the prospect be willing to write a check for the sales call you just completed? The prospect would pay if you brought valuable expertise to the table, or offered a customized solution to a problem, or showed how to look at a problem in a new way. Such contributions create value for the prospect. The value creator's key to success lies not in persuading but in understanding the customer.
- *You must know your customers better than they know themselves.* The consultative seller must go to the customer with precisely the information the customer needs – so solid, extensive research is a life-or-death matter. Research should tap your sales representative well. These folks know the best sales messages but often don't know they know them, because they haven't kept records that tell you the content and frequency of value messages they hear from customers.
- *Get your technical pros out of their pocket protectors and onto your sales team.* The increasing complexity of many products and services makes it impossible for any one person, whether sales representative or product-design whiz, to know all he or she can do for a buyer. That means consultative sales are becoming less one-to-one and more group-to-group. This blurs the distinction between who is in sales and who isn't. Indeed, what may be required of the consultation-path selling is team involvement, both before and after the sale. The team can include sales representatives and a mix of folks from purchasing, design, engineering, finance, information technology and other formerly behind-the-scenes areas of the organization.
- *Talk is cheap; sellers today have to be multimedia communicators.* Here is a turn-of-the-millennium fact of sales life: you don't get the same face time with buyers you once got, and you can look forward to less in the future. Somewhere there may be a purchasing decision maker who has a moment to spare for your sales team, but today's technology lets him spend that moment on something other than your sales pitch. Ever-fancier technology allows prospects to erect ever-higher barriers to the sales call. Now they can say, "Just fax something", or "E-mail it", or "FedEx it". The result? The rapport that many sales professionals can so easily establish in person must increasingly come from the written, printed or electronically transmitted word.

That means the people who can demonstrate their sales skills in writing will probably do better than those who can't.

DEVELOPING CUSTOMER LOYALTY

In the rush to build Internet businesses, many executives concentrate all their attention on attracting customers rather than retaining them. That's a mistake. The unique economics of e-business make customer loyalty more important than ever. Loyalty may not be the first idea that pops into your head when you think about electronic commerce. After all, what relevance could such a quaint, old-fashioned notion hold for a world in which customers defect at the click of a mouse and impersonal shopping bots scour databases for ever better deals? What good is a small-town virtue amid the faceless anonymity of the Internet's global marketplace? Loyalty must be on the fast track toward extinction, right?

Not at all. Chief executives at the cutting edge of e-commerce care deeply about customer retention and consider it vital to the success of their online operations. They know that loyalty is an economic necessity. Acquiring customers on the Internet is enormously expensive, and unless those customers stick around and make lots of repeat purchases over the years, profits will remain elusive. They also know that it is a competitive necessity. In every industry, some company will figure out how to harness the potential of the Web to create exceptional value for customers, and that company is going to lock in many profitable relationships at the expense of slow-footed rivals. Without the glue of loyalty, even the best-designed e-business model will collapse.

Contrary to the common view that Web customers are fickle by nature and will flock to the next new idea, the Web is actually a very sticky space in both the business-to-consumer and business-to-business spheres. Most of today's online customers exhibit a clear proclivity toward loyalty. Web technologies, used correctly, reinforce that inherent loyalty. If executives don't quickly gain the loyalty of their most profitable existing customers and acquire the right new customers, they will face a dismal future catering to the whims of only the most price-sensitive buyers.

We have heard new economy pundits argue that the Internet has overturned all the old rules of business. But when it comes to customer loyalty, the old rules are as vital as ever. Loyalty is still about earning the trust of the right kinds of customers – customers for whom you can deliver such a consistently superior experience that they will want to do all their business with you. The Web does, however, raise new questions and open new opportunities – it places the old rules in a new context.

The Economics of E-Loyalty

The high cost of acquiring customers renders many customer relationships unprofitable during their early years. Only in later years, when the cost of serving loyal customers falls and the volume of their purchases rises, do relationships generate big returns. The bottom line: increasing customer retention rates by 5% increases profits by 25% to 95%. This general pattern – early losses, followed by rising profits – is actually exaggerated on the Internet. At the beginning of a relationship, the outlays needed to acquire a customer are often considerably higher in e-commerce than in traditional retail channels. That means that the losses in the early stages of relationships are larger for electronic retailers.

In future years, though, profit growth accelerates at an even faster rate. And since it is relatively easy for Web stores to extend their range of products, they can sell more and more kinds of goods to loyal customers, broadening as well as deepening relationships over time. The evidence indicates, in fact, that Web customers tend to consolidate their purchases with one primary supplier, to the extent that purchasing from the supplier's site becomes part of their daily routine. This phenomenon is particularly apparent in the business-to-business sector.

In addition to purchasing more, loyal customers also frequently refer new customers to a supplier, providing another rich source of profits. Referrals are lucrative in traditional commerce as well, but the Internet amplifies the effect. Online customers can, for example, use e-mail to broadcast a recommendation for a favorite Web site to dozens of friends and family members. Many e-tailers are now automating the referral process, letting customers send recommendations to acquaintances while still at the e-tailers' sites. Because referred customers cost so little to acquire, they begin to generate profits much earlier in their life cycles.

The combination of all these economic factors means that the value of loyalty is often greater on the Internet than in the physical world. For all companies doing business on the Web, the implication is clear: you cannot generate superior long-term profits unless you achieve superior customer loyalty.

A Matter of Trust

To gain the loyalty of customers, you must first gain their trust. That has always been the case, but on the Web, where distance is conducted at a distance and risks and uncertainties are magnified, it is truer than ever. Online customers can't look a sales clerk in the eye, can't size up the physical space of a store or office, and can't see and touch products. They have to rely on images and promises, and if they don't trust the company presenting those images and promises, they will shop elsewhere. Price does not rule the Web; trust does. When customers do trust an online vendor, they are much more likely to share personal information. That information enables the company to form a more intimate relationship with customers, offering products and services tailored to their individual preferences, which in turn increases trust and strengthens loyalty. Such a virtuous circle can quickly translate into a durable advantage over competitors. In addition to generously rewarding trust, the Internet opens new opportunities to build trust.

Focusing on the Right Customers

When many executives and entrepreneurs look at the Web, they see an opportunity to break free from one of the core constraints of the traditional business world: the need for focus. Because a Web site is accessible to any online customer anytime, anywhere, there is a huge temptation to try to attract as many potential buyers as possible. That temptation is reinforced by the vast up-front investments in site development and process design that companies often have to make in launching an e-business. Executives presume that these fixed costs should be amortized over as many customers as possible. So they become caught up in a frenzy of indiscriminate customer acquisition, gauging their success by the sheer number of page views, unique visitors, and sales they rack up. The fact that careful customer selection has always been a foundation of business success gets completely ignored.

A lack of focus makes building loyalty much more difficult. Customers want Web sites that are simply designed, fast to load, and easy to use, but the broader the array of customers a company attempts to serve, the more complex its site inevitably becomes. In trying to be all things to all people – to accommodate all levels of technical expertise, all service requirements, all price sensitivities, and all degrees of brand preference – it must constantly add new features and functions. As it does, its site becomes slower to load and more complicated to use. Customers flock in, but, confused by what they find, they rarely return.

An indiscriminate approach to customer acquisition also undermines profitability – a fact that is often overlooked in e-commerce, as investors and executives focus their attention on traffic statistics. The simple arithmetic of loyalty economics makes it clear that in most Web businesses, customers must stay on board for at least two to three years just for a company to recoup its initial acquisition investment. Yet, a large percentage of new customers – up to 50% in some sectors – defect before their third anniversary with an e-commerce site. Any company pursuing a strategy of grabbing customers as quickly as possible without regard to their potential for long-term relationships is in for a very bad surprise.

In identifying which customers to attract – and which to avoid – the first step is to clearly assess the different categories of online customers. Contrary to common perception, the majority of online shoppers are not out to score the absolute lowest price. The largest single segment of online customers are seeking convenience above all else. They want to do business with a site that makes their lives easier, and they are willing to pay more for that convenience. Price rational but not price obsessive, they also have a strong inclination toward loyalty. After all, returning to a familiar site is much more convenient than scouting out a new one. Another large group of customers are influenced primarily by brand. They too are looking for stable, long-term relationships. If a company assumes that the customers it is losing to dot-coms are motivated solely by price – and thus not worth defending – it is probably mistaken.

The way a site is designed and marketed has a large impact on the types of customers it attracts. The mix of customer segments varies widely among Web competitors within the same market. Some sites attract a rich mix of loyalty-oriented customers and others primarily attract the price butterflies who flit from site to site seeking bargains. The loyalists find sites mostly through referrals. The butterflies, by contrast, are lured by promotional discounts and general advertising. If a company is spending most of its marketing dollars on indiscriminate banner advertisements and online coupons, with little investment in building communities and promoting referrals, it is probably building long-term losses into its customer base.

Learning About Loyalty

While the Internet may seem like an anonymous space, in reality it is far easier to track customers, their purchase histories, and their preferences online than in a conventional business setting. Customers in brick-and-mortar stores leave no record of their behavior unless they buy something – and even then the data are often sketchy. But in virtual stores, their shopping purchase patterns are transparent. Every move they make can be documented electronically, click by click. If a customer exits a Web site when the price screen appears, it's a fair bet that he is price-sensitive. If he jumps from page to page without ever initiating a transaction, he is probably frustrated at being unable to find what he wants.

By providing such rich data, the Internet offers companies unprecedented opportunities for getting to know their customers in depth and for customizing offerings to meet their preferences. Very few companies, however, are actually doing much to realize that potential. Less than 20% even track customer retention rigorously, let alone try to systematically learn from customer defection patterns. Instead, they are fixated on building their Web capacity and increasing their visitor counts, click-throughs, and online sales. As a result, they overlook opportunities for upselling and cross-selling and end up capturing a much smaller share of customers' overall purchases than they might have. The average site achieves less than 30% of its full sales potential with each customer.

The real value of tracking measures of loyalty is that it allows companies to see beyond today's fads to the underlying drivers of business success. The five primary determinants of loyalty don't consist of technological bells and whistles, but rather old-fashioned customer service basics: quality customer support, on-time delivery, compelling product presentations, convenient and reasonably priced shipping and handling, and clear and trustworthy privacy policies. Of course, the drivers of loyalty will vary for each business and will evolve over time. But executives who don't set clear loyalty targets and measure their progress will inevitably drift toward weak retention performance as their organizations focus their energy in less productive areas. The long-term economic consequences of such a passive approach to loyalty will be dire.

Integrating Your Web Site With the Rest of Your Operations

Many companies have been tempted to split their Web businesses from the rest of their operations – in hopes of cashing in on investors' enthusiasm for dot-coms or of making it easier to attract the kind of talent required to manage Web activities. In the short run, such a strategy may create benefits. Over the long run, however, it is likely to erode customer loyalty. After all, when a customer does business with a company, she doesn't distinguish between a transaction on the Web and one in a physical store or branch – they are both elements of her total experience with the company.

In this view, the tool becomes a tool, not a strategy. Its unique capabilities are used to improve communications with customers, to enhance organizational learning about customers' needs and increase responsiveness, to reduce customers' transaction costs, and to enhance convenience – all of which are vital for developing strong and durable relationships. But these capabilities are not exercised in isolation. They are plugged into the full range of corporate capabilities.

In the end, loyalty is not won with technology. It is won through the delivery of a consistently superior customer experience. The Internet is a powerful tool for strengthening relationships, but the basic laws and rewards of building loyalty have not changed. By encouraging repeat purchases among a core of profitable customers, companies can initiate a spiral of economic advantages. This loyalty effect enables them to compensate their employees more generously, provide investors with superior cash flows, and reinvest more aggressively to further enhance the value delivered to customers.

What is changing is the pace at which these economic rules are playing out, and the speed with which companies must improve their products and services if they hope to keep customers loyal. Customers' tolerance for inconsistency and mediocrity is rapidly disappearing. In the past, convenient store locations, aggressive sales forces, and a general lack of information shielded companies from the penalties of providing anything less than the best product and service quality. Customers were loyal by necessity, not choice. Thanks to the Internet, those shields have been dismantled. Customers can compare suppliers in real time, all the time. Building superior customer loyalty is no longer just one of many ways to boost profits. Today it is essential for survival.

LEVERAGING ONLINE COMMUNITIES

Consumer brand companies need new management skills, and brand managers must understand online behavior if they wish to develop strong, sustainable, and beneficial online communities around their brands. The popularities of communities on the Internet has captured the attention of marketing professionals. As consumer-goods companies create online communities on the World Wide Web for their brands, they are building new relationships with their customers and enabling consumers to communicate with each other. Many famous brands, such as CNN[11], Disney[12], Shell[13], Pentax[14] and Bosch[15], host online communities through bulletin boards, forums and chat rooms, To extend the brand relationships established with their loyal customers into communities of brand consumers, strategists need to examine the long-established user communities in order to learn what makes them thrive. Strategists must also address the many issues surrounding brand-based online communities and incorporate the leadership and communication skill sets necessary to manage such communities.

If brand relationships are to be cultivated and managed over time, then the challenge for consumer brand owners is to devise a way to communicate that:
- customizes messages as it identifies the individual by name,
- rewards the individual for his or her continued support and interest,
- recognizes the passage of time and a strengthening of the relationship.

If mass-market consumer brand organizations are to unlock the potential of the Web to help them form genuine relationships with their customers – relationships that are reinforcing, competitively distinctive and long lasting – they need to look seriously at how relationships have formed up until now on the Internet. Brand managers need to understand the bases for dialogue that can lead to strong relationships, which in turn provide the foundations for online brand communities.

---

[11] http://community.cnn.com
[12] http://family.go.com/boards
[13] http://www.shell.com
[14] http://www.pentax.com
[15] http://www.boschtools.com

Communities of users, known as user groups, have a long history in the business-to-business world. The groups provide a useful forum for users to share experiences, solve problems, meet peers at conferences and events, and explore other companies and career opportunities, as well as keep current with technology and industry gossip. User groups are formed either spontaneously by buyers or they are formed at the initiation of the vendor. For vendors, user groups offer many attractive links with key buyers and users. Vendors can contact them about new product design and product enhancements, and users often test new products. They also act as opinion leaders, providing insights into future trends and new application areas.

Brand-based online communities have demonstrated the potential benefits of dialogue flowing between consumers via two utilities: real-time chat taking place in chat rooms and asynchronous discussions in discussion forums or bulletin boards. The popularity of interactive communication gives the brand Web site an abundance of free content from the consumer community. Both the content and possibility of forming relationships with other buyers and with the brand's managers act as a magnet, drawing consumers back to the site on a frequent and regular basis. This enables further commercial opportunities for the brand owners and legitimizes the investment in Web site development and maintenance. By making sure that consumers can interact freely with each other and build a friendly online community, marketers can follow consumers' perceptions about and feelings toward the brand in real time. Interactive online media will enable marketers to sense market forces with unprecedented accuracy and efficiency.

New technologies are enabling the task of turning electronic discussions into useful managerial information. Tools like Artificial Life's[16] STAn, a smart text analyzer, are designed to help companies retrieve and analyze information from online discussions using fuzzy logic technology, neural networking and statistical analyses.

Established communities on the Internet provide the potential brand community developer several measurements for success. These sites thrive because they offer their participants:
- a forum for exchange of common interests,
- a sense of place with codes of behavior,
- the development of congenial and stimulating dialogues leading to relationships based on trust,
- encouragement for active participation by more than an exclusive few.

Management Issues for Brand-Based Online Communities

Consumer product companies must address the issues of brand focus, community control, authenticity and ethics, community size and composition, and ultimately the objectives, management and skills involved in running these community sites.

How Do You Attract Members to Your Online Community?

The key is finding a related issue that captures people's attention. People must care about the issue, have opinions about it, and be enthusiastic enough to share their views. Advantages may well accrue to the first movers. The site must offer members not

---

[16] http://www.artificial-life.com

only entertainment, but also a sense of involvement and even ownership. Communities require a truly bottom-up view of brand-building, whereby the customers create the content, and are, in a sense, responsible for it. This view contrasts markedly with many brand strategists' traditional top-down view of business, where products and services are created by organizations and sold to customers.

How Many Members Do You Want, and How Active Should They Be?

The larger the community, the more likely it is to lose an essential intimacy. Good communities have fractal depth – that is, they are capable of being segmented into subcommunities centered on specific topics of interest. The higher order issue, which will be the key attraction of the brand community, must be capable of hosting many related interests and strong enough to give coherence and overall added value to each specific interest group.

Should There Be Links to Other Sites?

Related but non-competitive sites would be harmless, such as a travel agency offering links to country or city sites. Links could be made to competitors' sites depending on how general was the point of interest.

How Much Control Should the Brand Owner Exert Over Content?

In the consumer brand-based online community, it is likely the consumer will want to control the relationship. When building communities, marketers will have to treat their target market accordingly. To provide the best experience, brand sites will have to make consumers feel more like community members or partners and encourage them to initiate multilateral relationships. By overly controlling the discussion or dialogue within communities, brand sites face the risk of losing the interest of their members and losing the creativity inherent in their audience. Decisions about how much control a brand host should exercise over its online community will reflect, or may ultimately influence, the brand's personality.

If consumer-goods brand owners are to use their online communities as a reality check on the success (or otherwise) of their activities, they will have to develop a tolerance for the excesses and opinions of their participants. The policy on control is a tricky one to gauge. If the online brand community were to develop a sense of injustice and pit itself against the management, then the brand owners would have an ugly situation on their hands. Not to allow negative comments, however, might create a sterile environment that would drive away participants.

How Does Anonymity Affect Your Online Community Site?

One of the key contradictions of the medium is that for all its potential as a means of communication for social networking, socializing via the Internet can be anonymous. People can and do hide their real personalities and invent new ones for themselves. The facelessness of participation certainly facilitates interventions in a community, allowing it

71

to seem as if messages were sent by legitimate members of the brand community. Clearly, there are issues of both brand-community authenticity as well as ethics to be considered here. Decisions and policies need to be made at the highest organizational levels. If the brand lives by the quality and integrity of the ingredients in its product or service offering, it must have equally high standards in its interactions with its virtual community members.

New Skills Needed to Manage Online Communities

Exercising the delicate balance between controlling and letting go will require a new set of skills within the brand organization. Brand-community management brings together three skill sets that exist separately in the non-digital world but are rarely sought after by traditional marketing management. These are the skills associated with community leadership and development, with supervision of volunteer managers, and with editorial expertise. In the electronic world of community brand management, these skills must coalesce either within the same person or at least within the community brand-management team.

These three skill sets – leadership, managing volunteers, and editorial skills – will help the volunteer and professional managers as they undertake their new activities and responsibilities in the brand-based online community. In addition to these skills, constant communication between the membership and its volunteer leaders, and between the volunteer managers and the professional managers, is necessary to make the communities work.

Community Leadership and Development

Community leaders must have the necessary skills to create a purposeful and attractive community vision, to attract and shepherd new members, to stimulate member involvement and participation, and to nurture the community spirit and keep it refreshed and relevant to members' needs over time.

The skills required include the following:
- Creating, communicating and coordinating the vision, purpose and nature of the community, both internally and externally.
- Understanding the prime motivations for community participation.
- Ensuring a pleasant and engaging experience from first contact to lasting relationship, while meeting corporate and community security and information needs.
- Managing the delicate balance between attracting new members and maintaining community intimacy.
- Using political, diplomatic and decision-making skills.

Managing Volunteers

Volunteers serve at many community Web sites, providing a means of:
- keeping community management close to its roots (i.e., the membership base),
- keeping the costs of managing thousands of individualized and personalized relationships within sensible limits,

- recognizing and rewarding the desires and abilities of many deeply committed community members to increase their involvement with the community and the brand.

Volunteers function as chat-room hosts and discussion moderators and editors for specific bulletin boards, where they delete unsuitable material or repetitive questions and answers. The key to trouble-free operation lies in managing the tensions that inevitably arise when paid, full-time professionals interact with unpaid, part-time volunteers. The potential for conflict lies in unclear goals, feelings of exploitation, and an inability to detect when either group is treading on the other's toes. Appropriate objectives, structures, training, open channels of communication, frequent contact, systems for arbitration, and early detection of overloads are essential for the smooth operation of the volunteer-professional interface.

The skills required include the following:
- Recognizing the talents that volunteers must have to succeed in stimulating participation.
- Recognizing the determinants of trust and credibility within the community.
- Understanding volunteer motivations and limits to volunteer capacities.
- Establishing a reward system, mentoring, and training for volunteers.
- Managing the key volunteer activities.
- Managing the relationships among professional managers, volunteers, and community members.

Editorial Expertise

Community members interact primarily through their own text-based content. To attract people into the Web site and then entice people to participate, the community editor-in-chief will have to develop new sources of content. To keep the audience's interest, the editor must be able to create or acquire articles from internal or external sources, to choose appropriate reference material, to compile directories, and to archive material on the Web site. The editorial task is also one of ensuring that the brand personality is portrayed consistently and communicated correctly through the site design.

The skills required include the following:
- Understanding the interplay between serious and entertaining content, freedom of speech, and the brand community values.
- Sensing membership concerns.
- Balancing opinion leadership and stimulating healthy debate among the membership.
- Identifying topics of interest, managing guest/expert appearances, soliciting third-party input.
- Creating and managing the archive, and tracking community development for members and brand management.

Linking Community Strategy to the Total Brand Strategy

Ultimately, a company's brand-based Web community strategy must be part of its total brand strategy. The various communication vehicles used by brand managers are widely acknowledged to work better when they are in harmony, either by providing the same core message to different audiences or different expressions of the same message. The integration strategy determines how the various aspects of the brand can be made to cohere and benefit the total brand. Once given a voice, the brand community will act as the living manifestation of the brand's personality and relationships with consumers. The obligations inherent in a brand relationship, now vocalized by the online community participants, will have to be fulfilled.

Responsibilities and Activities for Total Brand Strategy

Professional Managers

- Set broad competitive goals for the brand.
- Plan how to develop the brand.
- Devise advertising and marketing communications approach.
- Establish overall sales strategy.

Responsibilities and Activities for Online Community Strategy and Management

Professional Managers

- Set broad goals for the community and implement development.
- Attract visitors to the Web site.
- Oversee calendar and special events.
- Train and supervise volunteer managers.
- Administer archiving of content.
- Monitor evolving areas of interest.
- Set editorial guidelines.
- Ensure site coherence.

Volunteer Managers

- Welcome new members.
- Encourage participation.
- Identify interesting new topics.
- Nurture shared values.
- Arbitrate minor infractions.

Community Members

- Mutual interaction and relationship building generates content and stimulates repeated visits.

Keys to Creating and Sustaining Online Communities

Before long, the ability to create and manage virtual communities will become a distinguishing feature of nearly every successful business. Community interactions occur wherever people people are connected over computer networks – whether these people are buying, selling, collaborating, or merely seeking diversion. These interactions can have a big impact on business strategy and operations. And they pose unforeseen threats as well as opportunities. For example, customer communities eliminate the information gaps that companies traditionally relied upon to maintain profit margins. But along with such threats come remarkable opportunities. By developing new value-adding communities, or better managing those that already exist, companies can greatly enhance their prospects for success in the age of e-business. Online communities require a wide range of supporting activities, from making sure the enabling technologies are available and working, to gathering and acting upon member feedback. Three kinds of activities appear critical to a community's continued viability: 1) member development; 2) asset management; and 3) community relations.

An online community can be a powerful ally in confronting some of today's most challenging business issues. But success requires effective execution in member development, asset management and community relations. By understanding and using these key elements, executives can begin to build communities that will support their business model, regardless of what that model happens to be.

Member Development

Communities need critical mass to remain active and hold the attention of members. Member development must be an ongoing effort. A clearly defined community focus helps coordinators conduct market research to identify potential members as well as the content, tools and services that will draw them in. Another effective approach is to work with individuals who influence community members or play leading roles in the community. They can become effective evangelists and a focal point for community formation. Community organizers need to know and cultivate such opinion leaders. Finally, there is no substitute for one-on-one promotion among potential members. There are many approaches: direct e-mail, phone, or fax; online and offline presentations to related groups or gatherings; and encouraging recruitment activities by existing members.

Asset Management

The assets of an online community include:
- content, both externally and internally generated,
- alliances with other groups,
- the knowledge and experience of experts,
- the community infrastructure (hardware, software, interface and other design elements).

The commitment of the members to the community is itself an asset. One way to sustain this commitment is to provide a blend of services, content and relationships that is difficult to find elsewhere. This in turn creates the kind of virtuous cycle that drives a successful community.

The community coordinator is responsible for maintaining the community's assets. Start by identifying those assets and creating a plan to manage them. Asset management activities include:

- Creating member profiles and topic-specific subcommittees to make the expertise within the community more visible.
- Maintaining a balance between experts and novices in the community.
- Capturing the information members need and creating structures and taxonomies that make the information easily accessible.
- Creating processes that facilitate discussion and other forms of contribution.
- Creating a critical mass of functionality that encourages use of community spaces.

Community needs, like those of individual members, are constantly shifting. Community organizers must gather feedback from members about what they find most beneficial. This can be done through one-on-one interviews, surveys, electronic feedback forms, rating tools, or simply by monitoring discussion groups. Members can also share in asset-management efforts. As a community matures, volunteers often come forward to help create and maintain assets that are pertinent to specific subgroups. Organizers can harness this discretionary energy to build the value of the community.

Community Relations

The main reason people participate in communities is to interact with other people. Where there is little or no face-to-face interaction, nurturing and strengthening connections can be a delicate balancing act. It calls for both a solid structure of norms and guidelines and the flexible reading between the lines of online moderation and facilitation. Most communities have a strong element of self-policing; when conflicts arise or members behave inappropriately, other members step in. Explicit rules and guidelines provide a reference point for members who want to play this role. But formal moderation is often required, and it takes skills and experience to do it successfully. For communities where discussion is a core activity, moderators are usually experienced or rigorously trained. Managing community relations involves tending to connections between people, rather than the assets the community creates. As such, informal or social interactions are typically valued and promoted.

PROVIDING CUSTOMER SERVICE ONLINE

Everyone knows that it usually costs companies less to conduct business over the Web than through traditional channels. An online banking transaction, for example, costs just two cents, compared with 36 cents for an ATM transaction and $1.25 for a teller-assisted transaction. So it is not surprising that many companies are desperately trying to attract consumers to the Internet channel. What is surprising, however, is that most have had dismal results. In retail brokerage, for instance, only 2% of households trade online. And the figures for the airline industry are even worse: less than 0.1% of households purchase tickets through airline Web sites.

Why are the numbers so low? In large part, it is because many companies have bought into the myth that the Internet is a self-service channel. They assume they should let their online customers help themselves to whatever product or service they need – be it reserving their own airline tickets or configuring their own automobiles. The problem is that when a company does less, the customer ends up doing more – and most customers don't want to do more. In many cases, self-service Web sites just leave customers frustrated and annoyed.

A better approach to electronic commerce is when a company uses technology to shoulder many of the tasks involved in shopping and buying, relieving the burden on the customer. This model recognizes that although customers like having choices, they don't want too many. They appreciate it when companies offer pre-screened alternatives geared to their needs. Companies should focus on customer service, not self-service.

You can help your company adopt this strategy by taking the following four steps. First, deconstruct the entire transaction process – from the identification of the customer need to order fulfillment. Second, distinguish between those functions that are currently performed by your company and those performed by your customer. Third, pinpoint which of the customer functions you can take responsibility for – establishing the boundaries of your company's reach into the transaction – and assess the costs and benefits of taking on each task. Finally, find ways to expand your reach beyond a single transaction to create more value for the customer.

The Web promises not only to reduce corporate transaction costs but also to enhance customer convenience. To fulfill that promise, though, companies need to move beyond the self-service myth. Making it easy and enjoyable for visitors to use your Web site will translate into more customers, greater loyalty and higher profits.

Traditionally, service has been thought of as an exchange in which an employee serves a customer. That definition has been expanded to include self-service, in which a customer serves himself or herself. The Internet enables customers to engage in a higher degree of self-service than ever before possible. In order to conduct self-service on the Internet, customers need to have the ability to navigate around a Web site with ease, and to acquire information from it.

For some Internet businesses, the information itself is the product. These are "pure information" Internet firms such as *The Wall Street Journal Interactive Edition*. For these businesses, the quality of the service delivered largely depends on the quality of a Web site's navigational tools and design, and the quality of information that is provided. Many of these organizations serve their customers almost purely through the Internet, delivering completely technology-intermediated service.

However, many e-commerce business-to-business and business-to-consumer firms deliver more than pure information. These firms offer products and services through their Web sites. Because of the physical nature of the products and services they are selling, they rely on more than a technology-intermediated service delivery system. Their service delivery systems must also include customer support and logistics. While going to the Internet increases their degree of self-service, it does not eliminate the need for customer support for the occasions when customers need help, even if that help is now provided only on an exception basis. While customer-support needs are reduced, logistics needs often increase as all products or services must be packaged and delivered to the customer. For organizations selling physical goods and services over the Internet, the components of service quality begin with Web site navigation and information. However, customer support and logistics must be added as they are critically important when necessary, even when only used by exception.

Ironically, it may be the less glamorous components of service quality, customer support and logistics, that are the least easily duplicated, and thus the greatest sources of competitive advantage for Internet organizations delivering a physical product or service. This point has important implications for the economics of these firms. This is because while customer support and logistics are the least easily duplicated, they are also the least scalable. In contrast, navigation and information are the elements of service quality for an e-commerce firm that are most easily scalable, but they are also those most easily duplicated.

Venture capitalists investing in Internet businesses often look for what they call infinite scalability. This refers to a business's ability to serve numerous additional customers at extremely low incremental cost. The need for infinite scalability to justify high valuations creates a problem for Internet firms relying on high-quality customer support and logistics. In order to deliver infinite scalability, these firms need to reduce their dependence on human resources, which increase variable costs. Internet firms have attempted to do this by automating customer support and discouraging customers from interacting with employees, overtly or covertly. Yet in order to develop a sustainable competitive advantage, those same firms must rely on human resources to deliver high-quality customer support and logistics. This dual need to have front-line human resources for competitive advantage, and at the same time not to have them to enable infinite scalability, creates a contradiction many Internet firms are beginning to face.

E-commerce involves a customer experience cycle that includes four components: navigation, information, customer support, and logistics. Navigation refers to ease of access, or helping customers to get around a Web site. Information refers to providing information in sufficient depth to enable or encourage customers to make a purchase decision. Customer support refers to helping customers with questions about either the goods and services for sale or how to use the Web site. Logistics refers to the handling, packaging and delivery of the physical goods or service to the customer and arranging for payment. When all four elements are executed well, they produce customer loyalty through repurchase or word-of-mouth referral, also called viral marketing.

Many e-commerce firms have focused on making their Web sites attractive and easy to use (navigation). Some have spent considerable resources on providing excellent information about their products and services. Few have focused on customer support or logistics, many believing that these functions are best outsourced. Customer support and logistics are important to many e-commerce organizations. Amazon.com, arguably the leading e-commerce firm, has spent millions on call centers and warehouses. The surprise may come from just how important customer support and logistics are, and the effect of their importance on the ability of these companies to be infinitely scalable. E-commerce companies failing to pay adequate attention to customer support and logistics will encounter trouble. In fact, analysis of competitive advantage in services generally, and e-commerce in particular, suggests that this inference may understate the importance of customers support and logistics.

It is easier to replicate excellent navigation and information than excellent customer support and logistics. Customer support and logistics may thus prove to be a sustainable source of competitive advantage for e-commerce firms, just as they have for bricks-and-mortar firms such as L.L.Bean. Navigation and information are more easily replicable because they are available to the world at large to study. They are also relatively predictable: once developed and implemented, they remain effective throughout their useful lives with little additional input. The frequency with which e-commerce firms make improvements to their Web sites also suggests that changing navigation and information is relatively easy. In contrast, customer support and logistics involve a series of processes that are difficult to infer from their output. Their execution involves front-line, entry-level employees on an ongoing basis. This increases their operational variability, and thus the difficulty of managing them. Changing customer support and logistics is particularly difficult as it requires getting individuals to change their behavior, one of the most challenging of all management tasks.

When navigation, information, customer support and logistics are well designed and executed, a virtuous cycle develops in which the whole is greater than the sum of the parts. This virtuous cycle creates high customer value, resulting in customer loyalty. Loyalty dramatically reduces the cost to acquire a customer. If one element of the cycle is mishandled, the loyalty generated may be dramatically reduced. Thus if an e-commerce firm is to benefit fully from excellent navigation and information, it must also deliver a high level of customer support and logistics.

The Relationships Among Navigation, Information, Customer Support, And Logistics

The four elements in the customer experience cycle – navigation, information, customer support, and logistics – all interact. Excellence in one can lead to reduced demand for others. Alternatively, poor design and/or execution of one can result in greater use of the others, and consequently increased costs. Excellence in all four can result in greater customer loyalty, which generates increased volume, driving down unit costs.

When navigation is simple, intuitive and quick, customer support costs are reduced because fewer customers contact the company with questions about how to use the Web site. This may sound obvious. Yet more than half of all interactions with customers – telephone calls, e-mails and online chats – at several prominent e-commerce firms involve questions about the use of the Web site. While these interactions will never be eliminated, efforts to improve navigation at Web sites expecting increased volume may pay off handsomely as these efforts will incur relatively fixed costs, while the interactions they preempt result in largely variable costs.

The benefits of improved navigation extend beyond those associated with lower costs. As navigation improves, more customers are able to get information about the products and services they want. When they arrive at this information, many will be less exasperated and more likely to buy. As e-commerce attracts more and more users, navigation will become increasingly important because many of the newest users will have less experience with computers and the Internet. Like navigation, information also has the ability to improve service quality and reduce both customer support and logistics costs. Good information increases the confidence buyers have in their potential purchases, encouraging informed decisions. When the information buyers need to make a decision is easily accessible, they do not need to interact with employees to request it, reducing customer support costs. Finally, at some e-commerce firms, superior information also helps to lower logistics costs. Thus information has the ability to enhance service quality, and reduce customer support and logistics costs simultaneously.

Logistics, executed well, has the ability to reduce customer support costs. In bricks-and-mortar retailing, a failed or late delivery often results in customers contacting customer support, increasing its costs. Logistical problems in e-commerce have a similar effect. Customers' desire for information on a troubled e-commerce transaction may be even greater than for similar bricks-and-mortar transactions because customers have no tangible evidence of an Internet-based organization's existence.

When all four of the elements in the customer experience cycle are designed and executed well, customers are more likely to be loyal, engaging in repurchase and/or positive word of mouth. This contributes to increased volume. Volume, in turn, reduces all costs on a per-unit basis, particularly those related to navigation and information which are largely fixed.

Service Operations And Infinite Scalability

The virtuous, or self-reinforcing, positive cycles among the elements of the customer experience cycle suggest that excellent navigation, information, customer support and logistics can both improve service quality and reduce costs. Because customer support and logistics are two components of e-commerce that do not lend themselves to infinite economies of scale, their importance to an e-commerce venture may help to explain how infinite its scalability is. Customer support and logistics need to be analyzed to determine their importance to a service. Such an analysis should consider their quantity, complexity and predictability.

Thus we can derive a scalability continuum, containing four categories of e-commerce services and products that lend themselves to different degrees of scalability. A pure information provider, such as a search engine or an online newspaper, deals with few customer support or logistics issues. Thus its scalability is very high. Commodity items with standardized handling procedures such as books or toys have somewhat less scalability, as more complex logistics are required and some customer support may be necessary. Airline tickets have common handling issues (due to e-ticket usage), but, as unique services, often require customer support. This reduces scalability further. Finally, we have products and services such as antiques and paintings sold through Sothebys.com that are both unique, requiring customer support, and awkward, requiring customized logistics.

For firms that are very high on the scalability continuum, the need for customer support and logistics does not present a scalability problem. At these firms, information is the core service. Customer support and logistics are relatively insignificant, both from the customers' perspectives and from the firm's perspective. Thus these firms do not rely on customer support and logistics to differentiate their offering. Their differentiation tends to come from the quality of the Web site navigation and the quantity of information they provide.

In contrast, firms that sell physical, non-information services such as travel, or goods such as books, toys or antiques, require significantly more customer support and logistics. The degree to which they need more customer support and logistics is inversely proportional to the degree to which they are scalable and the degree to which their economics will be revolutionized by the Internet. Customer support and logistics are particularly important to these firms as they rely on them for differentiation. The services and goods they sell are rarely theirs exclusively. For example, there are numerous Internet bookstores, travel agents and sources for art and antiques. Thus it is not what they sell, but rather how they sell it that provides differentiation. While many of these firms appear to be looking to navigation and information to provide differentiation, given the relative ease with which competitors can copy these attributes, they are unlikely to provide sources of sustained competitive advantage.

The vast majority of e-commerce firms not working to differentiate themselves through service may be working toward a position of cost leadership. Cost leadership can be a successful competitive strategy. However, given the Internet's ability to provide information inexpensively, a cost leader will also need to be a price leader in order to generate the significantly greater volume that will translate into higher profit. Clearly, there can be only one price leader in an industry. Thus this is not a sustainable strategy for many firms.

The continued importance of human resources in e-commerce is not entirely negative. While the need for front-line human workers often makes infinite scalability unlikely at best, it also suggests that e-commerce firms can leverage human resources for competitive advantage, just as their bricks-and-mortar brethren do. Given the relative ease firms have copying Web site design and even content, e-commerce firms without genuinely differentiated products will ultimately rely on their ability to differentiate their service offerings, largely through the limited human-to-customer service they provide. Customers will want to know that if they need help using a Web site, want additional information, or if something goes wrong in the delivery or performance of their purchase, the service they need to remedy the situation will be easily and readily available.

The implications are clear. Service remains important to much of e-commerce, and front-line human capital, people, often remain important to delivering service. Managers and investors need to consider the roles those people play in delivering service, and the effects this has on scalability and competitive advantage. They can then value e-commerce organizations considering both the benefits and disadvantages that continued dependence on front-line servers create.

SERVICE MARKETING IN ELECTRONIC COMMERCE

In many of the world's advanced economies, services today account for a far greater proportion of gross national product than manufactured goods. In fact, they comprise more than 75 percent of GDP and jobs in the United States. Yet only in recent years have marketing academics, practitioners, and even service firms begun to give serious attention to the marketing of services, as distinct from products. Service marketing is generally considered more difficult, complex and onerous because of the problems created by unique service characteristics.

The 1990s, however, saw the emergence of a phenomenon which will dramatically change this thinking forever: the World Wide Web. Most service problems don't really matter on the Web; services are no longer unmanageably different. Cyberservice not only overcomes previously conceived limitations of service marketing, it creates hitherto undreamed-of opportunities for the marketers.

Service is any act or performance that one party can offer to another that is essentially intangible and does not result in the ownership of anything. Its production may or may not be tied to a physical product. What makes services different from products? What unique characteristics do they possess that products do not? Four of these characteristics are intangibility, simultaneity, heterogeneity and perishability.

How does the Web handle these differences? Cyberservice overcomes many of the traditional problems of service marketing by giving the marketers unprecedented control over the previously capricious characteristics of services. As an interactive medium, the Web combines the best of mass production (based on the manufacture of products) and customization (typically found in services). The ultimate tool for mass customizing, it can treat millions of customers as though each were unique. Innovative firms find a number of ways to use their Web sites to manage the difficulties traditionally associated with service marketing.

Cyberservice overturns the traditional hierarchy between the two kinds of corporate offerings – products and service. How does the Web achieve this? The answer lies in its three unique characteristics: the ability to quantize, search and automate. Quantization of services – breaking them down into their smallest constituent elements – allows unparalleled mass customization by recombining those elements into unique configurations. Searches facilitate hyper-efficient information markets, matching supply and demand at a level previously unattainable. Automation allows users to bypass service bottlenecks, returning power and choice to the customer and overcoming the traditional limitations of time and space.

Thus the traditional challenges to the service marketer are quickly being ameliorated and transformed into singular opportunities by cyberservice. The irony is that in the near future, products may become more troublesome to marketers than services.

Managing Intangibility

Unlike products, services are performances or experiences that are intangible or impalpable; they cannot be seen, held or touched. The main problem this creates for service marketers is that there is nothing to show the customer. Experience and credence qualities are crucial. Service marketers have to make sure their customers know the services exist. To do so, they can use the Web to provide abundant evidence of the services that are available, make the service tangible, offer samples in cyberspace, and multiply memories for the customer.

Providing Evidence

Giving customers evidence of what they will get when purchasing a service has long been a stratagem employed by successful service marketers. Cyberservice puts evidence management into overdrive. One of Ford Motor Company's most innovative U.S. dealers is planning to install live video cameras in its service bays and relay a live feed to its Web site. Customers will be able to visit the service center and check the progress of their car's service. By opening up the center for continuous customer inspection, the dealer is proving the quality of its service.

Making the Service Tangible

Although services are considered intangible, effective Web sites can – and should – lend a tangible dimension to them. There is a simple but critical reason for this: When you can't really see what you are buying, you look for clues, or what psychologists call cues.

When managing Web sites, three critical elements must be remembered

- *Quality.* A site must have good quality text, graphics, video, and sound. Just as in the case of conventional service tangibles, when a customer sees a Web site and not the firm, the site becomes the firm.
- *Frequency of update.* Surfers generally won't visit a Web site unless it changes regularly. No matter how engaging it is on first impression, the site will fail if it is not perceived as up-to-date.
- *Server speed.* In the pre-cyberservice days, speedy service counted. In the Web environment, the same goes for server speed and ease of navigation. Just as customers won't wait endlessly in line for a bank, a fast food restaurant or a travel agent, they won't wait forever to access a slow Web site on a sluggish server; they will simply move on. Immediacy is central to service and a defining expectation in cyberspace.

Sampling in Cyberspace

Giving customers a sample of one's wares goes a long way toward persuading them to buy the product. Traditionally, sampling is much more difficult with services because of their intangibility. But a Web site has the potential to change that.

Multiplying Memories

People tend to rely more on the testimony of others for services than for products. But in the case of a product, the customer actually has something to show for it, whereas service customers are usually left with just a memory. Vivid Travel Network[17] is a collection of Web sites based in San Francisco that link and integrate travel information resources from all over the world. One key feature of the service is that it brings together people with similar travel experiences and interests. Those who have visited a location relive their experiences by writing about them and engaging in discussions and recollections with others who have also been there. At the same time, they provide valuable and highly credible word-of-mouth information to prospective visitors by allowing vast networks to multiply those memories.

Managing Simultaneity

In the case of goods, production and consumption do not occur at the same time or place. But when services are performed, both producer and consumer generally have to be present. Service marketers can manage simultaneity on the Web by customization,

---

[17] http://www.vivid.com

treating the customer as a part-time employee, making innovation a part of customer participation, and reducing customer service errors.

Customization

Because a service is produced and consumed simultaneously, it is possible for the provider to customize it to a far greater extent than can be done with most products. The Web excels at customization. Because its capacity is based on information technology, data storage and data processing, rather than on employees and physical location, it can customize on a scale that traditional service providers would find impossible to match.

Managing Customers as Part-Time Employees

To obtain services, customers generally have to come to the service facility itself. Clients enter banks, vacationers visit travel agencies, university students attend classes in classrooms. Once inside the service facility, customers generally have to do a bit of work – indeed, sometimes a substantial amount of work. Often, the quality of the service they receive is almost as dependent on them as on the efforts of the service provider.

The Web site of a well-known international service firm illustrates how the medium can manage customers profitably as part-time employees. Federal Express allows customers access to its system through its surprisingly popular Web site[18]. A customer can track a shipment traveling through the system, request a pick-up, find the nearest drop-off site and request invoice adjustments. Previously, FedEx has employed a large team of service agents and a major telephone switchboard to deal with such inquiries. Now, 900,000 tracking requests are handled online each month, half of which would otherwise have been made on the more expensive and time-consuming telephone system. Not only does the company save in costs, but customers seem to prefer this form of service delivery.

Innovation as Part of Customer Participation

If we understand that in service settings the customer is a necessary co-producer and participant in the service creation process, then we can become aware of many possible service innovations that can create advantages in competitive markets. Customers willing to do some work can help create enjoyable environments in which to do it, and service firms can devise efficiencies that lead to considerable cost reductions.

Reducing Customer Errors

When customers are part of the production process, their errors can directly affect the service outcome. One third of all customer complaints are related to problems caused by the customers themselves. Ways must be found to make the service component, as well as the producer component, fail-safe. Customer errors can arise during preparation for the service encounter, the encounter itself, and its resolution. Cyberservice reduces or avoids customer errors in each stage. Customers can be reminded of what they need

---

[18] http://www.fedex.com

84

before the encounter – what to bring, what steps to follow, which service to select and where to go. An advantage of cyberservice is that customers can be led repeatedly and precisely through a process.

Managing Heterogeneity

Products tend to possess a sameness or homogeneity that is not achieved by accident. Manufacturing lines make homogenous products and have quality control procedures in place to test them as the come off the line, ensuring that defective products don't reach the market. Services, however, vary in output. Mistakes happen in real-time, thereby creating a number of challenges for the service marketer. There are a few things the service marketer can manage on the Web to overcome the problems occasioned by service heterogeneity. Indeed, the Web offers unique opportunities in this regard.

Service Standardization on the Web Site

Some service marketers are reluctant to standardize activities because they believe it tends to mechanize and dehumanize interactions between people. In some circumstances this is true, but it doesn't mean managers should not look for opportunities to produce service activities as predictably and uniformly as possible. The real skills of service marketers become apparent in their ability to decide what should be standardized and what should not.

Electronic Eavesdropping on Customers' Conversations

Every day, customers discuss products and services on the Internet. Newsgroups and listservs provide forums for customers throughout the world to pass along comments on a company's offerings. Bad news especially travels at megabits per second to millions of customers, as Intel discovered when the flawed Pentium chip was detected. There are three types of customers doing the talking: external customers, competitors' customers, and internal customers or employees.

Companies can eavesdrop on these electronic conversations and respond whenever appropriate. They can collect and analyze comments to learn more about their customers and competitors. Internally, they can set up electronic bulletin boards to foster communication from their employees. Cyberservice means listening to more customers more intently and reacting electronically in real time. It also means everyone in the organization can eavesdrop as well. Key insights can be broadcast on internal bulletin boards so that everyone understands what customers truly want. There has never been a better opportunity to get closer to customers and focus on their needs.

Service Quality

Whereas good quality can be controlled into – and bad quality out of – the manufacturing process for goods, heterogeneity makes this much more difficult for services. Quality must be carefully measured and managed. In the last ten years, tremendous progress has been made in the accuracy and pertinence of service quality measurement.

Interactive Web-based questionnaires are a convenient and inexpensive way to collect customer perceptions of service quality or some other aspect of a service. The real payoff to Web-based questionnaires is in reducing the length of the feedback loop so that quality problems are rapidly detected and corrected before too many customers are turned away.

Managing Perishability

Because services are produced and consumed simultaneously, they cannot be inventoried. To understand and minimize the effects of service perishability, astute service marketers are using the Web to manage two factors: supply and demand.

Managing Supply on the Web Site

Managing supply in a conventional service setting requires running all those production factors that affect a customer's ability to acquire and use the service. Thus, it traditionally includes attention to such variables as opening and closing hours, staffing, and decisions on how many customers will be able to use the service at any particular time. On the Web, these issues are circumvented, for a Web site gives the service marketer the ability to provide 24-hour service anywhere.

Directing Demand on the Web Site

Service marketers also cope with service perishability by managing demand. They use aspects of the service marketing mix, such as promotions, pricing and service bundling, to stimulate or dampen demand for the service. Most service firms are characterized by a high fixed cost component as a proportion of the total cost structure. Finally, some service marketers make good use of service bundling: putting together inclusive packages of services in a way that allows customer value to exceed what would have been spent purchasing each component separately.

ELECTRONIC COMMERCE AND GLOBAL MARKETING

The Internet promises to revolutionize the dynamics of international commerce and may be a major force in the democratization of capitalism. Small companies will be able to compete more easily in the global marketplace, and consumers in merging markets, in particular, will benefit from the expanded range of products, services, and information to which the Internet will give them access. The Internet removes many barriers to communication with customers and employees by eliminating the obstacles created by geography, time zones and location, creating a frictionless business environment.

The long-term international growth of the Internet raises the opportunity for cross-border information flows and transactions. However, transactions are currently concentrated in a limited number of product categories, even within the United States, due to:

- the distinctive demographic profile of current Internet users,
- the type of product information most easily presented electronically, given limitations in bandwidth,
- trade regulations,
- transaction security concerns.

In addition, legal restrictions restrict cross-border transactions; many software products cannot be sold internationally for security reasons due to their inclusion of encryption technologies. But these constraints will likely be overcome as Internet use diffuses and adopter profiles become more heterogeneous, as bandwidth and software capabilities expand, and as data security issues are resolved.

Is the Internet potentially revolutionary or just another marketing channel like home shopping or direct mail? The answer depends on how much added value there is in Internet communications and transactions compared to existing alternatives. The value added will vary across country markets and according to company type. Because distribution channels tend to be less developed, less direct, and less efficient in emerging markets than in the United States, the Internet may offer special opportunities in these markets. In addition, the differences in speed of, control over, and access to communication and distribution channels between the Internet and traditional media and distribution channels internationally will offer different mixes of opportunities and challenges to large multinational companies (MNCs) and to small businesses.

A company's choice of evolutionary path depends on whether it is an established multinational company or a start-up company created to do business solely on the Internet. Existing multinational companies tend to adopt the information-to-transaction model, whereas start-up companies tend to use the transaction-to-information model. The multinational company starts by offering information to address the needs of its existing customers. It then collects information from its existing customers for market research purposes. It then uses the Internet to provide customer support and service. Then it adapts the Internet to provide internal support and service to employees within the organization. Last, it uses the Internet to execute transactions. On the other hand, simple economics require Internet start-ups to begin with transactions and then continue to use the medium to build a brand image, provide product support, and win repeat purchases. They then use the Internet to collect data for market research purposes.

Whichever of the two business models a company pursues, the specific functions embodied in a Web site, whether targeted to internal or external users, need to generate revenue or reduce costs. As a multinational company or start-up develops its site to incorporate a broader range of functions, it needs to assess how the functions influence the global business model. For example, transaction capabilities can have both revenue-generation and cost-reduction potential, depending on whether the company is attracting new customers and sales or transferring existing sales to a more profitable medium. Similarly, providing information to internal and external audiences can increase revenues by facilitating incremental sales or increased margins. The dissemination of information via the Internet can also reduce costs by replacing communications through less cost-efficient channels.

		Primary Business Impact	
		Cost Reduction	Revenue Generation
Customer Focus	Internal	Technical, Legal, and Administrative Support Database Management Internal Research Company Information	Marketing and Sales Support/Information
	External	Customer Service Transactions	Product Information Promotions Database Development Market Research Transactions

Table 3-2: Drivers of Internet Business Models

While the Internet offers many benefits to both existing multinational companies and start-up companies, the challenges of an inadequate technological infrastructure, concerned public policy makers, and, especially for multinational companies, existing distribution and organization structures all seem formidable. Any company eager to take advantage of the Internet on a global scale must select a business model for its Internet venture and define how information and transactions delivered through this new medium will influence its existing business model. The company must also assess who its diverse Web audiences are, what specific customer needs the medium will satisfy, and how its Internet presence will respond to a changing customer base, evolving customer needs, competitor actions and technological developments. For international marketers, achieving a balance between the new medium's ability to be customized and the desire to retain coherence, control, and consistency as they go to market worldwide will be a major challenge.

The Impact on Markets: Effects on Efficiency

Standard Pricing

Advances in Web browsers and servers facilitate rapid, frequent price changes and levels of price discrimination to a much finer degree than are currently achieved in alternative media, such as magazines and direct mail. Prices can be customized, not only by country market, but at the level of the individual user. When a user accesses a Web site, the page she receives when she clicks on a link can be made dependent on her IP address, which is embedded in the commands sent from her browser to the server. This means instant customization of information and prices across borders, furthering the potential for more efficient markets.

In addition, smart agents, software programs that can search the Internet for products meeting prespecified criteria, may further combat attempts at price discrimination by uncovering different prices. The Internet will lead to increased standardization of prices across borders or, at least, narrow price spreads across country markets.

Changing Role of Intermediaries

The Internet can connect end users with producers directly and thereby reduce the importance of intermediaries. The ubiquitous availability of the Web enables buyers, particularly in emerging markets, to access a broader range of product choices, bypass local intermediaries, and purchase their goods on the world market at lower prices. However, if intermediaries can perform a different mix of services, made necessary by the Internet, they will continue to play critical roles and extract value. While the Internet makes direct contact between end users and producers more feasible, this may also be less efficient over the long term and across a broad range of products. The potential for information overload is enormous. An intermediary's value-added may no longer be principally in the physical distribution of goods, but in the collection, collation, interpretation and dissemination of vast amounts of information.

Making Markets

There are new opportunities for businesses to serve primarily as market makers, assisting buyers and sellers in locating one another, in negotiating terms of trade, and in executing secure transactions. The two principal market-making vehicles are auctions and exchanges. Exchanges prescreen buyers and sellers, introduce them to one another, and assist in the transaction process, but do not help them agree on a price. Exchanges are examples of businesses in which there is true value-added from the international scope of the operations.

Efficient Capital Flows

The efficiency of international capital flows and foreign direct investment may also increase. Many start-up companies benefiting from this increased access to capital and investment opportunities are small and located in emerging markets. Improved access to capital will be another factor in leveling the playing field between large and small businesses competing internationally.

Internal Implications: The Intranet

While the early audiences for most Web sites have been external customers, the potential for serving internal customers may be equally as great. Creating internal networks to facilitate communications and transactions among employees, suppliers, independent contractors and distributors may be the Internet's principal value for multinational companies. Internal Web servers have a number of advantages over classic client-server solutions:
- they are cheaper, faster and easier to set up than client-server network systems, given the existing use of TCP/IP for outside communications,
- vendors are quickly developing new products specifically for this market,

- the architecture is already established and built into personal computers,
- the platform offers room for growth and flexibility,
- Web-based internal networks can also offer sufficient security based on encryption technologies and allow companies to adjust levels of access based on a user's status.

Companies can use the traditional "one to many" or broadcast model to communicate corporate policies and product or market news to worldwide divisions. Similarly, companies can provide employees worldwide with immediate and up-to-date access to company databases, phone directories and reports. In the "many to one" model, multinational companies can use the internal system to ask questions or collect information from divisions and individual employees. In the "many to many" model, multinational companies can use the network to enable real-time, synchronous discussion among operating units. Several intranet applications of these communication models are in use, often aimed at expediting relatively simple but costly and time-consuming tasks like information distribution.

More complicated two-way communications take fuller advantage of the new technologies. Companywide bulletin boards permit multiparty dialogue on specific problems. As expertise on intranet usage spreads from the MIS department to marketing and other functions, companies can bring together functional departments located at sites around the globe to learn, share and solve problems. They can also use these real-time forums as training vehicles for selected employees worldwide. In addition, companies are testing intranets as tools for internal transactions.

External Implications: Global Product Reach

The global expansion of the Internet will facilitate both finding markets for new products and developing products for new markets.

New Product Diffusion

New product announcements on the Internet will spawn immediate demand. To respond and to avoid competitive preemption, manufacturers will have to be prepared to distribute and service new products overnight. At the same time, using sophisticated technologies, companies may find it easier to test multiple new product variations simultaneously if they can control the information flow between test markets. When able to discriminate by a visitor's Internet address, companies can target variations of new products at different groups and get instant feedback on the value of specific features and appeal of various prices.

Local Adaptation and Customization

Marketers are finding it easier to adapt their products inexpensively to local or national preferences, due to factory and marketing customization. The Internet's new communication capabilities may speed this trend. However, if the global community is able to communicate more openly, the global mass-market concept will thrive as consumers retain their desire to share in the latest trends around the world.

90

Niche Products

Small companies offering specialized niche products should be able to find the critical mass of customers necessary to succeed through the worldwide reach of the Internet. The Internet's low-cost communications permits firms with limited capital to become global marketers at the early stages of their development. Indeed, the risk that entrepreneurs in other parts of the world will preempt their unique ideas demands that they do so.

Overcoming Import Restrictions

Many Internet retailers are finding that they can offer products to consumers directly via their Web sites for a delivered cost significantly lower than most international consumers find in their local retail outlets. However, with the Internet stimulating cross-border product flows, government import regulations may become stiffer. Information flows have come under similar scrutiny.

Understanding Global Consumers

The Internet promises to be an efficient new medium for conducting worldwide market research. Marketers can test both new product concepts and advertising copy over the Internet for instant feedback. They can also test varying levels of customer support to help managers define country market priorities and adapt the marketing mix. Marketers can also establish worldwide consumer panels to test proposed marketing programs across national, regional or cross-cultural samples. Tracking individual customer behavior and preferences will become easier over time. Moreover, the Internet permits new types of measurement tools that will expand the data available to marketers, including:

- *Online Surveys*. Marketers can post surveys on sites and offer incentives for participation. Internet surveys are more powerful than mail surveys because of the medium's branching capabilities (asking different questions based on previous answers) and are cheaper than either mail or phone surveys.
- *Bulletin Boards*. Companies can monitor and participate in such group discussions in many countries simultaneously.
- *Web Visitor Tracking*. Servers automatically collect data on the paths that visitors travel while in the site, including time spent at each page. Marketers can assess the value of the information and correlate the observed traffic patterns with purchase behavior.
- *Advertising Measurement*. Since servers automatically record the link through which each Web visitor enters a site, marketers can accurately assess the traffic, as well as sales, generated by links placed on other Web sites.
- *Customer Identification Systems*. Both business-to-business and business-to-consumer marketers are installing registration procedures that enable them to identify individuals and track purchases over time.
- *E-mail Marketing Lists*. Many sites ask customers to sign up voluntarily on a mailing list for company news. The audience generated appears very different from that

garnered through traditional direct marketing. Internationally, information can be disseminated quickly to the audiences on these lists at minimal cost.

Challenges for International Marketers

The growth of the Internet as a facilitator of international commerce presents different challenges and opportunities to small Internet start-up companies and to multinational companies. Some of the obstacles are unique to each company, while others confront all marketers striving to succeed globally on the Internet. Multinational companies usually already do business internationally, but may have to revise their operations, strategies, and business models if they want to exploit the opportunities offered by the Internet. The start-up doing business primarily through the Internet must be prepared to operate globally from the outset, which can strain its resources. The company must have:

- twenty-four hour a day order taking and customer service response capability
- regulatory and customs-handling expertise to ship internationally
- in-depth understanding of foreign marketing environments to assess the relative advantages of its own products and services
- sufficient staff with multilingual skills
- access to information on local laws and trends.

Global Branding

A major challenge for multinational companies is the management of global brands and corporate name or logo identification. Consumers may be confused if a company and its subsidiaries have several Web sites, each communicating a different format, image, message, and content. Developing one site for each brand – while costly and limiting to cross-selling – is preferable when the brands have distinct markets and images. New Internet users tend to explore the sites of familiar brands first. Trust is a critical factor in stimulating purchases over the Internet. As a result, sites with known brand names enhance the credibility of the site sponsor, as well as the medium. Recognizing the importance of brand names, many multinational companies are establishing Web sites for each brand.

New Competition

The Web will reduce the competitive advantage of scale economies in many industries and make it easier for small marketers to compete worldwide. Aadvertising as a barrier to entry will be reduced as the Web makes it possible to reach a global audience more cheaply. Paying to place links on pages with audiences that mirror or include a company's target customers is less expensive than traditional media. Postings on Internet discussion groups on topics relevant for specific products or markets is another way for small marketers to attract visitors to their sites. Increased advertising efficiency will be available to more marketers. As the role of intermediaries evolves, gaining visibility and distribution will become easier for small companies. The traditional networks of international distributors and subsidiaries that multinational companies set up are less efficient barriers to the entry of smaller companies than they used to be - except perhaps in the case of products that require significant after-sales service. These existing networks may even impede multinational companies' effective, timely response.

However, providing on-site, after-sales service will be difficult for manufacturers of products sold directly via the Internet. Local distributors currently fulfill this role but will be unlikely to take it on without profiting from the accompanying sale. Multinational companies must develop policies for providing such service without disrupting the existing channel arrangements.

Competitive Advantage

For companies marketing on the Internet, technology is a more important source of competitive advantage than size. A small company can quickly become a big player internationally by leveraging technology in ways that respond to customer needs. What does this mean for large multinational companies? The advantages of size will erode. As a result, many will need to proactively invent new ways of using the Internet to address customer needs and also to connect their worldwide operations.

Organizational Challenges

The Internet presents especially serious organizational challenges for multinational companies attempting to convert their global businesses to the new medium because its speed and worldwide presence make its audiences intolerant of inconsistencies and slow response. The services that a multinational corporation offers on the Internet should be available to buyers in all countries to prevent confusion and distraction.

A multinational company must set up a worldwide task force of executives to coordinate the presentation of its corporate identity on multiple, interconnected Web sites. It might appoint a particular office or operating unit that has been a leader in using the Internet as the center for home page development. It also must have a system for regular updating of Web site information, especially if price changes or inventories go out of stock. Managers of Internet task forces must keep informed about developments around the globe.

A specialized customer service staff may be needed to deal with Internet traffic. Internet users have high expectations for timely, efficient response, due to their knowledge of the company's expanded capabilities. A company's Internet center should also analyze the server data that tracks customer site access and transactions. Marketers will need to integrate their marketing communications and distribution for Internet customers with their existing strategies.

Disseminating Information

News of product quality problems and cross-border differences in quality, price, and availability will be hard to contain. There will inevitably be a need for a worldwide approach to crisis management. Controversies, especially those surrounding global brands, will be impossible to contain at the national level. There are other implications of the rapid information flow. Third-party search agents can collect pricing information through robots from various sources around the world, so consumers can compare prices and products. This is especially important in emerging markets where such sources of information are widely available.

Maintaining Web Sites

The creation of a Web site is not a one-time effort. The current speed of technological innovation in Web site design and the increasing competitiveness of the medium require global marketers to continually assess their Internet sites' perceived value among target groups across countries. Sites must offer valuable, changing content that will not only attract new customers from many countries but also encourage them to return. Given that individuals around the world will have different product information needs, levels of brand familiarity, and bandwidth capacity, fulfilling such diverse needs on a single site will be challenging. With new technologies and the proliferation of Web design and management companies, the temptation to customize content will have to be weighed against the value of maintaining a consistent worldwide image. In addition, companies will have to choose how to maintain, grow, and manage their sites. Should they outsource? Or should they strive to create proprietary content and software?

Language and Cultural Barriers

The Web promises to reinforce the trend toward English as the lingua franca of commerce. Very few multinational companies offer translations of their Web site content into local languages. Several translation services have opened on the Internet. However, cultural barriers remain. When setting up a traditional business operation in a foreign country, managers usually have numerous conversations with local partners and visit the country several times. With a virtual business, the need for such contacts is minimized, and cultural differences may not be as apparent. To avoid cultural pitfalls, many small entrepreneurs without broad contacts use Internet discussion groups to become familiar with local customs, trends and laws.

Government Influence and Involvement

Foreign government support and cooperation will be critical in determining how the international Internet business environment will evolve. Will foreign governments allow the free flow of trade and ideas? Will they be able to agree on issues such as data security and taxation on transactions. Who will lead in developing the infrasructure, educating users, and providing access to the Internet for businesses and consumers?

Early initiatives by some governments, trade associations, and telecommunication companies bode well for future expansion. Some governments in Asia have aggressively led in development of the Internet infrastructure in their countries to further economic growth and to retain control over external access and internal usage. The United Nations has established a "Global Trade Point Network" that assists small and medium-size companies eager to expand globally by linking interested entrepreneurs with information resources on trade regulations, trade associations and local markets. In Europe, small businesses are likely to establish an online presence through regional cooperatives and state organizations that promote local business. In the United States, individual small businesses have rapidly exploited the new opportunities on their own. While joint development efforts reduce costs and risks, they also limit an individual company's freedom to innovate and invest in aggressive marketing on the Web.

Numerous issues remain to be resolved:

- Defining the scope of import tariffs and export controls.
- Delineating the boundaries of intellectual copyrights.
- Standardizing regulations on the use and sale of personal information.
- Defining the roles of national governments in limiting the flow of ideas.
- Creating cross-national laws for regulated industries such as gambling, financial services and liquor.

An equally daunting obstacle is the poor state of the current infrastructure and the regulation of the telecommunications industry abroad. Countries need to invest in better telecommunications infrastructures and to promote internal competition before they can take full advantage of the opportunities the Internet offers for global commerce.

Chapter 4

Advertising in Electronic Commerce

TYPES OF WEB ADVERTISEMENTS

A major source of revenue on the Web today is advertising. While the Web is much more than an advertising medium, that is likely to remain one of its primary functions. Four kinds of Web advertising can be distinguished:

- *Banner ads* are "teasers", typically small, rectangular ads placed on high-traffic Web sites. While the ad provides exposure to the advertising message by itself and thereby increases awareness of the product, the goal is usually to have the user click on the banner and be linked to the advertiser's site.
- *Target ads* refer to the destination sites to which those who click on banner ads are sent. They are larger ads, often consisting of a whole page or a complete Web site, which advertise the marketer's products.
- *Sponsorship* is an alternative to advertising. Companies running Web sites get a steady source of income (typical sponsorship deals range between $250,000 and $1.5 million) without the complexity of repetitively selling advertising space, while the company advertising gets preferential treatment in getting its message across to its target segment. A good example of a highly sponsored site is BabyCenter[1], which has a number of "Sponsored Educational Areas" with sponsors such as Johnson & Johnson and Proctor & Gamble.
- *Promotion* can be used on the Web to increase brand awareness and product trial through, for example, competitions, price discounts, and offers of free samples. A number of services exist on the Web to deliver promotional incentives to site visitors. Examples are Netcentives, Hot Coupons, Coupons Online and Freeshop.

The following two tables show who advertises on the Web and with whom they advertise. Table 4-1 illustrates the top 10 ad spenders. Table 4-2 illustrates the top 10 ad-supported sites. Seven names appear on both lists. This suggests that, at this early stage in the building of an audience for this medium, much of the advertising carried on the Web may be for the medium itself, not for the other products and services that, ultimately, will justify its existence.

---

[1] http://www.babycenter.com/

Rank	Site	Ad Spending ($ millions)	Company Type
1	Microsoft	40.3	Software
2	IBM	19.4	Hardware
3	Excite	15.7	Search engine
4	Yahoo!	10.7	Search engine
5	AOL	9.4	Online Service
6	Ziff-Davis	7.7	Publisher
7	Lycos	7.5	Search engine
8	CBS Sports Line	7.2	News
9	Infoseek	6.5	Search engine
10	Ford	6.5	Car manufacturer

Table 4-1: Top Online Advertisers for Year-to-Date July 2000

Rank	Site	Ad Revenues ($ millions)	Company Type
1	Yahoo!	69.5	Search engine
2	AOL	53.0	Online service
3	Infoseek	43.7	Search engine
4	CNET	32.8	Online service
5	Excite	27.6	Search engine
6	Lycos	26.8	Search engine
7	ZDNet	24.3	Online service
8	MSN	20.0	Online service
9	CMP Net	17.9	News
10	Webcrawler	15.4	Search engine

Table 4-2: Leading Ad-Supported Sites for Year-to-Date July 2000

How do advertisers compare the cost and benefit of advertising on the Web to the cost and benefit of other media? The usual measure of cost used by advertisers and their agencies to compare one advertising medium to another is cost-per-thousand audience member impressions (CPM).

Media	Vehicle	Cost	Reach	CPM
TV	30 second spot on "NBC Evening News"	$60,000	5.5 M adults age 18-49	$10.9 per thousand adults
Consumer magazine	Full-page, four-color ad in Cosmopolitan	$92,155	2.5 M paid readers	$36.86 per thousand paid readers
Website	Banner on InfoSeek	$10,000 per month	500,000 page views (guaranteed)	$20 per thousand page views
Online Service	Banner on one of CompuServe's major topic menu pages for one month	$10,000 per month	750,000 visits	$13.33 per thousand visits

Table 4-3: CPM Rates for Various Media

Some of the qualitative factors that advertisers take into account when comparing different media are presented in the table 4-4.

Media Factors	TV	Radio	Magazines	Newspapers	Web
Total audience coverage	+++	+	+	+	+
Selectivity of audience	+	++	++	+	+++
Prestige of medium	+	+	+++	+	+++
Ability to demonstrate	+++	+	+	+	+
Emotional impact	+++	+	+	+	+
Ability to intrude	+++	++	+	+	+
Ability to convey news, information	+	+	++	++	+++
Ability to change content quickly	+	++	+	+++	+++
Opportunity for audience response	++	+	++	++	+++

Table 4-4: Comparison of Qualitative Factors Across Types of Media

Because CPM advertising simply counts exposure – how many times an ad appears on a Web site – it does not take advantage of the medium's ability to detect viewer response. As a result, clickthrough pricing for advertising has become popular. When advertising is priced per clickthrough, the advertiser pays only when a response is elicited. The Web site, however, depends on the quality of the advertising to earn revenue. A third way of pricing Web advertising is paying for action – per lead, per transaction, per dollar spent, etc. Because of the ease of following the actions of the customer on the Web, multi-tiered pricing schemes using more than one of these methods may become prevalent in the near future. One other method of advertising is the barter method, where companies (usually offering complementary or related services) agree to exchange icons or banner advertisements on each other's sites free of charge.

Web sites command a range of CPMs, depending on audience size and quality. These attributes in turn depend on the purpose for which the user visits the site. Individual sites also have varying CPMs depending on how the ad is placed – whether it is a general ad, or tied to a specific keyword or a specific page within the site. For example, Excite's prices range from $24 (general rotation) to $65 (keywords)[2].

It is common to distinguish between two kinds of sites: search engines and destinations. Search engines are the sites that users visit to find other sites. Consequently they provide advertisers with large volumes of traffic, but they are not selective, and therefore tend to earn low CPMs. Destination sites contain the content that users are searching for. They deliver lower levels of traffic, but audiences are more homogeneous. A third category of advertising site is the "start page" or "personalized home page". These sites offer users the ability to select a number of personal features, perhaps a Dilbert cartoon, the Philadelphia weather forecast and last night's basketball scores, to appear on a page each time the user starts a Web session. Examples are Netscape's "My Start" page and Microsoft Network. Customized start pages may provide both high volumes of traffic and the ability to target advertising, and are therefore likely to be the next competitive battleground, similar to the current competition among search engines. Search engines and start pages are also called portals as the user commonly encounters them in the beginning of a Web session. The attractiveness of search engines – many of which also offer start pages – to advertisers trying to reach a mass audience can be easily seen from table 4-5, which lists the most popular Web sites.

Rank	Domain	Percent Reach	Site Type	URL
1	AOL	61.9	Online service	http://www.aol.com/
2	Yahoo	52.8	Search engine	http://www.yahoo.com/
3	Geocities	32.5	Community	http://www.geocities.com/
4	Microsoft	31.8	Software	http://www.microsoft.com/
5	Excite	27.9	Search engine	http://www.excite.com/
6	Infoseek	18.9	Search engine	http://www.infoseek.com/
7	Tripod	17.7	Community	http://www.tripod.com/
8	Angelfire	16.4	Community	http://www.angelfire.com/
9	Lycos	14.8	Search engine	http://www.lycos.com/

Table 4-5: Web Domains Visited from Home (July 2000)

ATTRACTING CUSTOMERS TO YOUR WEB SITE

The explosive growth of the Internet and the appearance of the World Wide Web, together with the rapid expansion of public access to these media, have boosted the idea of doing business online and attracted a broad range of commercial interests. There are several reasons for firms to join the scurrying herd to create a Web site:

---

[2] http://corp.excite.com/MediaKit/pricelist.html

- to reduce the costs of matching buyers and sellers,
- to promote the image of a leading-edge corporation and increase visibility,
- to improve customer service,
- to enable market expansion,
- to lower stakeholder communication costs through online transactions and global information distribution.

The Web changes the nature of communication between firms and customers. Traditional advertising centers on the firm broadcasting a message. The flow of information is predominantly from the seller to the buyer. However, the Web puts this flow in reverse thrust. Customers have considerable control over which messages they receive because it is primarily by visiting Web sites that they are exposed to marketing communications. The customer intentionally seeks the message. The Web increases the richness of communication because it enables greater interactivity between the firm and its customers and among customers. Firms and customers can get much closer to each other because of the relative ease and low cost of electronic interaction.

Although there is some traditional advertising on the Web, especially that associated with search engines, in the main the communication relationship is distinctly different. This shift in communication patterns is so profound that major communication conglomerates are undergoing a strategic realignment. Increasingly, customers will use search and directory facilities to seek information about a firm's products and services. Consequently, persuading and motivating customers to seek out interactive marketing communication and interact with advertisers is the biggest challenge facing advertisers in the interactive age.

In the new world of Web advertising, the rules are different. The Web, compared to other media, provides a relatively level playing field for all participants in that:
- access opportunities are essentially equal for all players, regardless of size
- share of voice is essentially uniform – no player can drown out others
- initial set-up costs present minimal or non-existent barriers to entry.

Small companies with a well-designed home page can look every bit as professional and credible as a large, multinational company. People can't tell if you do business from a 90-storey office building or a two-room rented suite. Web home pages level the playing field for small companies. Differentiation – success in appealing to desirable market segments so as to maintain visibility, create defensible market positions, and forge institutional identity – is considered to be a central key to survival and growth for businesses in the new electronic marketplace.

Thus resolving the fundamental marketing issues for success in the electronic marketplace include adaptation of traditional goals:
- how to communicate effectively with customers and other stakeholders,
- how to position and differentiate a product or a brand,
- how to generate pull forces emanating from a company that attract and lure potential customers into repeatedly visiting a company's Web site.

An attractor is a Web site with the potential to attract and interact with a relatively large number of visitors in a target stakeholder group. While the Web site must be a good attractor, it must also have the facility for interaction if its powers of attraction are to have a long life span. Merely having attraction power is not enough. The strength of the medium lies in its ability to interact with buyers. Good sites offer interaction above all else; less effective sites may often look more visually appealing, but offer little incentive to interact. Many organizations have simply used the Web as an electronic dumping ground for their corporate brochures – this in no way exploits the major attribute of the medium – its ability to interact with the visitor. The best Web sites both attract and interact. For example, the BMW site shows pictures of its cars and accompanies these with textual information. More importantly, BMW allows the visitor to see and listen to their new models, redesign the car by seeing different color schemes and specifications, and drive the car using virtual reality.

The strategic use of hard-to-imitate attractors, building blocks for gaining visibility with targeted stakeholders, will be a key factor in online marketing. Creating an attractor will become a key component of the strategy for some firms. The attractor strategy model stimulates thinking about the audience to be attracted and the degree of interactivity with it, and it is a tool for linking attractors to a stakeholder driven view of strategy. Attractors are strategic information systems and must be aligned with organizational goals.

Web sites have the potential for creating competitive advantage by attracting numerous visitors so that many potential customers can learn about a firm's products and services or so that influential stakeholders can gain a positive impression of the firm. The advantage, however, may be short-lived unless the organization has some valuable and rare resource that cannot be displaced. A valuable, but not necessarily rare, resource for many organizations is the current information technology infrastructure. Practitioners may find it useful to re-examine their existing databases to gauge their potential for highly attractive Web applications. Building front-end Web applications to create an attractor (e.g., customer service) can be a quick way of capitalizing on existing investments, but competitors are likely to be undertaking the same projects. Information technology infrastructure, however, is not enough to create a sustained attractor. The key assets are managerial information technology skills and the ability to view information as the key asset that can create competitive advantage. Sustainable attractiveness is dependent on managers understanding what information to deliver and how to present it to stakeholders.

All organizations need to examine how they can attract visitors to their site, otherwise they have no measure of its value. There is every sign that a major shift in the communication patterns between organizations and their stakeholders is in progress. Attractors, an early product of this change, will play a key role in the efforts of organizations to interact with their stakeholders and now serve as an unprecedented platform for communication. In many ways, they will not only shape and direct dialogue between an organization and its stakeholders, they will actually redefine organizations.

TYPES OF ATTRACTORS

Organizations are taking a variety of approaches to making their Web sites attractive to a range of stakeholders. Web sites can attract a broad audience, some of whom are never likely to purchase the company's wares, but could influence perceptions of the company and certainly increase word-of-mouth communication, which could filter through to significant real customers. Other Web sites focus on serving one particular stakeholder – the customer. They can aim to increase market share by stimulating traffic to their site or to increase the share of the customer by providing superior service. An organization is not restricted to using one form of attractor. It makes good sense to take a variety of approaches so as to maximize the attractiveness of a site and to meet the diverse needs of Web surfers.

The Entertainment Park

Web sites in this category engage visitors in activities that demand a high degree of participation while offering entertainment. Many use games to market products and enhance the corporate image. These sites have the potential to generate experiential flow, because they provide various degrees of challenge to visitors. They are interactive and often involve elements and environments that promote telepresence experiences. These attractors are interactive, recreational, and challenging. The potential competitive advantages gained through these attractors are high traffic potential (with repeat visits) and creation of an image of a dynamic, exciting and friendly corporation. An example is GTE Laboratories[3] Fun Stuff part of its Web site, which includes Web versions of the popular games MineSweeper, Rubick's cube, and a 3D maze for Web surfers to navigate.

The Archive

Archive sites provide their visitors with opportunities to discover the historical aspects of the company's activities. Their appeal lies in the instant and universal access to interesting information and the visitor's ability to explore the past. The credibility of a well-established image is usually the foundation of a successful archive, and building and reinforcing this corporate image is the main marketing role of the archive.

The strength of these attractors is that they are difficult to imitate, and often impossible to replicate. They draw on an already established, highly credible feature of the company, and they bring an educational potential, thus reinforcing public relations aspects of serving the community with valuable information. The major weakness is that they often lack interactivity and are static and less likely to attract repeat visits. The potential competitive advantage gained through these attractors is the building and maintenance of the image of a trusted, reputable and well-established corporation. For example, Boeing's[4] site appeals to aircraft enthusiasts by giving visitors a chance to find out more about its aircraft through pictures, short articles on new features, and technical explanations.

Exclusive Sponsorship

An organization may be the exclusive sponsor of an event of public interest and can use its Web site to extend its audience reach. Thus, we find on the Internet details of sponsored sporting competitions and broadcasts of special events such as concerts, speeches and the opening of art exhibitions. Sponsorship attractors have broad traffic potential and can attract many visitors in short periods. They can enhance the image of

---

[3] http://info.gte.com/gtel/fun/
[4] http://www.boeing.com/

the corporation through the provision of timely, exclusive and valuable information. An example is Reebok's[5] site which includes interviews with the athletes it sponsors.

The Town Hall

The traditional Town Hall has long been a venue for assembly where people can hear a famous person speak, attend a conference, or participate in a seminar. The Town Hall has gone virtual, and these public forums are found on the Web. These attractors can have broad traffic potential when the figure is of national importance or is a renowned specialist in a particular domain. Town Halls have a potentially higher level of interactivity and participation. An example is CMP Publciations Inc.[6] a publisher of information technology (IT) magazines, where an IT guru posts statements on a topic and responds to issues raised by readers.

The Club

People have a need to be part of a group and have satisfactory relationships with others. For some people, a Web club can satisfy this need. These are places to hang out with your friends or those with similar interests. The club is an electronic community, which has been a central feature of the Internet since its foundation. Web clubs engage people because they are interactive and recreational. These attractors can potentially increase company loyalty, enhance customer feedback, and improve customer service through members helping members. An example is Apple's EvangeList[7], which is a bulletin board for maintaining the faith of Macintosh devotees.

The Gift Shop

Gifts and free samples nearly always get attention. Web gifts typically include digitized material such as software (e.g., screensavers and utilities), photographs, digital paintings, research reports and non-digital offerings (e.g., T-shirts). Often gifts are provided as an explicit bargain for dialogue participation (e.g., the collection of demographic data). For example, Kodak[8] offers a library of colorful, high-quality digital images that are downloadable. Many software companies distribute upgrades and complimentary freeware or shareware via their Web site.

The Freeway Intersection

Web sites that provide advanced information processing services (e.g., search engines) can become Web freeway intersections with surfers coming and going in all directions. They present significant advertising opportunities because the traffic flow is intense. Search engines and directories, news centers and electronic malls, can attract hundreds of thousands of visitors in a day. The goal is to create a one-stop resource

---

[5] http://planetreebok.com/
[6] http://techWeb.cmp.com/
[7] mailto:macway@solutions.apple.com
[8] http://www.kodak.com:80/digitalImaging/samples/

center. First movers who do the job well are likely to regain a long-term competitive advantage because they have secured prime real estate, or what conventional retailers might call a virtual location. An example is Yahoo[9], which provides a search engine and a hierarchical directory of Web sites.

The Customer Service Center

By directly meeting information needs, a Web site can be highly attractive to existing customers. Many organizations now use their Web site to support the ownership phase of the customer service life cycle. For example, FedEx[10] has its much cited parcel tracking service online. The Web site is a customer service center. When providing service to existing customers, the organization also has the opportunity to sell other products and services.

ATTRACTIVENESS FACTORS

Attractors require varying degrees of visitor interaction. A search engine simply requires the visitor to enter search terms. While the customers might make many searches, on any one visit there is little interaction. A Web site is entertaining only if the visitor is willing to participate (e.g., play an interactive game). The degree of customization varies across attractors from low (e.g., the digital archive) to high (e.g., a customer service center).

---

[9] http://www.yahoo.com/
[10] http://www.fedex.com/

104

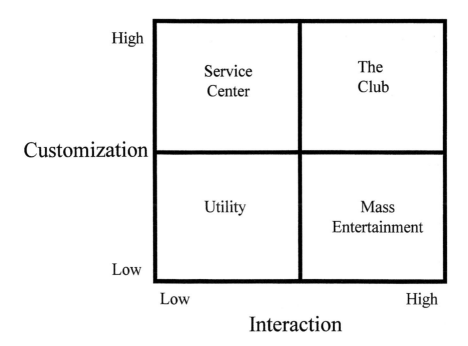

Figure 4-1: Attractors Grid

A *utility* (e.g., search engine) requires little interaction and there is no customization. Each customer receives the same output for identical keywords. A *service center* provides information tailored to the customer's current concern. In *mass entertainment* (e.g., an entertainment park), the visitor participates in an enjoyable interaction, but there is no attempt to customize according to the needs or characteristics of the visitor. The atmosphere of a *club* is customized interaction. The club member feels at home because of the personalized nature of the interaction.

The impetus with attractors should be towards customized service. The search engine, which falls in the utility quadrant needs to discover more about its visitors so that it can become a customer service center. InfoSeek[11] has already made a move to customize its search engine by releasing a desk-top utility that, among other things, saves frequent searches. Then the results of a search will be tailored to what is known about the customer and learned from past interactions. Similarly, mass entertainment should be converted to the personalized performance and interaction of a club. The service center can also consider becoming a club so that frequent visitors receive a special welcome and additional service. Indeed, commercial Internet success may be dependent on creating clubs or electronic communities.

Where possible, organizations should be using the Web to provide customized service by creating highly customized attractors. A potential of the Web is that it will

---

[11] http://guide.infoseek.com/

105

make mass customization workable. It will enable customized service to each customer, while serving millions of them simultaneously. Each customer will get more or less what they want, tailored to what is unique to them and their circumstances. This will be achieved, almost without exception, by information technology. The important aspect of this is that by mass customization, the firm will learn from customers. More importantly, customers are more likely to remain loyal.

SUSTAINABLE ATTRACTIVENESS

The problem with many Web sites, like many good ideas, is that they are easily imitated. Because the Web is so public, firms can systematically analyze each other's Web sites. They can continually monitor the Web presence of competitors and, where possible, quickly imitate many initiatives. Consequently, organizations need to be concerned with sustainable attractiveness – the ability to create and maintain a site that continues to attract targeted stakeholders. In the case of a Web site, sustainable attractiveness is closely linked to the ease with which a site can be imitated.

Attractors can be classified by ease of imitation, an assessment of the cost and time to copy another Web site's concept. The easiest thing to reproduce is information that is already in print (e.g., the corporate brochure). Product descriptions, annual reports, price lists, product photographs, and so forth can be converted quickly to hypertext markup language (HTML), graphical interface format (GIF) images, or an electronic publishing format such as Adobe's portable document format (PDF). Indeed, this sort of information is extremely common on the Web.

There are a variety of attractors, such as utilities, that can be imitated with some effort and time. The availability of multiple search engines and directories clearly supports this contention. The original offerer may gain from being a first mover, but distinctiveness will be hard to sustain. Nevertheless, while investing in easily imitated attractors may provide little gain, firms may have to match their competitors' offerings so as to remain equally attractive.

The key to imitatability is whether a firm possesses valuable and rare resources and how much it costs to duplicate these resources or how readily substitutes can be found. Back-end computer applications that support Web front-end customer service can be a valuable resource, though not rare. Information technology investment can create a competitive advantage, but it is unlikely to be sustainable because competitors can eventually duplicate the system. Sponsorship is another investment that can create a difficult to imitate attractor. Signing a long-term contract to sponsor a major sporting or cultural event can create the circumstances for a long-term attractor.

There are some attractors that can never be imitated or for which there are few substitutes. No other beverage company can have a Coke Museum – real or virtual. Firms with respected and well-known brands (e.g., Coca-Cola) have a degree of exclusiveness that they can impart to their Web sites. These attractors derive their rareness from the reputation and history of the firm or the object. History can be a source of enduring competitiveness, and, in this case, enduring attractiveness.

This analysis suggests that Web application designers should try to take advantage of:
- prior back-end information technology investments that take time to duplicate,

- special relations (e.g., sponsorship),
- special information resources (e.g., archive),
- established brand or image (part of the enterprise's history),
- proprietary intellectual/artistic capital.

STRATEGIES FOR ATTRACTORS

Adapting the notion that a firm should sell to the most favorable buyers, an organization should concentrate on using its Web site to attract the most influential stakeholders. For example, it might use an attractor to communicate with employees or it may want to attract and inform investors and potential suppliers. After selecting the targeted stakeholder group, the organization needs to decide the degree of focus of its attraction. First, identify the target stakeholder groups and make the site more attractive to these groups. Second, decide the degree of customization.

Broad Attraction

A broad attractor can be useful for communicating with several types of stakeholders. Many archives, entertainment parks and search engines have general appeal, and there is no attempt to attract a particular segment of a stakeholder group. A broad attractor provides content with minimal adjustment to the needs of the visitor. Thus, many visitors may not linger too long at the site because there is nothing that particularly catches their attention or meets a need.

Specialized Attraction

A specialized attractor appeals to a more narrow audience. Federal Express, for instance, with its parcel tracking system, has decided to focus on current customers. A specialized attractor is situation dependent. It may attract fewer visitors, but nearly all those who make the link find the visit worthwhile.

Personalized Attractor

The marketer's goal is to develop an interactive relationship with individual customers. Personalized attractors, an incarnation of that dream, can be customized to meet the needs of the individual visitor. There are two types of personalized attractors. *Adaptable attractors* can be customized by the visitor. The visitor establishes what is of interest by answering questions or selecting options. *Adaptive attractors* learn from the vistor's behavior and determine what should be presented. Firefly[12] is an early instance of a learning, adaptive Web site. It tries to discover what type of music the visitor likes so that it can recommend CDs. It is likely that Web applications will emerge that use the visitor's previously gathered demographic data and record of pages browsed to create dynamically a personalized set of Web pages.

One advantage of a personalized attractor is that it can create switching costs, which are not necessarily monetary, for the visitor. An adaptive Web site further raises

---

[12] http://www.ffly.com/

costs because the switching visitor will possibly have to suffer an inferior service while the new site learns what is relevant to the customer. Furthermore, an organization that offers an adaptable or adaptive Web site as a means of differentiation learns more about each customer. Since the capacity to differentiate is dependent on knowing the customer, the organization is better placed to further differentiate itself. Personalized attractors can provide a double payback – higher switching cost for customers and greater knowledge of each customer.

Chapter 5

Pricing in Electronic Commerce

THE EMPOWERMENT OF CONSUMERS

The Internet represents the biggest threat so far to a company's ability to brand its products, extract price premiums from buyers, and generate high profit margins. Everyone knows that the Web makes price comparisons much easier. But that is just one aspect of a much deeper problem. The real threat is what economists call *cost transparency*, a situation made possible by the abundance of free, easily obtained information on the Internet. All that information has a way of making a seller's costs more transparent to buyers – in other words, it lets buyers see through those costs and determine whether they are in line with the prices being charged.

Consider the information about costs that is available on the Internet. The Internet not only provides buyers with more information about prices, features, and quality than they have had in the past, it also reduces the search for that information to a few effortless keystrokes. Ferreting out the same information through traditional shopping requires a lot more time and energy.

The most prevalent form of information available on the Internet is about prices. Consumers know that they can often find lower prices for books, CDs, computers and airfares by searching on the Internet. But they can do much more than compare the prices of an Internet store against those of a traditional retailer. They can log on to price-comparison sites such as Pricescan.com and shopping agents such as Bottomdollar.com, to readily compare the prices and features of more than 10,000 products available on the Web. Every time a customer takes advantage of a cheaper price from an online discounter like Buy.com or Onsale.com, she unlearns long-held rules of thumb about how price and cost are related for the product she just purchased.

Besides making price comparisons easier, the Web offers a wealth of information about product quality and features and about the reliability of different suppliers. Prospective buyers can easily tap into online databases of reviews and ratings of any sort of product. They can go to a site like Epinions.com to read about the purchasing experiences of customers like themselves. And they can get information that once was proprietary. A site like Travelocity, for example, lets consumers enter the same flight-reservations database that travel agents monopolized in the past.

Cost transparency threatens both retailers and manufacturers. For retailers, it means customers will have a much better sense of a product's wholesale costs. That is already changing the way car dealerships operate. Car buyers routinely enter the showroom armed with detailed breakdowns of wholesale automobile prices that have been downloaded for free from any of a dozen Web sites. For manufacturers, cost transparency means consumers will be better able to infer a product's manufacturing costs, making it much harder to impose large price premiums. The threat, moreover, will be felt not just online. As consumers gain greater knowledge about cost structures, they will be able to use that information to deal with traditional merchants as well.

What can companies do to fight back? There are no easy solutions. As with so many issues, flexibility and the ability to innovate are the keys. Perhaps the most important weapon is knowledge – knowledge of what exactly the Internet makes possible and how that threatens to erode any seller's bottom line.

Seeing Through Costs

Sellers have a natural interest in keeping their costs opaque to the outside world. They want people to accept the notion that their prices are justified, and they spend a lot on advertising to convey the message that their brands offer unique benefits. This approach has been very effective for brands such as Nike and Calvin Klein, which have managed to find many buyers around the world willing to pay a handsome premium for sneakers and jeans.

Buyers, on the other hand, have a natural interest in knowing a seller's costs for a product or service – after all, they want to know if they are paying a fair price for what they are receiving. To the extent that buyers can determine what a fair price is, they can then search for the best bargain available and avoid overpaying for brands whose prices are clearly out of line. The problem is, it is virtually impossible for buyers to find out what a seller's real costs are. They are left to infer those costs by evaluating competing brands or offerings. People generally use the price of the cheapest brand as a benchmark in order to determine if more expensive brands really offer the quality that justifies their higher prices. Until now, the process of inferring costs has been difficult. Consumer have had some information at their fingertips – flyers and newspaper advertisements, for example – that have allowed them to compare prices, but even then only locally for the most part. And they have been able to discover more by traveling from store to store, but such legwork is time consuming and often frustrating. Costs have not been transparent in many cases because consumers have not been able to obtain the information they need to make accurate inferences.

In addition to learning from company behavior, consumers have to some extent been able to gain a better understanding of costs from third-party sources. For example, shoppers have long relied on consumer education magazines such as *Money* and *Consumer Reports* to learn about product prices, quality and features. On the Internet, there are almost unlimited sources of such information, and most of it is free. As cost transparency increases, so will the problems it causes for companies. Some of these problems are:

- Cost transparency severely impairs a seller's ability to obtain high margins.
- Cost transparency turns products and services into commodities.
- Cost transparency weakens customer loyalty to brands.
- Cost transparency can damage companies' reputations by creating perceptions of price unfairness. When costs become clearer, consumers may come to believe that sellers of their favorite brands have been ripping them off. That perception often leads to enduring distrust, and companies can find it difficult to win back their old customers.

How The Internet Makes Costs Transparent

The Internet is a much greater threat to major brands and prices than private labels have been. It is increasing cost transparency in several ways, as described below.

Internet technology erodes the "risk premium" that sellers have been able to extract from wary buyers. In the past, buyers had relatively few sources for knowledge about a brand's quality or about variations in quality from brand to brand. Lacking reliable information, buyers typically sought to minimize their risk of buying an inferior product by purchasing a well-known, nationally advertised brand. Manufacturers of national brands, in turn, charged a risk premium for guaranteeing a certain level of quality in their products. Through the Internet, people can always find expert advice about a product or service. A growing number of Web sites offer reliable and independent information about products and services, as well as stories about them from consumers around the world. Such easy access to information helps prospective buyers to see through a risk premium and make better decisions about the premium's justification.

The Internet makes a buyer's search much more efficient. Anyone can use Web-based shopping agents to quickly research products. For example, with a few clicks of the mouse, a consumer can find out who is selling washing machines, at what prices, with what features, and with what type of warranty. Thus an online shopper can know in a matter of minutes what the best deal is. The efficiencies of Internet-based searches are especially clear in the business-to-business context of industrial procurement

Buyer-led pricing and reverse auctions allow consumers to see the "price floor" more easily than they can with traditional shopping. Thanks to sites like Priceline.com and eBay, consumers have started to believe that the prices of even the best-known brands are open to negotiation. Priceline requires that buyers name the price they are willing to pay for airline tickets, home financing, cars, hotel rooms, and even groceries. It then lets companies decide if they want to meet the quoted price. A buyer whose price is accepted may be motivated to bid even lower the next time. Sooner or later he/she will come to know the price floor – the lowest price for which a company is willing to sell a product or service. If evidence were needed that the Internet has unfurled the flag of consumer supremacy, reverse auctions provide it. From a seller's perspective, these developments herald greater cost transparency and thus increased consumer reluctance to pay full prices – whether they are buying a product or service from an Internet site or from a traditional bricks-and-mortar merchant.

The Internet encourages highly rational shopping. Before the rise of electronic commerce, most companies attempted to build their brands by using sensory cues that required affective processing, or the words, images, sounds and smells that speak to people's emotions. That strategy has paid off handsomely for companies like Tommy Hillfiger and Budweiser, which have relied heavily on seductive visuals in advertisements to achieve a premium image – and thus to earn very high margins on their products. And strategies based on appealing to the senses are easy to maintain in physical stores through the use of beautiful displays, piped music and friendly salespeople. The Internet, however, presents a very different shopping experience, one that appeals to people's cognitive faculties. It encourages dispassionate comparisons of prices and features. It also puts shoppers in control – it is up to them to consciously navigate through the Internet's maze of pages and links. And although surfers' increasing use of multimedia will give companies new opportunities to provide sensory cues online, the solitary, information-rich nature of Internet shopping will continue to encourage people to make decisions based on reason rather than on emotion.

The Internet demands that companies with varying prices re-examine their price structure and policy. In the physical world, companies have discreetly practiced selective pricing for different markets. But after opening an online store, the same companies usually realize that this strategy will create resentment and perceptions of price unfairness among consumers who are charged higher prices – even if that pricing strategy is in place because of legitimate cost differences associated with serving different market segments.

The e-commerce paradigm that emphasizes building a customer base over making profits is changing the way customers think about costs. In this popular retail model followed by Buy.com, online stores hope to attract loyal customers by selling items at or below cost. The theory is that subsequent advertising and co-branding opportunities will more than justify the initial losses. Many companies are essentially giving computers to people who sign up for long-term Internet service contracts. The free PC is merely an accessory for the service – just as cell phones are accessories for wireless service. Such strategies send an interesting message to consumers: the price of a product can be lower than its costs when service charges are taken into account. Not surprisingly, computer prices have plummeted recently as people have inferred that the costs to companies of buying and selling these boxes are relatively small compared with the value they can derive from maintaining a large and essentially captive subscriber base.

Managing Cost Transparency

Cost transparency is the new reality and companies will not be able to avoid it. That does not mean, however, that companies should automatically cut their prices. They can take several steps to mitigate the effects brought about by the Internet's abundance of information. For example, companies can pursue pricing options that go beyond just cutting their prices. One strategy involves price lining, which is also called tiered pricing or versioning. Price lining is the well-known practice of offering different products or services at various price points to meet different customers' needs.

Companies may also implement dynamic, or smart pricing, in which the prices they charge vary from one market to another, depending on market conditions, differences in the costs of serving individual buyers, and variations in the way consumers value the offering. That is what Staples is trying to do with geographic segments by forcing shoppers to enter their zip codes before they can view prices. Companies that can pull off this approach can earn higher profits than those that have only one price for every market they serve. Major airlines, automobile dealers and car rental companies have long practiced dynamic pricing. Lately, the strategy has been touted as a pricing panacea for e-commerce businesses, but managers need to be aware of its pitfalls and risks.

Marketers seem to view the popularity of auction sites on the Web as proof that buyers really enjoy online haggling. And online auctions do represent companies' ultimate dream of collecting the highest amount that each individual buyer is willing to pay at a certain point in time, a practice that in theory would allow them to extract the maximum possible profit from the market. Smart pricing is also popular because today's technology makes it easy to do so. Even small and midsize businesses can make multiple price changes per day as market conditions and valuations shift. But the proponents of smart pricing appear to have overlooked its most obvious pitfalls. Because the Internet allows customers to easily share information with one another, smart pricing is likely to create widespread perceptions of unfairness that may prove devastating to businesses in the long run. Consumers will be unhappy if they believe they have paid more for a product than someone who was more persistent, more adept at bargaining, or just plain lucky. Companies should tread carefully when thinking about smart pricing. For most consumers, fixed prices are a security blanket that helps them feel they are being treated fairly – or at least no worse than the next customer.

As a better solution, companies should look toward improving the benefits that their products or services offer, There is no substitute for quality, and brand leaders can continue to enhance their offerings and then see to it that their superior quality is communicated to the public. Even in an era of cost transparency, the better products and services will still command higher premiums. Bundling – packaging a product with other goods and services – can make it difficult for buyers to see through the costs of any single item within the bundle. It focuses buyers on the benefits of the overall package rather than the costs of each piece. Some computer manufacturers, such as Gateway, are bundling their own Internet services with their machines as a way to mitigate the problem of free-falling computer prices. But the optimal way of counteracting cost transparency is through innovation. Consumers will reward makers of new and distinctive products that improve their lives. The lesson for traditional companies, like the large bookstore chains whose bricks-and-mortar superstores increasingly look like white elephants, is that they too, will have to innovate and create new experiences for customers to differentiate them from their online competition.

Better-quality products, creative-pricing strategies, imaginative bundling and innovative thinking can all help keep cost transparency from overwhelming a seller's ability to maintain brand loyalty and obtain relatively high profit margins. But contending with the Internet's vast reach and power will not be an easy fight. Those managers who best understand the dynamics of cost transparency on the Internet will be most prepared for the challenge.

PRICING MECHANISMS IN ELECTRONIC COMMERCE

The emergence of electronic commerce raises important price-management questions. Many observers see the Internet creating downward pressure on price levels. Potential buyers can speedily search the Internet, employing shopping agents to check prices. These low consumer search costs will lead to greater price competition and ultimately lower prices and better value for customers. The specter of price pressure and the resulting slashing of margins has cooled much of the enthusiasm for electronic commerce on the part of online vendors. The same technology behind customer search power enables other important phenomena driving how the e-commerce market operates. The Internet facilitates a buyer's acquisition of quality information for various products. The Internet enables suppliers to update prices dynamically in response to observed demand. The Internet allows a seller to create a meaningful market of potential buyers with price being the outcome of an auction process rather than pre-specified by the seller.

The Internet permits a prospective buyer to specify in detail the product's requirements and put fulfillment out to bid to an organized market of potential sellers. These impacts may be more fundamental than any effect of more customer information. They change how exchanges between buyers and sellers take place.

The Internet enables certain mechanisms of transacting business. The mechanisms are of three fundamentally different types. The first mechanism is the set price mechanism. Within this there are two subclasses. The first is the situation where set prices are updated only periodically. The second subclass is one in which the set prices are updated continually, for example, as the airlines do. The second mechanism is the negotiated price mechanism. In a negotiated price situation, there can either be a specified starting point for the negotiation (for example, the seller's asking price on a house, or the dealer's list price on a new car) or not.

The third mechanism relies on competition across buyers and sellers to produce prices. There are three subclasses of this mechanism. The first is an auction system, the seller does not specify a price, but rather, provides an item which buyers compete for the right to buy in a bidding process. The second is a reverse auction mechanism where the customer takes the lead in organizing the pricing process. An example of this is when the buyer develops a Request for Proposal (RFP) on an item or service and price is determined via a competition involving a bidding process among potential sellers. The third is an exchange mechanism in which there is a coming together of multiple buyers and multiple sellers and price is determined by the interaction of the exchange to clear the market.

One impact of the interactive nature of the Internet is that exchange mechanisms can be very efficiently organized. Sites such as eBay thrive on this mechanism. The challenge of managing price on the Internet is not only how to set price in an era wherein the customer has more information, but also how to select the most advantageous combination of market mechanisms via which to manage transactions.

The Set Price Mechanism

In the set price mechanism, the seller simply sets a fixed price, and the buyer is expected to accept or reject that price. Negotiation is not an option. The seller's attitude is "take it or leave it". This mechanism has some advantages such as low transaction costs (for example, no negotiation is conducted), and the perception of fairness since every buyer must pay the same price. Numerous Internet retailers, including Amazon.com and eToys.com have adopted fixed pricing mechanisms.

In traditional retail markets, buyer ignorance is often a source of profit for companies. Firms set prices with reasonable confidence that the majority of buyers are unlikely to spend a large amount of time and effort comparison shopping. But on the Internet, several factors have begun to bite into this ignorance premium. For one thing, potential buyers no longer have to physically travel from store to store in search of the best deal; rather, they can comparison shop a number of Web sites from the comfort of their own computer. In addition, a number of Internet search tools have made online comparison shopping even more efficient. These search agents (also called bots or spiders) can theoretically compare prices and features across every available retailer on the Internet. Some of the more popular tools include third-party price comparison sites, third-party price comparison agents, and retailer-price comparison agents.

Third-party price comparison sites, such as MySimon.com, Compare.Net and DealTime.com, perform automatic price and feature comparison in a matter of seconds. Potential buyers simply visit the site, indicate the item of interest, and the search agent scans product and pricing information from a list of hundreds of online sellers stocking the item. Many of these sites charge merchants a fee to be part of their searches. Other sites, such as MySimon.com earn a commission every time a buyer accesses a merchant site and ultimately buys an item through the search.

Third-party price comparison agents have been developed by companies such as ClickTheButton, DealPilot, and R U Sure. These agents offer shoppers better deals on whatever merchandise they happen to be viewing on a Web page. Once a user has downloaded software from one of these agent services, the software is activated anytime the user's Web browser is open. A consumer viewing a book on, say, Amazon.com, is then automatically given price comparison information on the same book from competing retailers.

Retailer price comparison agents have been provided by online merchants who have become resigned to the prospect of comparison shopping. These merchants offer their customers a comparison pricing feature within their own Web sites, as a means of building trust. Online computer merchant NECX, for example, offers buyers a price comparison feature. Click on the price comparison button, and the buyer finds the competitors' price of the item being considered at NECX. In some cases, these competitive prices are lower than NECX's and for those shoppers wishing to take their business to one of these competitors, NECX even provides a direct link.

Classic economic theory predicts that if electronic tools allow consumers to comparison shop more easily, the end result will be greater price competition and ultimately, downward price pressure. A number of high-profile, zero-margin Internet businesses seem to be bearing this prediction out. Perhaps the most well-known of the zero-margin businesses is Buy.com. Currently the fourth largest retailer on the Internet, Buy.com pioneered the strategy of selling its products at or below cost to lure customers. The company is betting that it will eventually be able to make money by selling advertising on its Web site. In the meantime, its proprietary software works 24 hours a day to gather millions of prices for books, CDs, computer hardware and software, and other products from hundreds of competitors. All of this technology is designed to sniff out the cheapest bargains online and help the company deliver on its advertised promise to have the lowest prices on earth.

Onsale.com, the Internet auction company, launched an AtCost model built around a similar pricing strategy. Free-PC made a splash by giving away computers to consumers who agreed to view advertisements every time they used their computer. Today, it is possible to find merchants in almost every product category willing to sell products at or below cost. The long-term sustainability of zero-margin Internet businesses remains to be seen. Buy.com has moved to a more conventional pricing strategy of offering certain items at a loss to draw traffic and promote the sale of higher-margin items. Onsale.com, which has merged with Egghead.com, also appears to be moving toward a more conventional loss-leader pricing strategy, lowering prices on some items while keeping prices high on others. Some of the most popular online retailers do not offer the lowest prices. Amazon.com is a good example; it continues to grow marketshare despite dozens of competitors offering lower prices. Clearly, merchants are able to leverage other dynamics – such as branding and trust, the shopping experience, and lock-in – to maintain healthy margins on products.

Branding and trust may take on added importance in electronic markets for several reasons. First, buyers are often purchasing from sellers they have not seen and whose physical location is either unknown to the buyer or quite distant. Second, most online transactions are not instantaneous; they typically involve a delayed exchange of money and goods. Buyers usually have to submit their payment and then trust that they will receive their goods in a timely fashion. Third, a significant percentage of buyers may be purchasing goods online for the first time; this may lead to heightened concerns about being ripped off. For all these reasons, online consumers may still be willing to pay a premium to purchase a product from a retailer they are familiar with, rather than risk dealing with an unknown seller.

The most sophisticated shopping sites offer a number of features that contribute to the shopping experience, such as superior product information, sophisticated search tools, extensive product reviews from experts and other customers, product samples (for example, music clips, book chapters), product recommendation tools and convenient check-out services. All of these features contribute to the creation of a particular shopping environment that affects the likelihood that customers will enjoy shopping at the site. Firms that successfully leverage these features may be able to charge a price premium.

Lock-in refers to mechanisms that increase customers' switching costs. Sometimes lock-in occurs simply as a result of familiarity with a particular Web site. Rather than incurring the switching costs associated with learning how to navigate a new Web site, customers may choose to pay a higher price to avoid this inconvenience. In some cases, firms explicitly attempt to increase lock-in by creating additional incentives for repeat customers. Frequent buyer programs, such as that marketed by Netcentives, are a good example of this. Other, less obvious mechanisms include personalization features such as individualized shopping lists, customized interfaces, and "one-click" ordering accounts.

Dynamic Pricing

Dynamic pricing is not new. Airlines, for example, often have dozens of different fares paid by passengers on a given flight. These fares depend on a number of variables, including how early customers booked their flights, inventory of available seats at the time of booking, what restrictions they were willing to accept, their travel history, etc. The hotel and car-rental industries have followed suit, adopting the airline industry's yield management principles.

On the Internet, the opportunities for dynamic pricing are even greater, for at least two reasons. While the Internet has made it easier for customers to collect information about products and prices, it has also made it easier for sellers to gather information about customers. This information can be used to more accurately determine how much individual customers are willing to pay for certain goods. Menu costs refer to the costs associated with making price changes. For example, every time a traditional catalog retailer decides to change prices, it must incur the costs associated with reprinting its catalog. On the Internet, lower menu costs increase the likelihood that retailers will change prices more frequently. Add to these factors the fact that technology has made it easier for online retailers to check the prices of their competitors, and the end result is that online prices tend to be more dynamic than prices in conventional settings.

Dynamic pricing can be implemented in a variety of ways. Firms can simply update prices frequently. Firms can also engage in various forms of price customization, where different customers are charged different prices. On the Internet, price customization can take many forms. Some online retailers track the clickstreams of customers, instantaneously making special offers based on their online activity. Other retailers rely on their extensive customer databases to micromarket customized offers to customers based on their past purchase behavior, often using personalized email. Some online merchants are using price comparison technology to develop instantaneous price-matching systems. When a customer visits the Web site directly, the posted prices are fixed. However, if the customer uses a third-party search tool to compare prices among a number of competitors, the prices automatically drop.

This movement to price customization is pursued widely and when well implemented can offset the added customer information on prices. The ultimate form of price customization is customization directly to the buyer's willingness-to-pay. That is pursued on the Internet via auctions.

The Negotiated Price Mechanism

A vendor's willingness to negotiate can attract certain customer groups. It can also offer an additional way in which the vendor can customize the price to the individual buyer. The negotiation mechanism has some disadvantages compared to the set price mechanism. It takes longer to complete the transaction. The price aspect of the transaction can be highlighted dominating the buyer-seller interaction and squeezing out presentation of the product features and value. For negotiation to be effective, the customer contact person must have some degree of pricing authority.

The Internet provides an efficient mechanism for buyer/seller interaction alleviating each of these problems. For example, the seller can develop an intelligent agent to simulate the process of person-to-person negotiation. Several general purpose and many special purpose negotiation sites currently operate on the Internet. NexTag.com is a site which provides negotiation with a specified starting price for the negotiation.

The transition of the negotiation process to the Internet overcomes many of the disadvantages of negotiations in the real world. From a customer's point of view, negotiation can be done with multiple suppliers simultaneously. Because response is immediate in many cases, the transaction can close quickly, even with multi-supplier negotiation. The customer is always in control and not subject to unwanted persuasion attempts. The advantage to the seller is that the dialog about price provides information about the buyer which can be used to customize prices.

Examples of negotiation sites covering a range of products are Make Us An Offer and Hagglezone. Make Us An Offer offers real-time online haggling hosted by an animated artificially intelligent sales agent named Chester and positions itself as a solution to the delayed response time of other sites such as the auction site eBay, as bid responses are delivered within seconds. Hagglezone, where everything is negotiable, features six hagglers with unique personalities, moods and tendencies. A buyer can choose which haggler to deal with. Hagglezone emphasizes the fun/entertainment aspect of buying.

A common negotiation tactic in the real world is to stress the size of the order at issue or even increase the quantity of goods to be purchased as a mechanism to get the price down. Sites such as Accompany and Mercata aggregate the demand from different customers who are unknown to one another to use in negotiating lower prices.

It is not clear at this point in time how important these negotiation sites will be in the long run. Some buyers prefer the option to haggle. Sellers have the ability to automate the process on their side via intelligent agents, yielding more price customization opportunity. Thus, for at least some segment of the market, this mechanism will likely be operative as the market mechanism itself provides value to buyers.

Auctions And Exchanges

There are three types of auction mechanisms currently operating in cyberspace. In case of the *classic auction* model, competition across buyers leads to a price. In the case of the *reverse auction* model, competition across sellers leads to a price. In the case of *exchanges*, multiple buyers and sellers interact to set prices.

Classic Auctions

In the classic auction, a vendor puts items up for sale and would-be buyers are invited to bid in competition with each other. Bidding can take a number of forms, e.g., sealed bid or open bid. The most common format is the ascending-price format wherein the highest bidder wins the item. As more potential buyers become involved, there is upward pressure on prices. Classic auctions differ from other pricing mechanisms in several fundamental ways. In contrast to set pricing, classic auctions involve a flexible pricing scheme in which prices are tailor-made for each transaction. Moreover, in a set price system, the item may not be sold. In an auction, the price moves to a level where the item is sold. Auctions are basically demand aggregation models that function to deliver the best price for the seller, given the market demand the seller has been able to assemble.

Auctions now constitute some of the most popular sites on the Web. Their popularity has largely been driven by the fact that the Internet increases the economic efficiencies associated with auction models. More specifically, for suppliers, the Internet has not only lowered the search costs associated with finding a critical mass of buyers in the market, but it has also lowered the costs associated with making inventory available to buyers on an immediate basis. For buyers, the Internet has lowered the costs associated with accessing hard-to-find items, and finding other buyers who share common interests.

The Internet lowers the search costs for sellers looking for buyers. The Internet has produced a number of market-makers that have been able to pool together significant numbers of potential buyers without having to deal with physical search and travel costs. These market makers set up the infrastructure which individual sellers can plug into. In the Web universe, several factors make it easy to transform niche market segments into mainstream market segments. First, the global reach of the network provides a much greater pool of potential buyers to draw from. Second, reduced search costs make it easier to identify small pockets of people with highly-specialized needs. Finally, reduced communication costs make it easier to establish and sustain relationships with these market segments. The end result is a situation where firms are discovering that there is significant value associated with simply aggregating demand among these market segments. Some of the busiest sites on the Web are those fulfilling this market-making function in three settings: the consumer-to-consumer, business-to-consumer or business-to-business context.

The Internet lowers the costs associated with making inventory available to buyers immediately. When it comes to excess merchandise, the need to liquidate inventory has traditionally been a problem for suppliers. Internet auctions allow suppliers to make this inventory available to buyers on an immediate, and continually updated basis. Sellers who choose to dispose off surplus goods via auction must accept the uncertainty associated with dynamic pricing. However, for many sellers, this uncertainty is easily worth the cost-savings associated with quick inventory turnover. Online auctions generally move goods much more quickly than direct sales, catalogs or offline auctions. In addition, firms that use auction mechanisms to liquidate surplus goods are able to bypass liquidation brokers who tend to pay fire sale prices. As a result, auctions, particularly business-to-consumer auctions, are becoming an increasingly common mechanism by which firms adjust inventory levels.

For buyers, the Internet lowers the costs associated with accessing hard-to-find items. Internet auctions have significantly increased the options available to buyers in the market for hard-to-find items. The online auction houses not only aggregate demand for sellers, they aggregate supply for buyers. In this sense, they have become convenient one-stop shopping sources for buyers in this market. Moreover, buyer choices are not limited to the big auction firms. Niche auction companies have sprung up all over the Web, covering every product category imaginable.

The interactive nature of the Internet facilitates the creation of buying communities. Classic auctions on the Internet have a distinctly social component that most successful auction sites recognize and promote. They provide an online forum where buyers and sellers can become acquainted, discuss topics of common interest, and exchange information with one another.

Classic auction firms on the Internet can be categorized into three groups: consumer-to-consumer sites that conduct auctions in which both the sellers and the buyers are consumers; business-to-consumer sites that conduct auctions for businesses wishing to sell products to consumers; and business-to-business sites that conduct auctions in which both the sellers and the buyers are businesses.

The total consumer-to-consumer auction market on the Internet was estimated at about $2.3 billion in sales in 1999, and is expected to grow to $6.4 billion by 2003[1]. Typically, firms in this category do not own the goods up for auction; rather, they simply conduct auctions on behalf of a large group of sellers. For this reason, they do not have to deal with the logistics associated with shipping actual products. They simply act as electronic intermediaries, connecting sellers with a pool of buyers. For these firms, the bulk of their revenue tends to come from seller fees, although they occasionally collect

---

[1] Source: Forrester Research

additional revenue from advertisements and buyer fees. eBay is the leader in this category. It has over seven million registered users who at any given time can find up to three million items at auction.

One of the biggest challenges facing consumer-to-consumer auction businesses is dealing with fraud. Because these firms only serve as intermediaries, they exert little direct control over the sellers posting items. The most common complaint comes from buyers who pay for merchandise, only to have the seller disappear without delivering the goods. eBay, however, has implemented some elegant ways to address some of these potential hazards. On its site, regular sellers establish a reputation for reliable delivery and quality through a ratings system based on comments from previous buyers who have transacted with the seller. Bidders can not only browse through these comments and ratings, but they can also add their own feedback, based on their experience. Extensive chatboards also let eBay-ers share tips and gossip. In effect, the company relies on the users themselves to establish trust between buyers and sellers. Its fraud rate is subsequently very low: 25 out of every million transactions. Note that this reputation-building system not only promotes a sense of community, but it also increases the switching costs for both buyers and sellers.

eBay currently faces competition from a number of competitors, including Yahoo! auctions and Auction Universe. And, recognizing and opportunity to leverage its existing customer base, Amazon.com jumped into the auction business in the Spring of 1999. Traditional offline auction houses are also entering the fray. Butterfield's, a high-end auction firm, was purchased by eBay, while Sotheby's has forged an alliance with Amazon.com.

The total business-to-consumer auction market was estimated to be about 0.4 billion in sales in 1999, but is expected to grow to $12.6 billion by 2003[2]. Onsale, which has merged with Egghead.com was the first business-to-consumer auction site on the Internet and is still one of the largest. Other sites that fall into this category include uBid, BidOnline, and WebAuction.

Business-to-business auctions are expected to eventually make up most of the volume of the online auction market. In fact, many auction firms that started out as business-to-consumer firms (e.g., Onsale, uBid) are finding that an increasing percentage of their revenues is now being generated by business customers. In general, business-to-business auctions involve fundamentally different dynamics than consumer auctions. They typically involve larger amounts of money, firms are not seeking entertainment, and firms tend to be wary of jeopardizing long-term strategic relationships. AdAuction.com is an example of a business-to-business auction site. The company provides a venue for companies to buy and sell advertising space for all sorts of media: online, broadcast and print. Another example is TradeOut, which is a business-to-business liquidator auction.

In all of the classic auction categories, barriers to entry are relatively low, and competitors can launch new sites at a relatively low cost using commercially available software. However, the biggest hurdles involve building a potential bidder and seller base. Success literally breeds success; the large bidder base draws the suppliers which enhance the site's appeal to bidders. For smaller players seeking to enter the market, breaking this self-reinforcing cycle can pose quite a problem.

---

[2] Source: Forrester Research

But several firms are now offering these smaller players an alternative. These firms focus of helping other firms get into the auction business by using network synergies to quickly build a large buyer and seller base. FairMarket, a leader in this category, has created an auction network that connects a number of smaller auction sites hosted by some of the leading portals and vendors on the Web, including Microsoft (MSN), Excite, Lycos, AltaVista, Dell, CompUSA, Cyberian Outpost, MicroWarehouse and Boston.com. Each individual site is connected to a single massive database of merchandise. Besides developing the network, FairMarket provides a number of other services to its members. It hosts the servers, and creates the software and user interface for member auction sites. It also provides customer service, including fraud protection and security features. The company currently has a reach of 50 million users.

Reverse Auctions

In a reverse auction, a buyer communicates a need to a set of potential suppliers and suppliers bid on fulfilling that demand. The reverse auction has been a staple of purchasing in business-to-business situations for many years, often under the name of competitive bidding. The process entails the buyer drafting a request-for-proposal (RFP) specifying what is to be purchased. This request is transmitted to qualified sellers. Seller bidding can be of two general types. The first type is sealed bidding, in which each qualified supplier submits one secret bid and the buyer chooses on the basis of bids submitted in that round. The second type is open bidding, in which sellers interact in real time just as buyers do in a classic auction, except the bidding goes down over time and the lowest supplier price wins.

The Internet's interactive communication capability broadens the feasibility of economically efficient reverse auctions. The Web expands the scope of sellers participating. This creates an overall downward pressure on prices. Online analogs of business-to-business competitive bidding situations are gaining acceptance on the Web. Need2Buy, for example, is a special purpose site at which a buyer can engage in a ready-made reverse auction for electronic components. FreeMarkets is a firm dedicated to creating effective competitive bidding events for industrial buyers. The Internet makes possible the more efficient organization of reverse auctions – bringing in the maximum number of qualified suppliers, well-informed about the requirements. The real-time bidding process also helps the buyers. Overall, the net result is downward pressure on prices.

Reverse auction services are offered by MyGeek and Respond. Basically, these are buying services which broadcast a buyer's RFP to potential suppliers who respond via email. The customer can then choose the seller to transact with or not at all. An advantage of Respond is that it is able to accommodate a situation in which the buyer is only able to describe the item sought in generic terms. Buyers remain anonymous to potential sellers and can choose to follow up or not on emailed offers. A particularly high-profile variant in the reverse buying genre is Priceline.com.

As an Internet-based analog to the familiar real world competitive bidding, reverse auctions on the Internet have the potential to reduce acquisition costs significantly in many situations. For complex products, an integrated approach as proposed by FreeMarkets is necessary. Their work with very sophisticated purchasing organizations has already proven the value of developing the worldwide seller pool and providing the tools for real-time bidding which promotes competition. For commodity products, simple systems can be effective in expanding the seller base to promote lower prices for buyers.

Exchanges

Exchanges are electronic marketplaces where a group of buyers and a group of sellers interact to trade and set prices for transactions. The electronic product exchanges of the Internet have typically been organized around a particular industry. Metal Site has 18 sellers of metals interacting with many buyers. Fast Parts, patterned after the NASDAQ, serves the electronics manufacturing and assembly industries. ESteel, for the steel industry, facilitates negotiations between buyers and sellers. ChemConnect is the Internet's largest chemical and plastics exchange. The general process at an exchange is conceptually that for each item, a dynamically updated list of "offers to buy" and "offers to sell" is maintained. These buys/sells are matched up through a process.

A major advantage of these organized exchanges is that they bring together buyers and sellers on a global scale. The impact of this on the average price paid is not clear. A buyer benefits by having access to all the sellers on the exchange – not just those with whom she is familiar or in geographic proximity. For an individual transaction conducted at a given point in time, this expanding of the potential supplier pool should drive the price down. On the other hand, the exchange also opens up a host of new potential buyers to sellers. A seller needing to sell quickly will sell at a less distressed price than if his potential set were restricted to local, known buyers. A real benefit to both buyers and sellers is a reduction in the variability of prices across transactions. Prices on the exchanges are the product of marketwide economic forces impacting all buyers and sellers – not specific, highly variable, and relatively unpredictable, local conditions.

In general, on the Internet, commodity products will experience increased price pressure due to more buyer information about prices. The information available on the Internet cuts into the ignorance premium by reducing the asymmetry of information between the buyer and the seller. In contrast to the general price pressure befalling commodity products, the Internet can produce increased prices for those vendors who are selling a differentiated product. While the Internet can convey to consumers a fuller understanding of competitive products and prices, it can also provide another communication vehicle via which to create the perception of value in the consumer's mind. More customized information can be delivered in response to either consumers' explicit requests or their observed behavior.

The Internet is a disaster for those with a commodity-selling mentality. For them, the story of increasing consumer power over sellers resulting in price pressure and margin erosion will come true. The more sophisticated sellers will see the possibility of new market mechanisms for transacting with customers and take advantage of the opportunity to differentiate themselves not only by giving consumers products they want to buy but also by giving them choices about how they can buy them. For these marketers, the Internet will not be a story of buyer triumph over sellers through information, but rather, a mutually beneficial success story built on taking advantage of more efficient communication and the opportunity for a more intimate, personalized relationship.

Combining Multiple Online Transaction Mechanisms

Companies have always wrestled with two questions in tandem: what to sell and how to sell it. The question of how to sell is a big one, because in choosing one way, sellers almost always foreclose other possibilities. Commodity dealers selling on spot markets, for example, do not also offer continuous replenishment programs. Mass merchandisers with fixed prices do not invite negotiation. And auction houses do not sell through mail order.

Companies know that by limiting themselves to one main selling mechanism, they sacrifice a lot of potential customers and leave a lot of money lying on the table. But they've had no choice. Selling the same thing in different ways has traditionally been too complex and has required radically different physical setups. How, for instance, can a mall retailer bring together enough interested buyers to run a reasonable auction?

All that has changed in the age of the Internet, where business is increasingly unconstrained by the laws and limitations of the physical world. Consider the many different ways one could purchase a ticket on American Airlines' Web site. Travelers can book tickets through Sabre, the company's traditional reservation system, choose from a limited number of deeply discounted fares using NetSAAvers, secure special fares based on membership in one of a number of affinity programs, such as Senior TrAAvelers, arrange customized trips based on a personal profile stored in Personal Access, or select vacation packages, purchasing air tickets as part of a bundled offering.

Similarly, someone who goes to Dell's Web site can buy a customized computer using the company's famous online system configurator or bid in an auction for a popular setup. LandsEnd.com augments its fixed-price catalog with a Dutch auction for overstocks. Streamline.com offers buyers basic grocery ordering as well as a continuous replenishment option for staple items. All these sites are examples of markets that offer side-by-side, alternative ways for buyers and sellers to transact business.

It is easy to see why companies are moving quickly to offer more ways to buy. They recognize that the same buyer may want different transaction mechanisms under different circumstances. A clothes-horse may love certain purchasing methods when bargain hunting for basics, yet shun them when shopping for an outfit for a special occasion. A person may not care about ticket prices when traveling for business, but he may be the king of the cherry pickers when it comes time to plan a family vacation. Being able to offer multiple transaction approaches allows companies to win a larger share of existing customers' business as well as bring new types of customers into the fold.

The Internet-based markets have evolved in three stages. Stage one saw a great deal of innovation in online transaction mechanisms. Many companies experimented with mechanisms that had previously been unknown in their industries. iBeauty.com, for example, introduced continuous replenishment to the online health and beauty business, enabling automatic reordering of fragrances and cosmetics. Other companies pioneered entirely new transaction mechanisms. Priceline.com, for example, introduced the world to the "demand collection system" – where buyers post the price they are willing to pay and invite sellers to either accept or decline the business. Mercata pioneered electronic group buying. It allows individuals to gather into buying blocks, leveraging their combined purchasing power to drive prices down.

In Stage two, companies rushed to combine transaction approaches on their Web sites. Two-thirds of the leading e-commerce sites already employ multiple transaction mechanisms, and 30% support three or more mechanisms. Judging by the growing availability of off-the-shelf software for handling Web transactions, such as OpenSite's auction package, these numbers are sure to increase.

Now we are entering Stage three: the aggregation of many sellers onto the sites that already feature more than one selling mechanism. An early leader in this trend is Travelocity.com. Like the American Airlines Web site, Travelocity combines several transaction mechanisms. But unlike American Airlines, it provides access to travel services from a range of airlines, hotels and rental car agencies. Over the coming months, it is expected that many more markets will expand in just this way, as customers increasingly seek the convenience of one-stop shopping.

The rise of the integrated electronic markets was inevitable. By enabling frictionless movement among ways of doing business, they benefit both buyers and sellers. Nevertheless, this trend runs counter to the conventional wisdom about electronic commerce. Many observers predicted that the wide reach and low transaction costs of the Internet would push all transactions toward a single mechanism – open-market price competition. The evidence shows that the Internet economy is actually resulting in several different market mechanisms emerging, each of which may result in a different price for the same product.

Mechanism	Definition
Static Call	Online catalog with fixed prices
Dynamic Call	Online catalog with continuously updated prices and features
Product Tailored	Offerings are tailored to meet individual customer specifications
Price Tailored	Prices change based on purchase history or loyalty
Reverse	Buyer posts desired price for seller acceptance
Spot	Buyers' and sellers' bids clear instantly
Negotiation	Bargaining between one buyer and one seller
Seller Auction	Buyers' bids determine final price of sellers' offerings
Buyer Auction	Buyers request price quotes from multiple sellers
Barter	Buyer and Seller exchange goods
Continuous Replenishment	On-going fulfillment of orders under preset terms
Bundled	Seller combines multiple products into a prepackaged offering
Bulletin Board/ Clearance	Offerings limited by availability of product or by discount
Partnership	Integration of buyer and seller processes
Referral	Link to non-owned mechanism / commercial Web site

Table 5-1: Online Transaction Mechanisms

USING INTELLIGENT SOFTWARE AGENTS IN ELECTRONIC COMMERCE

Many buyers on the Internet routinely use software agents, such as those deployed by Evenbetter.com and mySimon.com, that automatically canvass the Internet looking for the cheapest price for a given product. Now e-businesses are deploying agents of their own. The online retailer Buy.com, for example, is reportedly using price-comparison software that automatically adjusts its prices to undercut competitors' prices. But if all online sellers deploy armies of such price-bots, would the result be self-destructive cyber price wars and digital mayhem? The question is hardly moot. Within the next decade, the Internet could be populated with billions of software agents exchanging information goods and services with one another and with people. As commerce increases on the Internet, a company's success may be determined as much by its skill in programming its bots as by the wisdom of its business strategy.

How might software agents set the prices of a commodity, such as a computer memory chip or a copy of John Grisham's latest novel. One simple bot uses trial and error to raise or lower prices incrementally in an effort to maximize profits. A more sophisticated agent makes pricing decisions based on detailed information about buyers' price sensitivity, use of shop-bots, and other characteristics. With this copious information, the price-bot applies a short-term optimization approach, dubbed the myoptimal strategy, and calculates the price that will maximize profits under the assumption that competitors' prices remain fixed.

If all price-bots rely on the trial-and-error strategy, their collective behavior will evolve toward tacit collusion in which they each maintain high prices and healthy profits. If one of the price-bots adopts the myoptimal strategy, however, it will garner higher profits at the expense of the trial-and-error agents. But if all price-bots make the switch, then endless price wars ensue. The bots continually undercut one another until the price reaches a lower limit, at which point they reestablish a higher price, touching off a new round of undercutting. Each price-bot actually fares worse than if all had just maintained a trial-and-error approach.

When all the agents are myoptimal, the one with the most up-to-date information on competitors' pricing reaps the greatest profits. Companies would therefore be highly motivated to program their bots to scan competing sites and databases constantly, with the advantage going to the fastest and most relentless repricers. In this scenario, suppliers' Web sites could be overwhelmed with price queries from competitors' price-bots – and the entire Internet could be gridlocked. To deter such abuse, sellers may have no choice but to charge price-bots and shop-bots for price information. This possibility hints at a powerful principle that could govern an agent-based economy. To ensure that information goods and services are neither overused nor under-provided, shop-bots and price-bots may evolve into full-fledged economic agents functioning as buyers, sellers and intermediaries to facilitate all facets of electronic commerce.

How might companies avoid destructive bot wars? This can be achieved by developing more intelligent price-bots that can adapt to their environment and anticipate the future. One promising approach is based on reinforcement learning, in which agents learn optimal pricing policies that maximize long-term profits. These forward-looking price-bots have outperformed trial-and-error and myoptimal agents. And when two forward-looking price-bots compete against each other, they refrain from excessive undercutting because they anticipate retaliation.

Also of great interest is the behavior of agent-based markets for complex products. For example, sellers' bots could not only set prices, but also determine product quality or configuration. For example, a bot could be used to create different versions of an online journal, each with a unique set of articles, and to adjust the prices accordingly – all in response to customers' demand patterns and competitors' actions. This will result in complicated cycles in which both price and product parameters oscillate indefinitely – an undesirable situation for both sellers and buyers.

To compete effectively on the Web, businesses will need to understand the market dynamics of large communities of software agents. Companies can use simulation studies to develop mechanisms and strategies that will help them avoid potential pitfalls such as price wars. Intelligently designed bots can help businesses capitalize on - and create – a flurry of information goods and services that will rise as quickly and pervasively as the growth of the Web, and that will affect the world even more profoundly.

Chapter 6

Business-to-Business Electronic Commerce

OVERVIEW OF BUSINESS-TO-BUSINESS ELECTRONIC COMMERCE

Business-to-business (B2B) commerce on the Internet is generating a lot of interest. Companies such as Ariba, Chemdex, Commerce One, FreeMarkets, Internet Capital Group and SciQuest.com have attained breathtaking stock market capitalizations. Venture capitalists are pouring money into more business-to-business startups. Even industrial stalwarts like General Motors and Ford have announced plans to set up their own Web markets.

The appeal of doing business on the Web is clear. By bringing together huge numbers of buyers and sellers and by automating transactions, Web markets expand the choices available to buyers, give sellers access to new customers, and reduce transaction costs for all the players. By extracting fees for the transactions occurring within the business-to-business marketplaces, market makers can earn vast revenues. And because the marketplaces are made from software – not bricks and mortar – they can scale with minimal additional investment, promising even more attractive margins as the markets grow. But as new entrants with new business models pour into the business-to-business space, it is increasingly difficult to make sense of the landscape.

Business-to-Business electronic commerce is poised for rapid growth. Forrester Research estimates this market at a whopping $327 billion in the year 2001. To understand the soaring popularity of online purchasing, one need only consider its value proposition. It is cheaper than traditional approaches – electronic processing of purchase orders costs less than paper processing and frees up valuable buyer and salesperson time for more productive activities. It is more convenient – online systems operate seven days per week, 24 hours a day, don't have the capacity constraints of call centers, and permit users to easily post and mail large attachments such as blueprints and Request For Quotations (RFQ). It is also faster than traditional paper-based purchasing. Finally, it virtually eliminates processing errors – which makes it even cheaper, more convenient and faster.

Online procurement brings dramatic changes to purchasing departments. Fewer buyers are needed to handle an equivalent volume of transactions. They become better decision makers because they have richer information about their purchasing economics. As a result, they can take on new, more strategic responsibilities. Less directly involved in transactions, they spend more time negotiating master contracts with suppliers and optimizing the entire supply chain.

A wide and somewhat confusing array of online purchasing tools is emerging. The good news is that these tools are not mutually exclusive; in many instances, they are actually complementary. The tools that are currently available fall into three broad categories: buyer-driven catalogs and bidding systems, third-party catalogs and trading exchanges, and supplier-driven extranets.

Buyer-Driven Solutions

Operating resource management (ORM) systems – software that manages the procurement of non-production goods, that is, all the things companies buy that don't flow directly into the products they manufacture – are creating a big buzz in the world of online purchasing. Historically, the procurement of non-production goods – a market that Giga Information Group estimates at $250 billion per year – has not been well managed. Operating resources can potentially be bought by every individual within an organization; by their very nature, these purchases are largely unplanned. And though they may represent smaller dollar-volumes than purchases of production goods, they typically occur more frequently, absorbing a disproportionate share of buyers' time and attention.

ORM systems are corporate intranets that permit employees to browse an online, customized catalog and automatically route orders for approval. The fanciest versions can, for example, access information from the human resources system about the buyer's position within the firm to help determine how much the buyer is authorized to spend and who else must approve the purchase.

Companies that have implemented such systems tout three benefits. First, the online catalog limits the range of suppliers to those with whom the company has a master contract, thereby eliminating what is commonly referred to as "maverick buying". Second, the automated order-entry and approval-routing features virtually eliminate order errors and accelerate the approval process. And third, the system captures valuable purchasing data that can be used to negotiate better contracts with suppliers.

Companies wishing to implement such a system first face a "make or buy" decision, and if the answer is "buy", the subsequent decision is whether to buy a software system or outsource the function entirely. A half-dozen small software start-ups such as Ariba[1] and Elekom[2] have developed ORM systems. A number of companies now offer complete outsourcing services. Among them is General Electric's (GE) Trading Process Network Mart (TPN Mart), an in-house service that GE offers externally as well. TPN Mart[3] hosts the electronic catalogs and buying guidelines of its customers and sends out their purchase orders using electronic data interchange on the Internet.

Several buyer-driven online procurement tools extend to production goods as well. With these tools companies can test their suppliers by subjecting them to competition. Existing suppliers may prevail, or buyers may identify new suppliers with whom they wish to work. Buyers post their production material needs on their Internet sites, inviting suppliers to contact them to submit a bid. Sony posts pictures and descriptions of parts that it needs. GE offers another service called TPN Post, which allows companies to post full RFQs on a secure site and then invites selected suppliers to view them and submit bids.

---

[1] http://www.ariba.com
[2] http://www.elekom.com
[3] http://www.tpn.geis.com

An intermediary called FreeMarkets Online[4] takes the online bidding process one step further. It stages an interactive, online bidding process among pre-qualified suppliers responding to a highly specific RFQ for custom parts. FreeMarkets claims that its clients save an average of 15% on their purchases.

Third-Party Services

Intermediaries have created catalogs that compile the offerings of multiple suppliers, can be conveniently accessed through one site on the Internet, and can be searched by buyers quickly and easily. Buyers are able, therefore, to avoid the time-consuming process of hopping from Web site to Web site in search of a qualified vendor. Nor do they have to worry about whether their paper catalogs are outdated. They can be assured that the information on the Web is current. Wiznet[5] gives buyers the ability to search the contents of 82,000 published supplier catalogs, view the relevant pages from catalogs with a match, visit the suppliers' Web sites, and send a secure electronic mail message to the supplier requesting additional information or a price quote. Third-party catalogs are not incompatible with buyer-driven solutions. Companies with ORM systems may find them helpful in identifying suppliers with whom to negotiate master contracts or to facilitate exception buying. In fact, a third-party catalog could conceivably become a module in an ORM system that employees access through the company intranet.

Intermediaries are also offering trading exchanges – sites that match buyers and sellers for particular products. The advantages that such a service offers over a third-party catalog are that orders can be fulfilled quickly because the product is usually already available, and that prices are based on what the market will bear. Examples include FastParts[6], an online spot market for new electronic components, and PartsMart[7], an online marketplace for spare PC parts.

Supplier Extranets

A growing number of suppliers offer Web sites that provide product information and allow online ordering. A subset of these even confirm payment and delivery. Supplier extranets facilitate efficient communication with buyers, accelerate product delivery, and lower the cost of goods. A Forrester Research survey of 50 companies indicates that Internet commerce was generating 42% of their revenue in the year 2000, up from a mere 15% in 1997.

What Businesses Purchase

To understand business-to-business marketplaces, it is useful to understand what businesses buy and how they buy. Businesses buy a diverse set of products and services,

---

[4] http://www.freemarkets.com
[5] http://wwwwiznet.com
[6] http://www.fastparts.com
[7] http://www.partsmart.com

ranging from paper clips to computer systems, from steel to machinery. At the broadest level, the purchases can be classified into *manufacturing inputs* and *operating inputs*.

Manufacturing inputs are the raw materials and components that go directly into a product or a process. Because these goods vary considerably from industry to industry they are usually purchased from industry-specific, or vertical, suppliers and distributors. They also tend to require specialized logistics and fulfillment mechanisms.

Operating inputs, by contrast, are not parts of finished products. Often called maintenance, repair and operating (MRO) goods, they include things like office supplies, spare parts, airline tickets and services. Operating inputs tend not to be industry specific. As a result, they are frequently purchased from horizontal suppliers – vendors such as Staples and American Express that serve all industries. And they are much more likely to be shipped through generalists such as UPS.

How Businesses Purchase

The second distinction in business purchasing is how products and services are bought. Companies can either engage in *systematic sourcing* or in *spot sourcing*. Systematic sourcing involves negotiated contracts with qualified suppliers. Because the contracts tend to be long-term, the buyers and sellers often develop close relationships. In spot sourcing, the buyer's goal is to fulfill an immediate need at the lowest possible cost. Spot transactions rarely involve a long-term relationship with the supplier; in fact, buyers on the spot market often do not know who they are buying from.

Classifying Business-To-Business Marketplaces

By applying this two-way classification scheme – *manufacturing inputs* versus *operating inputs* (the "what") and *systematic sourcing* versus *spot sourcing* (the "how") – we can classify business-to-business marketplaces into four categories (see Figure 6-1):

- *MRO hubs* are horizontal markets that enable systematic sourcing of operating inputs.
- *Yield managers* are horizontal markets that enable spot sourcing of operating inputs.
- *Exchanges* are vertical markets that enable spot sourcing of manufacturing inputs.
- *Catalog hubs* are vertical markets that enable systematic sourcing of manufacturing inputs.

What businesses buy

	operating inputs	manufacturing inputs
systematic sourcing	**MRO Hubs** Ariba W.W.Grainger MRO.com BizBuyer.com	**Catalog Hubs** Chemdex SciQuest.com PlasticsNet.com
spot sourcing	**Yield Managers** Employease Adauction.com CapacityWeb.com	**Exchanges** e-Steel PaperExchange.com Altra Energy IMX Exchange

How businesses buy

Figure 6-1: The business-to-business Matrix

In MRO hubs, the operating inputs tend to be low-value goods with relatively high transaction costs, so these business-to-business marketplaces provide value largely by increasing efficiencies in the procurement process. Many of the best-known players in this arena, including W.W.Grainger, Ariba and Commerce One, started out by licensing expensive "buy-side" software for e-procurement to large companies, which used the software on their own intranets. Now, instead of licensing their software to individual companies, the business-to-business marketplaces are hosting it on their own servers to provide an open market. These markets give buyers access to consolidated MRO catalogs from a wide array of suppliers. Newer entrants in this area include BizBuyer.com, MRO.com, PurchasingCenter.com and ProcureNet. Because MRO hubs use third-party logistics suppliers to deliver goods, they can disintermediate, or bypass, existing middlemen in the channel without having to replicate their fulfillment capabilities and assets.

Yield managers create spot markets for common operating resources such as manufacturing capacity, labor and advertising, which allow companies to expand or contract their operations at short notice. This type of business-to-business marketplace adds the most value in situations with a high degree of price and demand volatility, such as the electricity and utilities markets, or with huge fixed-cost assets that cannot be liquidated or acquired quickly, such as manpower and manufacturing capacity. Examples of yield managers include Youtilities (for utilities), Employease and eLance (for human resources), iMark.com (for capital equipment), CapacityWeb.com (for manufacturing capacity) and Adauction.com (for advertising).

Online exchanges allow purchasing managers to smooth out the peaks and valleys in demand and supply by rapidly exchanging the commodities or near-commodities needed for production. The exchange maintains relationships with buyers and sellers, making it easy for them to conduct business without negotiating contracts or otherwise hashing out the terms of relationships. In fact, in many exchanges, the buyers and sellers never even know each other's identity. Examples of exchanges include e-Steel (for the steel industry), PaperExchange.com (for the paper industry), IMX Exchange (for the home mortgage industry) and Altra Energy (for the energy industry).

Catalog hubs automate the sourcing of non-commodity manufacturing inputs, creating value by reducing transaction costs. Like MRO hubs, catalog hubs bring together many suppliers at one easy-to-use Web site. The only difference is that catalog hubs are industry specific. They can also be buyer focused or seller focused – that is, some catalog hubs essentially work as virtual distributors for suppliers; others work primarily for buyers in their negotiations with sellers. Examples of catalog hubs include PlasticsNet.com (in the plastics industry), Chemdex (in the specialty chemicals industry) and SciQuest.com (in the life-science industry). Because the products they offer tend to be specialized, catalog hubs often work closely with distributors to ensure safe and reliable deliveries.

Aggregation And Matching

As we think about the differences between systematic and spot purchasing, it becomes obvious that the market-making mechanism that is appropriate for MRO and catalog hubs is quite different from the mechanism used by exchanges and yield managers. business-to-business marketplaces create value by two fundamentally different mechanisms: aggregation and matching.

Business-to-business marketplaces that use the aggregation mechanism bring together a large number of buyers and sellers under one virtual roof. They reduce transaction costs by providing one-stop shopping. PlasticsNet.com, for example, allows plastics processors to issue a single purchase order for hundreds of plastics products sourced from a diverse set of suppliers. The aggregation mechanism is static in nature because prices are pre-negotiated. An important characteristic of this mechanism is that adding another buyer to the business-to-business marketplace benefits only the sellers. And adding another seller benefits only the buyers. The reason is simple: in an aggregation model, buyer and seller positions are fixed.

The aggregation mechanism works best in the following settings:

- The cost of processing a purchase order is high relative to the cost of items procured.
- Products are specialized, not commodities.
- The number of individual products, or stock-keeping units (SKUs), is extremely large.
- The supplier universe is highly fragmented.
- Buyers are not sophisticated enough to understand dynamic pricing mechanisms.
- Purchasing is done through pre-negotiated contracts.
- A metacatalog of products carried by a large number of suppliers can be created.

Unlike the static aggregation mechanism, the matching mechanism brings buyers and sellers together to negotiate prices on a dynamic and real-time basis. For example, Altra

Energy makes a market in energy and electricity by allowing industry participants to list bids and asks on specific quantities of liquid fuels, natural gas, and electric power. The matching mechanism is required for spot sourcing situations, where prices are determined at the moment of purchase. The matching mechanism can also take the form of an auction, as is the case with FreeMarkets.

In the matching mechanism, the roles of the players are fluid: buyers can be sellers, and visa versa. Therefore, adding any new member to the business-to-business marketplace increases the market's liquidity and thus benefits both buyers and sellers. While catalogs benefit only from the aggregation mechanism, exchanges benefit from both aggregation and matching. Therefore, successful exchanges will reap greater benefits from being first movers. In fact, it is likely that the first exchanges or yield managers will take on natural monopoly characteristics. That makes matching a more powerful business model than aggregation. At the same time, however, the matching mechanism is far more complex and far more difficult to scale.

The matching mechanism works best in the following settings:

- Products are commodities or near-commodities and can be traded sight unseen.
- Trading volumes are massive relative to transaction costs.
- Buyers and sellers are sophisticated enough to deal with dynamic pricing.
- Companies use spot purchasing to smooth the peaks and valleys of supply and demand.
- Logistics and fulfillment can be conducted by third parties, often without revealing the identity of the buyer or seller.
- Demand and prices are volatile

The Emergence of Reverse Aggregators

Reverse aggregators are a relatively recent development in the business-to-business arena. Reverse aggregators, which form groups of buyers within specific vertical or horizontal markets, reduce two major inefficiencies. By gathering together the purchasing power of many buyers – particularly small and midsize buyers – they can negotiate price reductions. In some industries, volume discounts can approach 20%. The purchasing business-to-business marketplace can reduce procurement transaction costs by outsourcing the procurement function.

A vertical reverse aggregator, such as FOB.com, pursues this in manufacturing inputs. A horizontal reverse aggregator does the same for manufacturing outputs (MRO procurement). BizBuyer.com and PurchasingCenter.com are some of the many firms pursuing this strategy. Traditionally, firms such as Ingram Micro have worked as forward aggregators by aggregating selling power for small value added resellers, providing them with virtual back-office functions and virtual economies of scale in purchasing as illustrated in Figure 6-2. By contrast, players like FOB.com have turned this supply chain on its head – they amass buying power for smaller buyers, as illustrated in Figure 6-3.

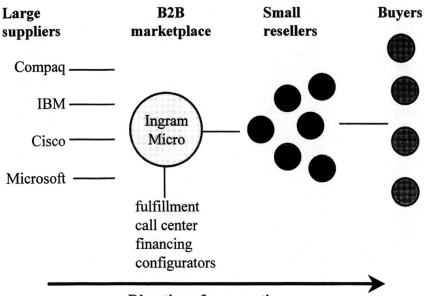

Large suppliers	B2B marketplace	Small resellers	Buyers
Compaq	Ingram Micro		
IBM			
Cisco			
Microsoft			

fulfillment
call center
financing
configurators

Direction of aggregation

Figure 6-2: The Forward Aggregator Model

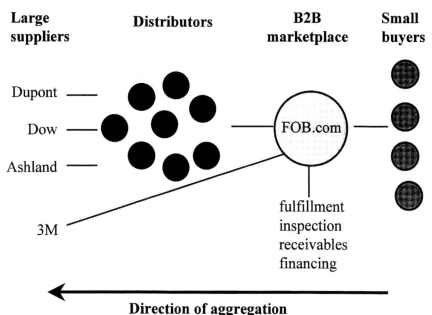

| Large suppliers | Distributors | B2B marketplace | Small buyers |

Dupont ——

Dow —— FOB.com ——

Ashland ——

3M

fulfillment
inspection
receivables
financing

Direction of aggregation

Figure 6-3: The Reverse Aggregator Model

Reverse aggregators have some advantages over neutral business-to-business marketplaces for the procurement of raw materials and components. For example, reverse aggregators can potentially use both spot and systematic sourcing, but exchanges are largely tied to spot transactions. A manufacturer looking for a long-term supply of steel is less likely to use e-Steel than to negotiate directly with a steel manufacturer. Even in those instances where manufacturers do source supplies on the spot market, some fraction of that sourcing is still likely to be systematic and relationship oriented. Not only will reverse aggregators be able to bring together buyers for spot purchases, they will also negotiate long-term contracts with suppliers. In many industries, reverse aggregators will have access to at least as large a market as exchanges and catalogs do.

Where will we see reverse aggregators emerge? First, these business-to-business marketplaces are likely to spring up in vertical and horizontal markets with fragmented buyers. The market need not be fragmented on both the buy and the sell side. Second, because the primary benefit that purchasing business-to-business marketplaces provide is demand aggregation, they will thrive in markets where there are a few large buyers and many small buyers. In these situations, larger buyers enjoy significant volume discounts, while smaller buyers don't have the purchasing power to negotiate with sellers, especially large sellers. Third, purchasing business-to-business marketplaces will be favored in products and services that can be easily broken down into smaller orders. The smaller the lot size the purchasing business-to-business marketplace can deliver, the greater its added value.

Why does the reverse aggregator opportunity exist? Can't the neutral business-to-business marketplaces destroy these new entrants? Neutral business-to-business marketplaces such as Chemdex, SciQuest and PlasticsNet in the relevant vertical markets or horizontal markets are unlikely to create reverse aggregators. That is because if a neutral business-to-business marketplace were to favor either the buyer or the seller side too heavily, it would risk losing its liquidity. In addition, neutral business-to-business marketplaces (especially exchanges) provide marketplaces for buyers and sellers to make spot purchases and sales. In other words, a manufacturer might use ChemConnect to find chemicals that it unexpectedly needs in the next month. That same manufacturer, however, is less likely to use ChemConnect for the chemicals that it buys under long-term contracts.

Biased Or Neutral?

Another important characteristic of a business-to-business marketplace is its bias. Most of the business-to-business marketplaces discussed so far are neutral – they are operated by independent third parties and don't favor buyers over sellers or visa versa. But a business-to-business marketplace can also be biased. When they favor sellers, biased business-to-business marketplaces act as forward aggregators that amass supply and operate downstream in a supply chain or as forward auctioneers that host auctions for buyers. "Forward" in this sense means that the process follows the traditional supply chain model, with the supplier at the start and the buyer at the end. Ingram Micro, for example, is a forward aggregator in the computer industry, and TradeOut.com is a forward aggregator of excess inventory. Biased business-to-business marketplaces that favor buyers act as either reverse aggregators or reverse auctioneers. "Reverse" here means that the business-to-business marketplaces attract a large number of buyers and then bargain with suppliers on their behalf. A reverse auctioneer, for example, hosts an auction where there are many sellers but just one buyer. Examples include FreeMarkets, a reverse auctioneer serving Fortune 500 companies, and FOB.com, a reverse aggregator serving small buyers in chemicals and other vertical markets. Biased business-to-business marketplaces can exist as aggregators in systematic markets or as matchers in spot markets.

Neutral business-to-business marketplaces, however, are the true market makers because they are equally attractive to buyers and sellers. That said, neutral business-to-business marketplaces face some daunting challenges. At first, they confront a "chicken and egg" problem: buyers do not want to participate unless there are a sufficient number of sellers, and sellers do not want to participate unless there are a sufficient number of buyers. To succeed, these business-to-business marketplaces must attract both buyers and sellers quickly, creating liquidity at both ends. Neutral business-to-business marketplaces also have to overcome the sellers' channel conflict. After all, sellers usually participate in these markets at the expense of their normal distribution channels. Chemdex solved this conflict by partnering with a large existing cataloger – VWR. VWR promised to send all its business through Chemdex in exchange for an equity stake in the company as well as a concession that Chemdex would not charge a transaction fee to VWR's largest buyers.

Finally, neutral business-to-business marketplaces need to be careful when taking equity investments from large buyers as well as from large suppliers; such investments can create a perception of bias.

By their very nature, biased business-to-business marketplaces do not have the "chicken and egg" problem; they just hitch their wagon to one side of the transaction. As a result, they have the potential to grow more quickly that neutral business-to-business marketplaces. They are also able to focus on smaller buyers or sellers because they can aggregate demand or supply. Furthermore, business-to-business marketplaces that are biased toward buyers typically do not have to overcome channel conflict.

Reverse aggregators do face some challenges, though. They are not attractive to large buyers that already enjoy substantial volume discounts. And they have to contend with high sales and marketing costs relative to neutral business-to-business marketplaces, because they focus on smaller buyers with lower revenue potential than the larger buyers targeted by neutral business-to-business marketplaces. Fragmented demand benefits reverse aggregators, but it also poses challenges for cost-effective customer acquisition.

Neutral and biased business-to-business marketplaces differ in another important way. Neutral business-to-business marketplaces are most likely to succeed in markets that are fragmented on both the buyer and seller sides. In such markets, neutral business-to-business marketplaces add value by reducing transaction costs (aggregating) and improving matching (providing liquidity). If only one side of the market is fragmented, the benefits are greatly reduced for the non-fragmented side. Biased business-to-business marketplaces, in contrast, can succeed as long as one side of the transaction is fragmented. In fact, reverse aggregators, such as FOB.com, add the most value when the supplier universe is relatively concentrated while the buyer universe is fragmented. In these situations, leveling the playing field for smaller buyers has significant value.

The Rise of Workflow Redesigners

Many of the business-to-business marketplaces make an existing process more efficient by automating transactions and by reducing interaction costs among buyers and suppliers. Now a new class of business-to-business marketplaces is emerging that go beyond automation; they also redesign workflow across businesses in specific industries. These workflow redesigners marry the efficiency gains from workflow automation to the effectiveness gains from the redesign of the processes by which businesses interact in business-to-business marketplaces.

GUIDELINES FOR INTRODUCING BUSINESS-TO-BUSINESS ELECTRONIC COMMERCE

Estimates of commerce to be captured in business-to-business (B2B) exchanges by 2004 range from $1 to $2 trillion. Although built on assumptions of thick margins, high volumes and low capital requirements, most business-to-business exchanges have experienced low transaction volumes and razor thin margins. It's not the end of the road for such ventures, but even the best of them are in for some rough riding – and the path to riches is narrow. In theory, a business-to-business exchange makes perfect sense. Buyers are exposed to new sellers, and sellers are exposed to new buyers. Product, search and transaction costs are reduced. Information exchange is enhanced. And as information is shared and leveraged across industry participants, supply-chain relationships are improved and costs dramatically reduced. We have seen this scenario played out on the business-to-consumer (B2C) side in the success of eBay and Priceline.

But most business-to-business exchanges rely on a few sweet spots in the market: areas in which supply and demand are fragmented, transaction costs are high, or the pricing mechanism is inefficient. But take away the sweet spots – that is, try to operate in suboptimal conditions characterized by highly evolved distributors, low margins and consolidated supply – and you've got a losing proposition.

How can exchange operators successfully navigate this narrow path to profitability? There are a few tips they can learn from previous experiences.

1. *Learn from the survivors of the shakeout in the business-to-consumer business.* Ally with scale players who are looking for expertise. The large consumer-products manufacturers, for example, have something to sell, but they lack speed, technology, and management teams dedicated to operating an online marketplace.

2. *Build value-added services around the core exchange.* Bring customers through the door on low-margin transactions, then keep them coming back for add-on, higher-margin sales of logistics, information, financial, or analytical services.

3. *Leverage the software you have created for the exchange.* Morph into a software house, an application service provider (ASP), or both. A lot of money has been poured into creating technology platforms for deep, vertical-industry problems. Become a solutions provider for industry-specific procurement or supply chains. The semi-custom software used to develop the platforms could be sold as a Web service through an ASP.

4. *Focus on supply chain savings.* As marketplaces deconstruct into a series of overlapping extranets, many exchange operators are discovering that most of the value lies here, rather than in buy/sell savings.

5. *Create a new structure.* Instead of independent exchanges backed by venture capital or a for-profit venture of two or three major players, consider industry consortia like VISA or MasterCard. Such a model allows all participants to realize the value of the exchange, but it doesn't fall victim to as many control issues or unrealistic economic expectations.

Some lessons which we can learn from the experiences of early entrepreneurs in the business-to-business segments are:

- *The race goes to the swift.* How you get started introducing online purchasing tools into your organization is less important than simply getting started. You should introduce Web technology to your purchasing department now so that your buyers become comfortable with it.

- *Develop a sense of how your organization can benefit from online purchasing.* Experiment with third-party catalogs and supplier sites. Map out your existing purchasing processes to understand what improvements to expect from automation. This information will help you forecast your return on future online purchasing investments.

- *Create a "requirements document".* If a buyer-driven catalog seems to be a good investment for your organization, writing a detailed requirements document will help identify both the purchasing functionality needed and the technology standards that your firm supports. Forging a true partnership among the parties involved in the implementation – information systems, the applications provider, the purchasing group and the systems integrator – is vital. Frequent communications ensure that the partnership functions well.

- *Pick a provider with staying power.* Being on the bleeding edge of online purchasing is not without risks. In the tumultuous world of the Internet, start-ups fail at least as frequently as they thrive, so it pays to ask yourself if your chosen online purchasing service provider will be a survivor. More important, consider whether you should undergo a large-scale systems implementation now or wait to see what other solutions may be coming down the road.
- *Be prepared for implementation challenges.* When you are first, you learn as you go. Put a buffer in your project plans.

STRATEGIC ISSUES IN BUSINESS-TO-BUSINESS ELECTRONIC COMMERCE

Issue 1: Establishing business-to-business relationships to sell competitively to consumers

Electronic commerce enables companies to develop stronger relationships with their various business partners and increase the value brought to market. Using Web-based electronic data interchange (EDI), electronic fund transfers (EFT), enhanced supply chain management, and replenishment models allows for swifter and more accurate transactions. Such high-velocity exchanges also support a faster cycle time. The ability to link with key business partners requires compatible software and network linkages and protocols. Securing these transaction flows often requires encryption or private networks.

Issue 2: Strengthening the value chain

Effective Web-based strategies can strengthen channel relationships. A manufacturer could use its Web site to help promote its channel partners. Working with existing channel partners as the new technology develops is critical to overall effective implementation, and suggests that in some situations the Web can effectively serve as a strategic method of communication and service. Stronger, more effective value chains can be leveraged to establish a competitive advantage.

Issue 3: Providing value through communication

The opportunity to give suppliers key information on order processing, current product demand, and inventory management has long been a method of establishing stronger business-to-business relationships. The Web extends these links by allowing firms to provide detailed partner information on product specifications, delivery notification, and process changes, keeping the information current and readily available. The use of the Web has resulted in greater speed-to-market and reduced coordination costs among partners. With information sharing, business partners can strengthen relationships as well as their competitive position.

Issue 4: Optimizing business-to-business service

Offering better service to key business partners is another capability of electronic commerce. FedEx helps its business customers monitor the progress of their packages and track delivery costs.

THE FUTURE OF BUSINESS-TO-BUSINESS ELECTRONIC COMMERCE

The use of the Internet to facilitate commerce among companies promises vast benefits: dramatically reduced costs, greater access to buyers and sellers, improved marketplace liquidity, and a whole new array of efficient and flexible transaction methods. But if the benefits are clear, the path to achieving them is anything but. The business-to-business market is still in its infancy, and its structure and players remain in rapid flux.

The high level of uncertainty is causing widespread anxiety among executives – and for good reason. Whether as buyers, sellers, or both, all companies have substantial stakes in the business-to-business marketplace. Their supply chains, their product and marketing strategies, their processes and operations – even their business models – will be shaped by the way business-to-business relationships are formed and transactions are carried out. Yet at this moment even the most basic questions remain difficult for companies to answer: Which exchanges should we participate in? Should we form a trading consortium with our competitors? Should we demand that our suppliers go online? What software should we invest in? Executives understand that the wrong choices could have dire consequences, but they also know that in the fast-paced world of the Internet they need to act soon or they will be left behind.

Most business-to-business activity to date has centered on online exchanges and auctions, and most observers have assumed that these electronic marketplaces would come to dominate the business-to-business landscape. Once you look beyond the hype, however, you quickly see that most Internet exchanges are floundering. They suffer from meager transaction volume and equally meager revenues, and they face a raft of competitors. The hard truth is that few of these exchanges will ever create the liquidity needed to survive.

The current business-to-business model has three fatal flaws. First, the value proposition offered by most exchanges – competitive bidding among suppliers allows buyers to get the lowest possible prices – runs counter to the best recent thinking on buyer-supplier relations. Most companies have come to realize that getting supplies at the lowest price may not be in their best economic interest. Other factors, such as quality, timing of deliveries and customization, are often more important than price in determining the overall value provided by a supplier. That is particularly true for the many manufacturers that have adopted lean, low-inventory production systems that depend on reliable, precisely scheduled shipments of supplies and components. Many companies have spent the last two decades methodically forging tighter, more strategic relationships with suppliers – many such affiliations have involved joint product design efforts, integration of complex processes and long-term service contracts. The online exchanges' focus on arm's-length, price-driven transactions flies in the face of all their hard work.

Second, the exchanges deliver little benefit to sellers. Yes, suppliers have access to more buyers with only a modest increase in marketing cost, but that benefit is overwhelmed by pricing pressures. Few suppliers want to be anonymous contestants in ruthless bidding wars, and for the highest quality, most innovative suppliers, price battles are anathema. As a result, the buyer-biased exchanges that characterize business-to-business today will not be able to achieve a critical mass of participants and transactions – they will be forever starved of liquidity. To be successful in the long run, business-to-business markets need to offer strong incentives to both buyers and sellers.

Third, the business models of most business-to-business exchanges are, at best, half-baked. In their rush to get online, the companies that run the exchanges haven't taken the time to study their customers' priorities in-depth, create distinctive offerings, or even map out paths to profitability. They have simply used off-the-shelf software to set up simple auctions as quickly as possible. Because the software is readily available and relatively cheap, the barriers to entry are low, and the resulting proliferation of new exchanges is undermining the margins of all players. Indeed, the influx of new entrants is leading to the same type of market fragmentation that exchanges were designed to overcome in the first place.

The current business-to-business model, propped up by cheap investment capital, is not sustainable. As the markets mature, they will have to evolve in ways that fix the problems of the existing system. New structures will enable buyers and suppliers to form tight relationships while still enjoying the reach and efficiency of Internet commerce. Rewards will begin to flow to sellers as well as buyers. And new business models will provide profits in a world of dirt-cheap transactions.

Formative Trends In Business-to-Business Electronic Commerce

Greater market liquidity and transparency have enabled more efficient pricing and more effective matching of buyers and sellers, and, most important, value has shifted from the product itself to information about the product. While the transfer of physical goods may remain the end result of a business transaction, the information that shapes the transaction – price, availability, quality, quantity, and so on – can now be separated and exchanged electronically. And that information is often more valuable to companies than the underlying goods.

From Simple to Complex Transactions

It is expected that there will occur a fragmentation of roles in the business-to-business world as markets are restructured to accommodate the complex goods and services that account for the bulk of most companies' spending. Most business-to-business exchanges focus on relatively simple transactions involving commodities, common maintenance items, or basic services such as cargo transport. Yet the vast majority of business spending lies in the more complex categories of components, services and capital goods. Here, purchase decisions hinge on many variables beyond price, and, as a result, companies usually rely on salespeople and other traditional channels, such as distributors and value-added resellers. Can the Internet provide a

141

mechanism for enabling complex transactions? MySimon, a consumer shopping service suggests how specialized shopping intermediaries may emerge in business-to-business markets to fill this need. Using decision-support software from Active Research, MySimon offers tailored purchasing advice in a variety of product categories while allowing buyers to compare the offerings of many vendors. It helps consumers sort through an array of purchase dimensions, decide which areas are important to them, and then see how well the available offerings match up with their requirements. MySimon renders obsolete the value-added role of the trained salesperson and goes beyond the role of a typical electronic retailer. Rather than selling the product, MySimon acts as a personal adviser to guide the customer to a source for purchase. The company generates revenues from vendor slotting fees and advertising.

With similar decision-support tools, more complex business-to-business sales will become feasible online. This trend is likely to be accelerated by the advent of extensible markup language (XML), a set of software standards for displaying and sharing detailed information such as pricing and product specifications over the Web. Purchase support could become a unique source of value and customer loyalty, with the actual transactions handed off to sites that compete solely on price and availability. Companies such as General Electric and Milatron are already moving to provide more of this decision-making information on the Web.

From Middlemen to Speculators

As the profit margins of business-to-business exchanges get pushed down by competition, some exchanges will start to take their own speculative positions, buying and selling large quantities of the goods traded in their markets. In this e-speculator model, running the biggest exchange still provides a source of competitive advantage, but, the advantage comes not from fees but from a superior window into the dynamics of the market. Ultimately, exchanges might even reduce their commissions to a price below zero; that is, they might pay for a flow of deals in order to gain valuable information about the market.

From Transactions to Solutions

The business-to-business landscape is well suited to solution providers. By using the Internet to bundle products with related information and services, creative companies can improve the effectiveness and efficiency of their clients' businesses. By doing so, they will be able to forge strong, long-lasting client relationships that will de-emphasize product price and exchange-based transactions. Early examples of solution sites are now appearing on the Internet. Some are operated by suppliers looking to counter the role of the exchanges; others are portals operated by third-party intermediaries.

From Buyer-Seller Exchange Transactions to Sell-Side Asset Swaps

Sell-side swap models are emerging in business-to-business e-commerce. In stark contrast to most existing exchanges, which tend to penalize sellers, asset swaps benefit suppliers by allowing them to better utilize their key assets – whether factories, trucks,

142

warehouses, or containers for shipping. At the same time, they enable buyers to tap a broader, more efficient supply base. The swapping model is particularly attractive in highly fragmented industries, where small-scale suppliers often lack a broad geographic reach and are highly vulnerable to fluctuations in demand.

New Business Models In Business-To-Business Electronic Commerce

As the trends play out, business-to-business commerce will be structured very differently from what it is today. Rather than being dominated by monolithic exchanges, it will encompass several distinct, independent business models.

Mega-Exchanges

Because scale and liquidity are vitally important to efficient trading, today's fragmented and illiquid exchanges will consolidate into a relatively small set of mega-exchanges that will occupy the center of the business-to-business universe. Although most transactions will flow through them, they will not generate much profit or shareholder value. As transaction fees fall or disappear entirely, the exchanges may turn into nonprofit collectives. Many business-to-business players will maintain stakes in the exchanges for the benefit of more lucrative e-commerce endeavors such as origination or speculation.

First-generation business-to-business exchanges, faced with boycotts by suppliers and antitrust scrutiny from regulators, are likely to evolve in two important ways. First, since the best method of achieving sufficient market liquidity is to enlist every participant's support, the exchanges will move away from being for-profit entities and move toward being collective industry efforts run for the benefit of all. Second, they will move beyond executing transactions to create the infrastructure and standards necessary to streamline communication between buyers and sellers. This will address pressing issues of efficiency, such as speeding up the flow of product information, automating billing and payment, and linking buyer and seller production processes more closely. And it will allow them to handle not only simple products but complex, custom components and services, which account for most business purchases.

Originators

Surrounding the mega-exchanges and plugged into them in various symbiotic ways will be the specialist companies. Originators, such as FreeMarkets, will structure and take orders for complex transactions, bundle them into large order requests, and send them to mega-exchanges for execution. The originator role will be most valuable in markets with relatively expensive products that are neither commodities nor completely customized, such as automotive and aircraft components, industrial equipment subassemblies, and complex services such as insurance. To be successful, an originator will need to concentrate initially on creating standards for trading complicated products and providing real-time support for customers online. An originator will be able to achieve an advantage by understanding a complex product category and customer decision-making parameters better than its competitors. It will also benefit by adeptly using configuration and decision-support software. Profits will come primarily from

143

commissions and from slotting fees paid by vendors and exchanges in return for preferential positions with the originator. Many of the niche portals already in operation will probably use their knowledge of narrow business communities to move toward an originator model.

E-speculators

Savvy e-speculators, seeking to capitalize on an abundance of market information, will tend to concentrate where relatively standardized products can be transferred easily among a large group of buyers. They will also look for price volatility, which will provide trading spreads. Expect to see e-speculators in markets for specialty chemicals, paper and certain basic auto parts. To thrive, an e-speculator will need to develop strong financial and risk-management skills. A speculator's advantage will come from having better, more timely market information than other participants. To get that information, it will have to partner closely with at least one mega-exchange or operate as the profit-making arm of an exchange. Speculators will likely earn profits not only by trading but also by creating and selling various hedging instruments.

Solution Providers

In many markets, a handful of independent solution providers with well-known brand names and solid reputations will thrive alongside mega-exchanges. A good number of them will leverage distinctive technical expertise to become indispensable to customers – and thus reduce the importance of price in buying decisions. Many will derive a substantial proportion of their profits from high-margin add-ons and consumables. The solution model will be most common in markets where the product itself represents a small portion of a customer's overall costs but heavily influences those costs, as in specialty chemicals, engineered plastics and cutting tools.

Sell-side Asset Exchanges

Many business-to-business transactions will consist of sell-side asset exchanges, in which suppliers will trade orders among themselves, sometimes after initial transactions with customers are made on the mega-exchanges. Sell-side swapping will be most valuable where markets are highly fragmented, both on the buyer and seller sides, where, for geographic or information reasons, demand and supply are often mismatched, and where suppliers can benefit greatly from keeping expensive fixed assets fully utilized. Industries with these characteristics include transportation, metalworking, plastic molding, farming and construction. A company seeking to pursue the asset-exchange model will need to have strong relationships with the supplier community, since success will hinge on its gaining a critical mass of supplier transactions. It will also need to be adept at understanding supplier problems. Sales of products and services that solve these problems are likely to be an important source of profits.

Skill Sets Required

Whether a company is hoping to play a role as a business-to-business service provider or simply needs to transact business with other companies, it will have to develop a deep knowledge of the emerging landscape and the various business models it will contain. The players' value and power will vary considerably depending on the industry and the products involved. Each company will have to create its own path to success – and not all products are suited to Internet transactions. Very complex, expensive items, such as aircraft or merger-and-acquisition advisory services, will continue to be sold primarily through personal relationships and multi-step purchasing processes. Radical changes in markets require radical responses. For many companies, traditional skills in such areas as product development, manufacturing, and marketing may become less important, while the ability to understand and capitalize on market dynamics may become considerably more important.

THE EMERGENCE OF PEER-TO-PEER NETWORKS

In the prevailing model of business-to-business commerce on the Internet, transaction flows through large, centralized exchanges. These exchanges play two valuable roles: aggregation and facilitation. As aggregators, they bring a group of dispersed trading partners together into a virtual marketplace. As facilitators, they provide software tools and protocols that enable the traders to do business electronically, exchanging information, processing offers and bids, coming to terms on deals, and following through on them.

The exchange-based business-to-business model has been a compelling one. It has attracted vast investments, intense corporate interest and reams of press coverage. But, unfortunately for the exchanges and fortunately for pretty much everyone else, its days may be numbered. A new and better business-to-business model – peer-to-peer networking – is emerging. It will enable all companies everywhere to locate trading partners on the fly and complete transactions swiftly, securely and efficiently, without the need for any central aggregator or facilitator. The basic technology for peer-to-peer networking is already available. Participants in a peer-to-peer network, whether individuals or companies, exchange information directly with one another, bypassing central exchanges. In some peer-to-peer networks, information about the location of files is stored in a central directory, but the files themselves remain on users' hard drives. In others, there is no center at all. Even the directory is disbursed among the users. In technical terms, the distinction between "client" and "server" evaporates; each computer on the network plays both roles simultaneously.

Peer-to-peer networks offer important advantages over the exchange-based model. First, and most obvious, they allow companies to avoid the fees charged by exchanges. Second, they reduce the complexity and expense of networking. It is much easier for a company to integrate its internal information systems with a single peer-to-peer program, or "peering portal", than with a bunch of different exchanges. Finally, while membership in exchanges is limited, often determined along industry lines, peer-to-peer networks have no bounds. A company can search as widely as it wants for new partners and products or for lower prices or better terms. More of the power of the open, ubiquitous Internet is harnessed in a business-to-peer model than in an exchange-based one.

If the underlying technology is available and if the benefits are compelling, why haven't businesses started moving to business-to-peer already? The answer is straightforward: peer-to-peer software hasn't yet progressed to the point where it can handle complex transactions. The data required to describe product specifications and business concepts are many and complicated. The processes facilitated by current peer-to-peer software – search and download are rudimentary. More work is required before business-to-peer partners will be able to agree on how to merge their complex business processes and embed them in software so they can be automated.

But the technical gaps will be filled quickly. As a start, it is not a difficult engineering feat to create programs that let companies share their lists of goods and services with one another. These "peering portals" will link with companies' internal inventory and production systems to ensure that listings are always accurate and up-to-date. Together, the peering portals of all the companies on the network will create a universal catalog of product and service offerings.

In addition, new Internet technologies, such as Extensible Markup Language (XML) and Resource Definition Format (RDF), are now enabling complex products and services to be defined and searched. XML allows a group of partners to agree on how any resource – a product, a production plan, a purchase order, a contract – will be described electronically. RDF is a highly flexible way to index collections of resources. These two advances make it feasible, for the first time, for companies to search for and exchange all types of information, to reach agreements, and to coordinate payments, shipments, and other processes without involving a lot of human, or digital middlemen.

Does this mean the end of digital intermediaries in business-to-business markets? Of course not. Third parties will still be needed to provide services that companies don't want to do themselves or trust one another to do. Running an auction is a great example of a function requiring an unbiased intermediary. Internet auctioneers such as FreeMarkets should continue to thrive in a business-to-peer world, even as the auctions become more efficient. The auctioneer's system will tie into the business-to-peer networks, automatically collecting data from companies' peering portals and hosting auctions in which both people and machines place bids.

All the technical requirements to shift business-to-business onto peer-to-peer networks are in place or will be shortly. The only real question now is timing. How quickly will companies come to realize the advantages that unbounded direct connections hold over centrally controlled exchanges? Judging by the speed of previous Internet advances, it probably won't take long.

Chapter 7

Rethinking the Value Chain

THE VIRTUAL VALUE CHAIN

Every business today competes in two worlds: a physical world of resources that managers can see and touch, and a virtual world made of information, which is referred to as cyberspace. The latter has given rise to electronic commerce, a new locus of value creation. Executives must pay attention to how their companies create value in both the physical realm and cyberspace. But the processes for creating value are not the same in the two worlds. By understanding the differences and the interplay between the value-adding processes of the physical world and those of the information world, senior managers can see more clearly and comprehensively the strategic issues facing their organizations. Managing two interacting value-adding processes in the two mutually dependent realms poses new conceptual and tactical challenges. Those who understand how to master both can create and extract value in the most efficient and effective manner.

Academics, consultants and managers have long described the process of creating value in the physical world, often referring to the stages involved as links in a "value chain". The value chain is a model that describes a series of value-adding activities connecting a company's supply side (raw materials, inbound logistics and production processes) with its demand side (outbound logistics, marketing and sales). By analyzing the stages of a value chain, managers have been able to redesign their internal and external processes to improve efficiency and effectiveness.

The value-chain model treats information as a supporting element of the value-adding process, not as a source of value itself. For example, managers often use information that they capture of inventory, production or logistics to help monitor or control those processes, but they rarely use information itself to create new value for the customer. However, Federal Express Corporation did just that by allowing customers to track packages through the company's Web site. Now customers can locate a package in transit by connecting online to the FedEx Web site and entering the airbill number. After the package has been delivered, they can even identify the name of the person who signed for it. Although FedEx provides this service for free, it has created added value for the customer – and thus increased loyalty – in a fiercely competitive market.

The value-adding processes that companies must employ to turn raw information into new information services and products are unique to the information world. In other words, the value-adding steps are virtual in that they are performed through and with information. Creating value in any stage of a virtual value chain involves a sequence of five activities: gathering, organizing, selecting, synthesizing and distributing information. A manager today collects raw information and adds value through these steps.

Organizations making money in the information realm successfully exploit both of their value chains. Rather than managing one series of value-adding activities, they are actually managing two. The economic logic of the two chains is different: A conventional understanding of the economies of scale and scope does not apply to the virtual value chain in the same way as it does to the physical value chain. Moreover, the two chains must be managed distinctly but also in concert.

Companies adopt value-adding information processes in three stages. In the first stage, *visibility*, companies acquire an ability to "see" physical operations more effectively through information. At this stage, managers use large-scale information technology systems to coordinate activities in their physical value chains, and in the process lay the foundation for a virtual value chain. In the second stage, *mirroring capability*, companies substitute virtual activities for physical ones; they begin to create a parallel value chain in cyberspace. Finally, businesses use information to establish *new customer relationships*. At this third stage, managers draw on the flow of information in their virtual value chain to deliver value to customers in new ways. In effect, they apply the generic value-adding activities to their virtual value chain and thereby exploit the *value matrix*. As companies move into the information world to perform value-adding steps, the potential for top-line growth increases. Each of the three stages represents considerable opportunity for managers.

Visibility

During the past 30 years, many companies have invested in technology systems to enable managers to coordinate, measure, and sometimes control business processes. The information collected by these systems about steps in the value chain has helped managers to plan, execute and evaluate results with greater precision and speed. In recent years, managers have been able to gain access to the information generated in the course of traditional operating activities, and that information helps them to see their physical value chains as an integrated system rather than as a set of discrete though related activities. In this way, they can gain new insight into managing the value chain as a whole rather than as a collection of parts.

When companies integrate the information they capture during stages of the value chain – from inbound logistics and production through sales and marketing – they construct an information underlay of the business. This integrated information provides managers with the ability to "see" their value chains from end to end. Companies such as FedEx, Wal-Mart, and Frito-Lay have transformed this kind of visibility into competitive advantage. The successful use of world-class information systems by each of these companies is now common knowledge.

Mirroring Capability

Once companies have established the necessary infrastructure for visibility, they can do more than just monitor value-adding steps. They can begin to manage operations or even to implement value-adding steps in cyberspace – faster, better, with more flexibility, and at lower cost. In other words, managers can begin to ask, 'What are we doing now in the physical world, and what could we do more efficiently or more effectively in cyberspace?' and, 'What value-adding steps currently performed in the physical value chain might be shifted to the mirror world of the virtual value chain?' When companies move activities from the physical world to cyberspace, they begin to create a virtual value chain that parallels but improves on the physical value chain.

Every manager knows that staying competitive today depends on achieving higher levels of performance for customers while incurring lower costs in research & development (R&D) and production. Traditionally, companies have gotten more for less by exploiting vast economies of scale in production while focusing on raising levels of quality. When scale economies do not apply, as in many service-sector businesses, managers seeking better performance at lower cost can tap the mirror world, in which the economics are altogether different. On the virtual value chain, companies may find dramatic, low-cost approaches to delivering extraordinarily high-value results to customers.

New Customer Relationships

Ultimately, however, companies must do more than create value in cyberspace. They must also extract value from it. They can often do so by establishing information-based relationships with customers. Once companies become adept at managing their value-adding activities across the parallel value chains, they are ready to develop these new relationships. In the world of high technology, examples of building customer relationships on the virtual value chain abound. Today, thousands of companies have established Web sites to advertise products or elicit comments from customers. Some companies have gone further and have actually automated the interface with the customer, thus identifying and fulfilling customers' desires at lower cost. Other companies view their challenge as that of managing each individual customer relationship in both the physical world and cyberspace. Those that succeed have an opportunity to reinvent the core value proposition of a business, even an entire industry.

The Value Matrix

The new relationships that companies are developing with customers spring from a matrix of value opportunities. Each stage of the virtual value chain – as a mirror of the physical value chain – allows for many new extracts from the flow of information, and each extract could constitute a new product or service. If managers want to pursue any of these opportunities, they need to put into place processes to gather the information, organize it for the customer, select what's valuable, package (or synthesize) it, and distribute it – the five value-adding steps unique to the information world. In effect, these value-adding steps, in conjunction with the virtual value chain, make up a value matrix that allows companies to identify customers' desires more effectively and fulfill them more efficiently.

By thinking boldly about the integration of the physical world and cyberspace, executives may be able to create valuable digital assets that, in turn, could change the competitive dynamics of industries. By thinking in terms of a virtual value chain and a physical value chain, the company's managers look at far more opportunities for creating and extracting value than they would have by considering the business exclusively from the point of view of a traditional physical value chain. Thinking about a business in terms of its value matrix can allow managers to go beyond changing the rules of the game: They can reinvent an industry.

Implications for Management

What all this means for managers is that they must consciously focus on the principles that guide value creation and extraction across the two value chains, separately and in combination. These two value-adding processes are fundamentally different. The physical value chain is composed of a linear sequence of activities with defined points of input and output. By contrast, the virtual value chain is nonlinear – a matrix of potential inputs and outputs that can be accessed and distributed through a wide variety of channels.

How can we make sense of this new realm of activity – the information space that allows for the creation of a virtual value chain and the exploitation of a value matrix? To succeed in this new economic environment, executives must understand the differences between value creation and extraction in the physical world and cyberspace; they must manage both effectively and in concert. More specifically, a company's executives must embrace an updated set of guiding principles because in cyberspace, many of the business axioms that have guided managers no longer apply. Five new management principles for managing an organization in cyberspace are mentioned here.

The Law of Digital Assets

Digital assets, unlike physical ones, are not used up in their consumption. Companies that create value with digital assets may be able to reharvest them through a potentially infinite number of transactions, thus changing the competitive dynamics of their industries. Providers of products or services that must price according to the traditional variable cost model – based on the consumption of the underlying materials – will have a tough time competing against companies that, by exploiting their virtual value chains, can price aggressively and still make margins.

New Economies of Scale

The virtual value chain redefines economies of scale, allowing small companies to achieve low unit costs for products and services in markets dominated by big companies.

New Economies of Scope

In cyberspace, businesses can redefine economies of scope by drawing on a single set of digital assets to provide value across many different and disparate markets.

Transaction-Cost Compression

Transaction costs along the virtual value chain are lower than their counterparts on the physical value chain, and they continue to decline sharply as the processing capacity per unit of cost for microprocessors doubles every 18 months. Lower transaction costs allow companies to control and track information that would have been too costly to capture and process just a few years ago.

Rebalancing Supply and Demand

Taken together, these four axioms combine to create a fifth. The world of business increasingly demands a shift from supply-side to demand-side thinking. As companies gather, organize, select, synthesize and distribute information in cyberspace while managing raw and manufactured goods in the physical world, they have the opportunity to sense and respond to customers' desires rather than simply to make and sell products and services. In today's world of over-capacity, in which demand, not supply, is scarce, managers must increasingly look to demand-side strategies.

Senior managers must evaluate their business – its strengths and weaknesses, its opportunities and risks – along the value chains of both worlds, virtual and physical. Today, events in either can make or break a business.

MANAGING THE VIRTUAL VALUE CHAIN

One of the profound consequences of the information revolution is its influence on how economic value is created and extracted. Specifically, when buyer-seller transactions occur in an information-defined arena, information is accessed and absorbed more easily, and arranged and priced in different ways. Most important, the information about a product or service can be separated from the product or service itself. In some cases, it can become as critical as the actual product or service in terms of its effect on a company's profits.

Everything about transacting business in cyberspace is different from what happens in the physical world. The *content* of the transaction is different: information about the products replaces the products themselves. The *context* in which the transaction occurs is different: an electronic, on-screen auction replaces a face-to-face auction. The *infrastructure* that enables the transaction to occur is different: computers and communication lines replace the physical marketplace.

The cyberspace transaction allows for lower costs (associated with inventory management), increased convenience (buyers can obtain the information on their desktop computers) and ubiquity (anyone can log on). The traditional marketplace – a bundle of physical locations, inventory and tangible products – has radically changed. Quite simply, in an information-defined transaction space, customers learn about products differently, buy them differently, and have them delivered differently. How they assign their loyalty can also be different. In a world where the traditional signposts of differentiation no longer matter – where "content" may not automatically mean "product" and where "distribution" may not automatically mean "physical location" – brand equity can rapidly evaporate.

As a result, information-defined transactions – value creation and extraction in cyberspace – are creating new ways of thinking about making money and are thus recasting the value proposition. Traditional financial analysis will not help calculate the value of a company's assets when those assets exist within a network of computers and communication connections. Similarly, the traditional marketing mix no longer applies.

In fact, old investment strategies may not even uncover the new threats to their conventional businesses.

Today, both physical-world and virtual-world transactions are occurring. Some companies operate solely in the physical world; others have begun to straddle the two realms. It is crucial to understand how companies survive at the cusp, working both physical-world and cyberspace transactions to their best advantage. Information-defined transactions are both inevitable and increasing in number and complexity, given the growing omnipresence of the microprocessor. As a result, companies must learn how to manage in – and take advantage of – this new arena.

A New Framework for Managing in Electronic Commerce

Companies that don't understand cyberspace will miss opportunities even as they build information-defined relationships with their customers. Thus, managers face two critical challenges: first, to recognize the full potential of cyberspace transactions in a coherent manner; and, second, to choose the best means to make money in this new arena.

Let us examine first how value is traditionally created and perceived. In cyberspace, brand equity is established and managed by manipulating content, context and infrastructure through the traditional marketing mix. The three elements are usually aggregated. Customers – and managers – see a brand as a representation of customer-perceived value that is provided by the product/service, as well as the communications programs, pricing strategy and channel activities related to that product/service.

For example, a newspaper is an aggregated collection of content (news, business, sports, weather, as well as other information), context (format, organization, logo, editorial style and rhetorical tone), and infrastructure (printing plant and physical distribution system, including trucks, door-to-door delivery, as well as news-stand sales). In order to create value for consumers, publishers must aggregate all content, context and infrastructure activities into a single value proposition.

In cyberspace, however, content, context and infrastructure can be disaggregated to create new ways of adding value, lowering costs, forging relationships with nontraditional partners, and rethinking "ownership" issues. In the new arena, content, context and infrastructure are easily separated. Information technology adds or alters content, changes the context of the interaction, and enables the delivery of varied content and a variety of contexts over different infrastructures.

Customer Loyalty in Cyberspace

Managing in cyberspace – and in the hybrid of the physical world and cyberspace – means combining content, context and infrastructure in new and creative ways based on the important premise that the interaction, or interface, between customer and company has radically changed. As a result, customer loyalty in cyberspace looks very different than it did in the physical world.

In mature electronic commerce environments, it is possible to mix and match content and context in ways that may at first seem unrelated to the core transaction. Once the consumer is in cyberspace and loyal to a particular context, the potential for related transactions may be limited only by the imagination of the strategic members involved. The implications and difficulties of managing in cyberspace become increasingly relevant as more and more products and services, marketing-management processes, and even markets themselves, move from the physical world to cyberspace.

Opportunities in Electronic Commerce

The first challenge for executives and strategic planners is to understand how the transition from the physical world to cyberspace is unfolding in key industries. Which competitors are establishing a presence on the networks? Who is using the network to market products or provide after-sales services? Which companies are adding value to their commodity products by providing superior information about that product or service? More than 400 million people have daily access to information services globally over the Internet, and usage is growing rapidly. Managers will need to understand what the implications of these virtual world presences are for their individual businesses.

The second challenge is to discover and act on new opportunities in cyberspace. This task may not be an easy one. Learning to manage in cyberspace requires a radical shift in thinking: from markets defined by physical place to ones defined by information space. Companies must carefully examine what they are offering, how they are offering it, and what enables the transaction to occur. Then they must decide which mix and emphasis will best serve their purposes.

What is critical to understand about cyberspace strategies is that they are dynamic. It is possible to develop a strategy that focuses primarily on one dimension. Creating content that has unique, innovative, or functional appeal can be very profitable. In cyberspace, which enables niche markets to be easily accessed, creativity will flourish. In addition, it is possible to develop a context-focused strategy. America Online does not have its own proprietary content or infrastructure. Instead, AOL creates an information-based context in which people consume, communicate and transact. There are, as the scramble to get onto the information superhighway suggests, fortunes to be made – and lost – in establishing new market contexts. It is also possible to develop a pure infrastructure strategy. Many local cable operators follow this strategy. Instead of focusing on content and context, they own the "wire" into the house – and they charge for it.

While a single-dimension strategy can be profitable, it may make sense early in the life of a market to launch a full proprietary system at all three levels and to hone in on one specialty later. No matter which product, it is important to understand and explore value creation in cyberspace. New cyberspace opportunities arise daily, and in order to seize them, managers need a coherent strategy that is not limited by the old physical world thinking.

THE CHANGING ROLE OF INTERMEDIARIES

Intermediaries exist to improve the efficiency with which products and services move through the channel. They go by many names: middlemen, retailers, wholesalers, distributors, agents, brokers and channel members. Because of their particular expertise, they are able to perform certain tasks more ably than a manufacturer could. They thus add value by reducing the transaction costs associated with bringing a product to market. Every market-related function that involves some type of transaction cost – from market research to promotion to customer service – can be handled by an intermediary. However, Internet technology is currently reducing many of these transaction costs and in so doing, is altering the role of intermediaries in the market.

The Changing Role of Geography

Traditionally, many of the market inefficiencies that intermediaries have had to deal with have involved geographic distance – the physical separation of buyers and sellers. In the Internet economy, however, the physical separation of buyers and sellers only comes into play when physical products need to be transported from one location to another. One of the implications of this is that many firms are beginning to reconsider who is capturing the margins and why. The threat of disintermediation is these industries is real.

Most channel functions involving the dissemination of information, including product information, customer orders, customer service inquiries and responses, and purchase orders can be carried out immediately and effectively via the Internet. Even though companies are ultimately in the business of providing physical products to customers, they can remove many of the inefficiencies associated with geography in a significant number of steps along the value chain. As a result, the roles of many of the intermediaries – whether they be dealers, retailers, financers or newspapers – are reduced.

The Relative Advantages and Disadvantages Associated With Firm Size

In traditional marketplaces, the size of the firm is generally considered to be positively correlated to three characteristics: efficiency, flexibility and market power. Efficiency results from increased economies of scale. Flexibility and market power tend to result from a variety of factors, including more complete product lines and stronger distribution networks. In the Internet economy, however, efficiency is more a function of velocity than mass, as businesses concentrate more and more on the flow of information and the speed at which connections between suppliers and customers are made. Thus, Internet technology allows even the smallest of businesses to go global. Companies no longer have to achieve critical mass in order to provide products and services efficiently to customers around the world. Even small companies that specialize in the delivery of products as opposed to information have been able to grow at a rate disproportionate to their physical size.

By contrast, many large, well-established companies have had trouble taking advantage of network efficiencies, in part because they are boxed in by existing channel structures. To date, larger firms have dealt with these types of channel conflicts in a variety of ways:

- *By reinforcing their commitment to existing channels.*
- *By "creeping" onto the Web*, hoping to satisfy customers who prefer this channel without attracting enough attention to create channel backlash.
- *By biting the bullet*, even if it means risking ongoing relationships with channel partners.

- *By simply abandoning traditional channels in favor of new ones.*

The Growth of "Infomediaries"

The claim that Internet technology leads to outright disintermediation is overly simplistic. In many cases, network technology encourages the existence of "infomediaries", who are able to take advantage of new market frictions. Network economies spawn two types of infomediaries in particular: those who play the role of "information broker" or "market-maker" and those who perform information-handling tasks for others.

In the Internet economy, the obstacles associated with trying to profit from niche interests are dramatically reduced. Reduced search costs make it easier to identify small pockets of people with highly specialized needs, while reduced communication costs make it easier to establish and sustain a much greater pool of potential people to draw from. As a result, the Web has literally become a universe of niche markets, filled with enthusiast clubs, niche subcultures, niche affinity groups, etc. Not surprisingly, firms are discovering that there is potential profit associated with simply bringing these communities of value together. Some of the busiest sites on the Web fulfill this "market-making" function.

In other cases, market-makers have lowered the transaction inefficiencies associated with search costs, i.e., that difficulty that buyers and sellers have had "finding" each other in a large, disorganized open market. These inefficiencies can be particularly high in fragmented markets where prices are difficult to compare. A related category of infomediaries consists of players who assist others in handling the information clutter associated with commercial activity on the Internet. For example, a number of companies currently offer data warehousing and data mining services for online firms interested in acquiring knowledge about visitors to their sites. Other infomediaries offer everything from aggregated data-handling services to technology-based buying aids.

A few of the ways in which Internet technologies are affecting channel structures have been outlined above. The impact of these technologies has already been such that it is possible to conceptualize the new marketplace as consisting of two worlds: a physical world of resources that managers can see and touch, and a virtual world made from information. The differences between these two marketplaces are outlined in Table 7-1.

Traditional Marketplaces	Cyberspace
Information exchange is costly	Information exchange is cheap
Physical location is important	Physical location can be irrelevant
Efficiency is driven by mass	Efficiency is driven by velocity
Large companies have flexibility	Small companies have flexibility
Emphasis is on market segments	Emphasis is on market niches
Intermediaries fill the channel	Infomediaries fill the channel

Table 7-1: Traditional Marketplaces vs. Cyberspace

155

Hypermediation

When the notion that you could sell things over the Internet first arose, there was a widespread belief that it would mean the death of the middleman. Producers of goods and services would use their Web sites to connect directly with consumers, bypassing wholesalers and retailers altogether. We would enter a great era of "disintermediation", which would drain profits from distributors and redirect them back to the manufacturers. Like many of the early assumptions about electronic commerce, this one has proved wrong. With few exceptions, manufacturers have not been able to do much direct selling over the Web. In the virtual world as in the physical world, people want a broad selection of goods when they go shopping; they do not want to be limited to a single product line.

It is now becoming clear that, far from experiencing disintermediation, business is undergoing precisely the opposite phenomenon – what is referred to as *hypermediation*. Transactions over the Web, even very small ones, routinely involve all sorts of intermediaries, not just the familiar wholesalers and retailers, but content providers, affiliate sites, search engines, portals, Internet service providers, software makers, and many other entities. And it is these middlemen that are positioned to capture most of the profits.

Two characteristics of electronic commerce make hypermediation possible and even inevitable. First is the sheer volume of activity. People make billions of clicks on the Web every day, and because each click represents a personal choice, each also entails the delivery of value and thus an opportunity to make money. The second characteristic is efficiency. Most physical businesses wouldn't be able to make money on penny transactions; it would cost more than a penny to collect a penny. But the incremental cost of an online transaction is basically zero. It doesn't cost anything to execute a line or two of code once the code has been written. The pennies taken in by many intermediaries are almost pure profit.

If volume and efficiency make microtransactions attractive, they make microbusinesses attractive too. Just as microtransactions don't look like much individually, so microbusinesses seem insignificant at first glance. But, again, volume changes everything. One microbusiness is no big deal. Millions of them, sucking billions of dollars of profit out of the e-commerce system, is a very big deal.

So what does hypermediation mean for the future of online business? The lion's share of the profits in e-commerce is likely to flow to two very different types of intermediaries. One type is the owner of specialized content sites. These content sites will draw people interested in the particular subjects they cover, often using discussion boards or other interactive features to encourage return visits. As affiliates of big electronic retailers, they will also serve as gateways to purchases, gaining a share of all sales. Some of these content sites will be large – America Online has long pursued such a business model – but most will be small and intimate. When people first venture onto the Internet, they tend to head for the big-name sites – Amazon, Yahoo, and the like – because those are the easiest to find. But as they become used to the Web and more familiar with searches and other navigation aids, they start to seek out sites tailored to their particular interests. For content sites, specialization is more important than scale.

The second type of intermediary who will gain a lion's share of the profits in the Internet economy is the infrastructure company – the search engines like Inktomi and Google, the advertising networks like DoubleClick and Engage, the affiliate networks like Be Free and LinkShare, the backbone providers like Akamai and Exodus. Here, scale will often be important. In some cases, the network effect will lock out small new competitors – at least for a time. But even more important than scale will be technical prowess. The technologies underpinning the Web are still in their infancy. Every day we see the arrival of some new company with a neat piece of code that changes something about the way the Web works. Those companies are well aware that every click is a potential source of profit. They are focusing their energy and creativity, not to mention millions of dollars of venture capital, on figuring out new ways to turn clicks into transfers of cash.

ELECTRONIC COMMERCE AND INTERORGANIZATIONAL INFORMATION SYSTEMS

Today, many of the most dramatic and potentially powerful uses of information technology involve networks that transcend company boundaries. These interorganizational information systems enable firms to incorporate buyers, suppliers and partners in the redesign of their key business processes, thereby enhancing productivity, quality, speed, and flexibility. New distribution channels can be created and new information-based products and services can be delivered. In addition, many interorganizational information systems radically alter the balance of power in buyer-supplier relationships, raise barriers to entry and exit, and, in many instances, shift the competitive position of industry participants. To grasp the potential of electronic commerce, the nature of information-technology-enabled market relationships must be fully understood.

A market can be viewed as a network of interactions (such as the exchange of products, services and payments) and relationships. While only two basic roles are required in any exchange – buyer and seller – a number of industry participants may join forces to perform the required activities of a given role. This is especially true within the value-chain network where advertisers, suppliers, distributors, retailers, bankers and others often work together to perform the activities required to design, manufacture, distribute, market, sell and maintain a product or service. In addition to these operational tasks, the value-chain network must also carry out interorganizational coordination, control, and resource management activities so that operations are performed effectively and efficiently.

All managers must answer two fundamental questions as they consider how best to position their firm within its major markets:

- As we organize to deliver our products and services, which activities should we keep inside the boundaries of our firm and which should we source from the outside?
- How should we relate to our customers, suppliers, distributors and other external business partners?

These two questions help frame our understanding of market interactions and the relationships among industry participants.

Which Activities Should We Keep Inside?

A firm performs many activities, such as research and development, manufacturing, logistics, marketing and sales, after sales service and distribution, in order to deliver its products and services. These activities can be organized in three basic ways. First, activities can be incorporated within a single, vertically integrated firm. Second, one or more selective activities can be sourced from an external party or partners. Finally, a virtual corporation can be created within which a firm retains only those activities that are considered a core competency and the management systems required to coordinate business processes within and across organizational boundaries.

Traditionally, managers have chosen to locate an activity within their organizational boundary (i.e., vertically integrate) when a significant cost (or risk) was involved in managing it on the outside. Costs and risks increased when:

1. a firm was required to make significant investment in physical facilities, people, or management systems to coordinate and control activities with outside suppliers, distributors, or other parties,
2. the services or activities were critical to the effective and efficient delivery of the firm's products and services, or
3. a high degree of uncertainty would surround the ongoing nature of the relationship, which, in turn, would make it difficult to define the interorganizational relationship in a comprehensive, structured contract and/or to create an efficient set of interorganizational governance mechanisms.

Several visionary leaders have found that they could use information technology to help manage the risks and cost of interorganizational coordination and control. By establishing electronic linkages with suppliers, distributors, and even directly with customers, they were able to integrate and coordinate interorganizational activities much more efficiently, to monitor operations more closely, and to communicate with external organizations more interactively. A growing number of firms are establishing information-technology-enabled networked organizations that take the selective sourcing model to the extreme. They are forming virtual corporations by contracting out the majority of the activities of production, eliminating intermediaries in the distribution channel, and retaining within their organizational borders only a few selective core competencies and the management systems needed to coordinate and control the network of relationships.

Information technology has played a major role, allowing participating firms to streamline, integrate and time-synchronize interorganizational operations and management processes. Information technology facilitates the process of business integration by:

1. providing common standards and procedures that support integration and coordination, and
2. creating an electronic information and communication platform that supports collaboration and control.

How Should We Relate to External Industry Participants?

All firms make choices about the nature of the relationship they wish to pursue with customers, suppliers and other external industry participants. These choices fall along a continuum from transaction to contract to partnerships.

	Transaction	Contract	Partnership
Basis of Interaction	Discrete exchange of goods, services, and payments (simple buyer / seller exchange)	Prior agreement governs exchange (e.g., service contract, lease, purchase agreement)	Shared goals and processes for achieving them (e.g., collaborative product development)
Duration of Interaction	Immediate	Usually short term; defined by contract	Usually long term; defined by relationship
Level of Business Integration	Low	Moderate	High
Coordination and Control	Supply and demand (market)	Terms of contract define procedures, monitoring, and reporting	Interorganizational structures, processes, and systems; Mutual adjustment
Information Flow	Primarily one way; Limited in scope and amount; Low level of customization	One or two-way; Scope and amount are usually defined in the contract	Two-way (interactive); Extensive exchange of rich, detailed information; Dynamically changing; Customizable

Table 7-2: Market Relationships

Transactions involve the simple exchange of products (goods and services) and payments, usually during a specific time period and with limited interaction between the parties involved. In a transaction relationship, the seller's primary goal is to sell a product in sufficient quantity, at a price that generates a specific profit margin. The buyers' goal is similar – they wish to purchase a product in sufficient quantity, at the lowest price possible. Transaction-based interactions are possible when buyers are reasonably certain that the products or services conform to their specifications and the price is clearly defined. There is little need for information exchange (beyond the terms of payment). Simple one-way mass advertising is most often used to inform potential buyers about product features and price; and aggregate information on supply, demand and price are used to coordinate and control the activities of buyers and sellers over time.

In *contractual relationships*, the resources to be provided or activities to be performed by each party, and the length of the relationship, are clearly documented. The formal terms of the contract become the basis for defining the authority structures, systems, and processes that will be used to coordinate and control the relationship. A simple contract is often viewed as a set of well-defined transactions extending over a predefined period. Once the contract and the necessary coordination and control mechanisms are in place, the relationship proceeds as a series of simple transactions unless one party defaults on the terms of the contract. As contracts become more complex, and as activities become less routine and more critical to each party, the contractual relationship often takes on the features of a partnership.

Partnerships are required when the activities to be jointly managed are complex, uncertain and critical to the success of the firm involved. Partnerships require shared goals, complementary expertise and skills, and interorganizational process integration. The exchange of goods and services is ongoing, and the interactions and relationships must adapt to the changing priorities of the parties involved. Partnerships often require significant investments in systems and people for carrying out, coordinating, and controlling shared activities. Because information exchange is intense and interactive, information systems and networks can play a powerful role in supporting partnerships.

While the above discussion treats the three types of interorganizational forms and the three types of interorganizational relationships as if they were distinct, in reality, most firms adopt a hybrid approach that combines elements of more than one form or relationship. This is especially true as we view market activities on the Internet and advanced proprietary networks. For example, some simple transaction-based relationships incorporate features of a partnership with higher levels of information exchange and shared goals. Similarly, some long-term partnership agreements include short-term contracts. A partnership agreement may also specify a formal process through which the parties will identify problems and negotiate solutions.

Electronic Commerce: Evolution and Trends

There are some distinct trends in the way companies are using information technology to support electronic commerce.

- Managers are choosing to source an increasing number of products and services from outside the firm. Many use advanced networks and information systems to integrate, coordinate and control these activities. An increasing number are extending the selective sourcing model to create a virtual organization that operates as a seamless unit to deliver both physical products and services and to exchange information.

- Within virtual organizations, many independent companies are becoming increasingly specialized. Like Federal Express, they are becoming experts at performing their critical steps in a process. Increased expertise leads to increased power, but within a more limited sphere; still specialized experts must unite and act as one to deliver products to a more demanding global customer base. The result is a more complex, distributed, interorganizational authority and control system, which resembles those used to simultaneously manage both specialization and integration within traditional, hierarchical, vertically integrated firms.

- Relationships among firms are also becoming more complex and often blend transactional, contractual, and partnership elements. Pure transaction exchanges are becoming increasingly automated, and contractual agreements are becoming embedded within automated coordination and control systems. The ability of today's technology to support the intense, interactive exchange of information required of partnership relationships, along with the increased specialized expertise and power of market participants, is enabling firms to derive the benefits of partnership while preserving the efficiency and control of transactional and contractual relations.

- The technology's growing capability to simultaneously manage product/market complexity and speed of response is enabling firms to bypass costly channel intermediaries and link directly to suppliers and customers. This allows a firm and its partners to streamline, integrate and time synchronize value chain activities and to provide higher quality products and services at a lower cost. But, to achieve these advantages, firms must be able to integrate their respective information technology systems and interactively share information to enable them to directly coordinate and control value chain activities across organizational boundaries.

- There is increasing separation of the physical flow of goods and services from the flow of information. Those capturing information in a form that can be packaged and delivered can significantly enhance the value of their current products and services, and can capitalize on a range of new products and services. Those who maintain control, either singly or in partnership, of both the product/service and information flows gain a more powerful position within the market.

- Firms that were able to achieve proprietary control (individually or in partnership) of both the information systems and the network channel upon which they were delivered have assumed the powerful position of channel manager within their industries. These channel managers use the information generated by shared information technology systems to coordinate and control interorganizational processes from suppliers to end consumers. Increasingly, the features that differentiate industry participants that evolve toward powerful channel managers and those that devolve toward extinction are the ability to become a best-in-class provider of a core channel activity, while simultaneously managing and controlling interorganizational processes throughout the channel.

- With the rise of low-cost, third-party network providers, the cost of establishing and managing interorganizational information systems has decreased, threatening the sustainable proprietary advantages that can be gained through ownership of electronic market channels. Many argue that the emergence of ubiquitous network platforms such as the Internet will result in further erosion of the power of traditional channel managers as power shifts toward the consumer, giving rise to mass customization within commodity markets.

161

Guidelines for Implementing Interorganizational Information Systems

The cost and expertise required to implement interorganizational information systems has decreased markedly, enabling broader participation and a wider range of opportunities. Reliable, low-cost, third-party online information providers and network facilitators have emerged as viable alternatives to proprietary networks. The sources of proprietary advantage through electronic commerce are increasingly uncertain. Companies can now tap into a powerful platform for interorganizational information sharing where the low cost, ease of use, and global connectivity all offer the potential to expand opportunities for electronic commerce dramatically.

A thorough analysis of potential opportunities for electronic commerce requires that managers start with the basics – a deep understanding of their current business. They must clearly define the current competitive environment, market dynamics, and the company's long-term goals, strategies and core competencies. This deep understanding of today's businesses must then be married with a deep understanding of the features and functionality of the technology that can be used to add value to the current business and/or enable the firm to go to market in new ways. The lessons from the history of electronic commerce help frame the questions to be asked and the solutions to be sought.

- Is your company capitalizing on the potential benefits of electronic commerce? Could actions by competitors or new entrants leave you vulnerable? Are there actions you should take to preempt competitive actions by others?

- Are you harnessing the power of the information embedded within your products and services to add value to customers? Are there potential new information-enabled products and services that could substitute for, or enhance, your current offerings?

- Are you capturing the potential benefits of electronic channel integration? Can information technology be used to manage product and market complexity, thereby allowing you to eliminate channel intermediaries, simplify and streamline product/service delivery, and dramatically decrease costs? Are there opportunities to become a channel manager?

- Have you and your information partners jointly redesigned business processes and designed appropriate authority and control systems?

- Have you selected your partners wisely? Do you have a shared vision and common purpose? Do you bring equal, and complementary power and resources (particularly each partner's area of distinctive competence) to the relationship? Are you and your partners financially viable, and is the relationship financially and competitively sustainable?

- Is the technical infrastructure you have in place the right one to effect and manage the types of electronic commerce you are considering? Are you maintaining the appropriate balance between experimentation and control? Have you instituted appropriate levels of security?

Chapter 8

Business Models in Electronic Commerce

THE EMERGING MARKET STRUCTURE IN ELECTRONIC COMMERCE

Over the years, several organizations doing business through the Internet have come out with their own set of unique propositions to succeed. For instance, Amazon.com demonstrated how it is possible to dis-intermediate the supply chain and create new value out of it. Companies such as Hotmail and Netscape made business sense out of providing free products and services. On the other hand, companies such as AOL and Yahoo identified new revenue streams for their businesses. Similarly, companies such as Vertical Net engaged in building online communities.

The Internet economy has divided the overall market space into three broad structures: portals, market makers and product/service providers. A *portal* engages primarily in building a community of consumers of information about products and services. Increasingly, portals emerge as the focal points for influencing the channel traffic into Web sites managed by the product/service providers and other intermediaries. Companies such as AOL and Yahoo largely cater to the business-to-consumer segment. ZDNet and MarketSite.net are examples of portals serving the business-to-business segment.

The *market maker* is another emerging structure in the Internet market space. Market makers play a role similar to that of a portal in building a community of customers and/or a community of suppliers of products and services. However, they differ from portals in several ways. Market makers invariably participate in a variety of ways to facilitate the business transaction that takes place between the buyer and the supplier. Consequently, a market maker is often expected to have a high degree of domain knowledge. Unlike a portal, a market maker endeavors to provide value to suppliers and customers through a system of implicit or explicit guarantee of security and trust in the business transaction. Auction sites such as eBay are the early market makers in the business-to-consumer segment. Some examples of the large number of market makers evolving in the business-to-business segment include Chemdex (Chemicals), HosutonStreet.com (Electricity), FastParts (Electronic components), BizBuyer.com (small business products) and Arbinet (Telecommunications minutes and bandwidth). The predominant forms the market makers take in the business-to-business segment include organizing auctions and reverse auctions, setting up exchanges, and product and service catalogue aggregation.

Product/service providers deal directly with their customers when it ultimately comes to the Internet business transaction. Notable examples in this category of market structure include Amazon.com and Landsend.com in the business-to-consumer segment, and Cisco and Dell Computers in the business-to-business segment.

These emerging market structures reveal some of the characteristics of Internet-based e-commerce business applications. First, each of these structures addresses a key constituent in the business that is carried out over the Internet. Secondly, they exist in both business-to-business and business-to-consumer segments. Third, there is a high level of overlap and inter-dependency among the players in the three market structures. For instance, players in the product/service-provider market succeed in marketing their products and services through their Web site only when they catch the attention of prospective customers. In order to do this they may often need the support of a portal. Meanwhile, the revenue stream of a portal or a market maker depends to a large extent on its relationship with product/service providers. Finally, since the fundamental purpose for each of the three market structures is very different, they have different approaches to the value that they offer to their business partners and customers and the manner in which they organize their revenue stream.

Market Structure	Business-to-Consumer Segment	Business-to-Business Segment
Portals	AOL.com Askjeeves.com Compare.com MSN.com Personalogic.com Yahoo.com Orlando.com	Cnet.com ec-portal.com MarketSite.net Netmarketmaker.com Questlink SmartOnline.com VerticalNet
Market Makers	Autobytel.com Beyond.com Buy.com Cameraworld.com Careerbuilder.com Ebags.com Ebay.com Etrade.com NetMarket.com Priceline.com Travelocity.com Ubid.com	Agriculture Online AdAuction.com AsianSources.com Bloomberg ChemConnect Manheim Auctions MRO.com NetBuy.com PaperExchange.com PlasticsNet.com Ultraprise Works.com
Product/Service Providers	Amazon.com Egghead.com EthnicGrocer.com Landsend.com Stacianewyork.com	Cisco Compaq Dell

Table 8-1: Examples of Internet-Based Businesses in the Emerging Market Structure

COMPONENTS OF A BUSINESS MODEL

A business model is a unique blend of three streams that are critical to the business. These include the value stream for the business partners and the buyers, the revenue stream, and the logistical stream. The value stream identifies the value proposition for the buyers, sellers and the market makers and portals in an Internet context. The revenue stream is a plan for assuring revenue generation for the business. The logistical stream addresses various issues related to the design of the supply chain for the business.

Value Streams in Internet-Based Business

The long-term viability of a business largely stems from the robustness of the value stream, which influences the revenue stream and the logistical stream. Often, buyers perceive value arising out of reduced product search cost and transaction costs. Further, the inherent benefits of the richness and reach of the Internet provide an improved shopping experience and convenience. Suppliers perceive value arising out of reduced customer search costs, product promotion costs, business transaction costs, and lead time for business transactions. These benefits are likely to be substantial in the business-to-business segment.

The introduction of a market maker or a portal is likely to increase the value for both the suppliers and the buyers, creating a virtuous cycle for all three players. As more suppliers join in the market-making process, the buyers begin to see more choices. As more buyers join, the suppliers begin to experience the beneficial effects of a wider customer base and lower customer search costs. Then the buyers themselves benefit from the growing community of buyers. Finally, both the buyers and the suppliers begin to rely on the market. There are four possible value streams in an Internet-based business.

1. Virtual Communities

Communities have a distinctive focus that brings together people with common interests. WebMD/Healtheon is a community that caters to medical professionals. Community sites provide an ideal platform for the focused groups to generate value and knowledge and share it among the members. It is extremely difficult to replicate the value proposition of virtual communities because much of the value of these communities is member generated. Moreover, communities induce a high switching cost for their members and thereby provide first mover advantage for the organizations that host these communities.

2. Dramatic Reduction in Transaction Costs

An electronic marketplace is an inter-organizational information system that allows buyers, sellers, independent third parties, and multi-firm consortiums to exchange information about prices and service offerings. Moreover, the cost of product and price comparisons becomes negligible. A major impact is that they typically reduce search costs for both the buyers and the sellers.

3. Gainful Exploitation of Information Asymmetry

In situations that involve numerous buyers spread over large geographical areas and sellers who have perishable products and services, it is possible to exploit the benefits of information asymmetry into a value proposition. The sellers do not have perfect information on demand. Similarly, the buyers do not have perfect information on supply. Therefore, an intermediary can create value arising out of this information asymmetry. Priceline.com is an example of such a value stream in the business-to-consumer segment. Even in the case of non-perishable items, it is possible to exploit the information asymmetry by setting up online bids and service auctions.

In the business-to-business segment, information asymmetry often exists when there are several potential suppliers for an industrial bid. By enabling an online real-time bidding and negotiation process, it is possible to obtain substantial reductions in the final bid value. An intermediary who enables this process usually creates a value proposition and a revenue stream that is linked to the value of the reduction obtained for the buyer. FreeMarkets is an example of this category.

4. Value-Added Market-Making Process

Value streams in the Internet context are sometimes augmented by additional value propositions, which can become the main value-generating stream in some cases. Security and trust, for instance, are major concerns in Internet-based commerce and can be used to create a value proposition. When the market maker vouchsafes the transactions that take place under its domain, it provides significant value to buyers and sellers. For example, this role in the business-to-consumer segment is played by eBay. Providing financial instruments and establishing guarantees for the transactions, as well as addressing privacy and delivery reliability concerns, also have the potential for creating new value streams.

Organizations often build their model on the basis of one dominant value stream. The value derived from the others is incidental and supplementary to the main value stream.

Revenue Streams in Internet-Based Business

Value streams address the long-term sustainability of the business proposition and often set the context for identifying revenue streams for an organization. The revenue stream is nothing but the realization of the value proposition in the short term, usually on a yearly basis. The Internet economy has allowed organizations to exploit new revenue streams that are hard to replicate in a brick-and-mortar operation. Following are six such revenue streams.

1. Increased Margins over Brick-and-Mortar Operations

There are several reasons why Internet-based businesses invariably have increased margins. The most prominent are reduced transaction costs and reduced customer search costs. Cost reduction can also be achieved through dis-intermediation of the supply chain.

2. Revenue from Online Seller Communities

By providing free membership, market makers can build a community of buyers and get access to a host of information about their interests. Similarly, by promising an untapped source of buyers, market makers can also build a community of suppliers. Once the community of suppliers and buyers is in place, the market maker can then build a revenue stream by charging the suppliers a one-time membership fee and a variable transaction fee linked to the amount of business performed through the market maker.

3. Advertising

Portals and large business-to-consumer and business-to-business community sites such as Yahoo, AOL, CommerceOne, and Agriculture Online play a crucial role in funneling customers into the target Web sites. It is natural for these Web sites to host banner advertisements, which generate huge revenue to support their operations.

4. Variable Pricing Strategies

Organizations that sell electronically delivered products have unique characteristics of the information economy to exploit. High initial cost and nearly zero marginal cost characterize such information production and dissemination. Different consumers have different valuations for the same product, and thus have different willingness to pay. If willingness to pay is correlated to some observable characteristics of the consumers such as demographic profile, then it could be linked to the pricing strategy.

5. Revenue Streams Linked to Exploiting Information Asymmetry

An intermediary exploiting the information asymmetry between the buyer and the supplier generates a revenue stream often linked to the amount of savings accruing to the buyer. Several variations of the auction format are being used in this area.

6. Free Offerings

The fundamental philosophy behind free services is one of giving up today's revenues in return for assured future returns. Organizations such as Hotmail and Netscape identified several revenue streams arising out of giving out free products and services.

Logistic Streams for Internet-Based Business

The Internet economy allows an organization to position itself at an appropriate level of the supply chain depending on the nature of its business. Three distinctive logistical streams exist in the Internet economy and all three have evolved out of the need for creating the maximum value for the customers. Dis-intermediation is the process by which the logistical stream is shortened, leading to better responsiveness and lower costs. Internet-based business also calls for new forms of intermediation. Infomediaries and meta-mediaries seek to add value to the logistical stream by addressing certain problems arising out of the information overload and transaction cost inefficiencies. Players in the product/service provider market are able to exploit the dis-intermediation stream for their business model. Portals utilize the infomediation stream and market makers utilize the meta-mediation stream.

1. Dis-Intermediation

Due to the nature of certain products and services, the Internet has made it possible to shrink the supply chain by a process known as dis-intermediation. Consequently, transaction costs have been reduced and responsiveness to customer requirements has improved considerably. These improvements often lead to price reduction and/or increased margin and sales turnover. The success of Amazon.com over Barnes & Noble has demonstrated the benefits of this logistical stream. In the business-to-business segment, the success of Dell Computers and Cisco Systems is largely attributed to this phenomenon.

2. Infomediation

In the market for information, the number of sources and suppliers of information, as well as the amount of information, is much higher than a single information seeker can comprehend. This is primarily due to the spectacular growth of Internet sites. This has necessitated a crucial role for intermediaries to address the information requirements of users. Examples of information intermediaries are primarily portals consisting of search engines and electronic product catalogue aggregators.

3. Meta-Mediation

Meta-mediation is a process that goes beyond aggregating vendors and products and includes additional services required for facilitating transactions. Certain markets in the business-to-business segment are characterized by fragmented supply chains leading to high vendor search costs, high information search costs, high product comparison costs and huge workflow costs. Under these conditions, meta-mediation adds value to the buyers, sellers and the intermediary.

SELECTING AN APPROPRIATE BUSINESS MODEL

The process of arriving at an appropriate business model involves choosing the right mix of alternatives. The following factors affect the choice of a business model:

1. Role in the Market Structure

Organizations can narrow down their choices by understanding the role that they play in the Internet economy. Table 8-2 illustrates the alternatives available for organizations in each market structure.

Business Model Building Blocks	Market Structures		
	Portals	Market Makers	Product / Service Providers
Value Streams			
Virtual Communities	Yes	Yes	Yes
Dramatic Reduction in Transaction Costs		Yes	Yes
Gainful Exploitation of Information Asymmetry		Yes	
Value-Added Market-Making Process	Yes	Yes	
Revenue Streams			
Increased Margins over Brick-and-Mortar Operations			Yes
Revenue from Online Seller Communities	Yes	Yes	
Advertising	Yes	Yes	
Variable Pricing Strategies			Yes
Revenue Streams Linked to Exploiting Information Asymmetry		Yes	
Free Offerings	Yes	Yes	Yes
Logistical Streams			
Dis-Intermediation			Yes
Infomediation	Yes		
Meta-Mediation		Yes	

Table 8-2: Potential Applications of Business Model Streams for the Three Market Structures

2. Physical Attributes of the Goods Traded

Goods traded over the Internet can be either informational goods (that can be transported electronically) or physical goods (that need physical transportation by a logistics provider). This influences the choice of an appropriate revenue stream. Informational goods are characterized by high initial costs to produce the first copy and almost no cost to make additional copies. This allows such firms to employ revenue streams such as variable pricing strategies, free offerings, and a combination of a one-time fee and a variable transaction-based fee. Organizations trading hard goods often have to resort to unique options that provides increased margins and/or premiums over brick-and-mortar operations. The choices with respect to logistical streams are obvious

170

for an organization trading informational goods. Such organizations eventually gravitate towards dis-intermediation.

3. Amount of Personal Involvement Required in the Buying/Selling Process

The choice of the logistical stream for physical goods is significantly affected by this factor. Goods traded over the Internet broadly fall into two categories: experience goods and economy goods. Experience goods require greater personal involvement in the buying process. Dis-intermediation of the supply chain is a risky strategy for such goods. On the other hand, the use of infomediaries and meta-mediaries greatly enhances the value by facilitating the process. Moreover, they can also play a significant role in reducing search costs and transaction cost inefficiencies. On the other hand, commodity goods are ideal candidates for dis-intermediation. The driving force in this case is to reduce the costs by eliminating portions of the value chain that do not seem to add any value. Many MRO supplies and commodity goods traded in the business-to-business segment fall in this category.

CATEGORIES OF WEB SITES

There are many ways to categorize Web sites and ways of making profits. These typologies are not exclusive. The choice of which to use depends on the situation faced.

Classification by Corporate Purpose

Most large U.S. corporations have some kind of Web site. These sites conform to several standard types.
- **The corporate presence.** The goal of these sites is communication with a range of constituencies including investors, suppliers, employees, regulators and customers, and often includes an annual report and company overview.
- **The promotional presence.** The second, more common site, exists to promote the company's products and services. Examples are Disney.com and Hilton.com. Proctor & Gamble has sites for a number of brands[1]. Once a site exists, a marketer usually promotes it to generate traffic. The most common way to do so is to buy or barter advertising banners on other sites.
- **The transactional presence.** Sites may include areas for transaction. Individual sites can function as freestanding stores (for example Amazon.com[2] is a virtual bookstore), be part of a virtual mall or collection of stores (for example marketplaceMCI[3]), or allocate part of a site to transactions (for example Firefly[4], a recommendation and chat service).
- **The conversational presence.** Sites can foster communication with their visitors, or they can encourage visitors to converse with one another. Most sites have a feedback feature that enables visitors to send e-mail comments to the site administrator. Some

---

[1] http://www.olean.com and http://www.sunnyd.com
[2] http://www.amazon.com
[3] http://www2.pcy.mci.net/marketplace/
[4] http://www.ffly.com

sites offer a weekly e-mail newsletter (for example, cnet[5]). Some allow the visitor to send questions to a database and receive answers. Some let the visitor ask for and receive software. For example, Nickelodeon[6] invites children to download computer games, and Microsoft[7] distributes software that transforms its word processing software into a Web page maker. A site can try to be the focal point for a community of like-minded people. Some sites set up bulletin boards on which visitors can post messages for each other, and others host chat groups at which visitors can meet and talk to people with similar interests (for example, Fox[8]).

Classification by Source of Income

There are a number of different ways for a site to contribute to a firm's income.

- *Advertising Support Model.* If we look at sources of revenue on the Web today, the advertising support model – including sponsorship – dominates. It is a major source of revenue for search engines.
- *Subscription Support Model.* A Web site which delivers value to customers, and has some assets that are not easily imitated, is likely to be able to command a subscription or membership fee commensurate with the value it delivers. For example, the Wall Street Journal Interactive[9] is a popular Web edition of the newspaper.
- *Cost Elimination Model.* The Web delivers information at an extremely low variable cost. For marketers for whom information delivery is a big element of the value proposition to customers, a presence on the Web can be justified purely on cost grounds. Examples are Fedex's[10] service for tracking shipments on the Web and General Electric's[11] Web purchasing center. Electronic Data Interchange (EDI) has been an important technology for extracting cost from industry supply chains. The Internet can be viewed as a low cost EDI system.
- *Sales Revenue Model.* Some sites earn a margin or fee on sales of a product or service.
- *Information Trading Model.* In this model, the Web site learns something about a visitor's interests or purchase intentions, and sells the information to a retailer or manufacturer. This includes the selling of leads.

Classification by Stage of the Adoption Process

Websites can try to cater to various stages in a customer's product adoption process. The AIDA (awareness – interest – desire – action) process is a common categorization of consumer adoption stages. While the Web may not be the ideal medium for each of the AIDA stages for a specific product and target segment, the customer must migrate through each stage.

---

[5] http://www.cnet.com

[6] http://www.nickelodeon.com

[7] http://www.microsoft.com

[8] http://www.fox.com

[9] http://www.wsj.com

[10] http://www.fedex.com/us/tracking/

[11] http://www.ge.com

- *Awareness.* Web advertising can create awareness of a product among people who have not encountered it before. Banner advertising is commonly used to build awareness.
- *Interest.* Clicking through from a banner advertisement to a Web site takes a prospect from awareness to interest.
- *Desire.* If the marketer succeeds, the person notices that the product fulfills his or her need, creating a desire for the product. For example, a Web site may have a Frequently Asked Questions (FAQ) section, which will convince the customer, or the site can be used to have a dialogue with the customer and answer inquiries.
- *Action/Adoption.* Web sites can be used to take orders and also for order fulfillment in the case of information products.
- *Retention.* The company still has the job of retention – making sure the product is satisfactory to the customer and that he or she will become a repeat purchaser. Web sites can, for instance, answer concerns, give ideas on how to use the product more often, or create a sense of community in which usage of the product is a prerequisite for membership.

At each stage of the process, a marketer can try to move the customer to or from the Web for the next stage, or continue into the next stage within the same medium. For example, awareness of a new product can be created through television advertisements, and a Web site – with its address presented in the TV advertisement – used to provide the customers with further information to create interest. Likewise, the marketer can create desire by answering inquiries on the Web site, but refer the customer to a retail store (or a toll-free phone number) for the purchase transaction.

Classification by Function

The early winners on the Web have been the search engines, such as Yahoo!, Lycos, Infoseek, and sites offering visitors content, such as ESPNet and SportsZone. These sites attract visitors and "sell the traffic", much as billboards do. Business models that thrive in the quieter environment of online services may be better indicators of the longer-term appeal of interactive media to users than those that succeed among the early users of the Web.

- *Service Provider.* Here, a member feels that the marketing partner is providing a service. American Express' ExpressNet is an example.
- *Community Areas.* A mutual fund community is an example. The site promises to deliver objective editorial content relevant to mutual funds. Users can inquire further by brand or by subject to obtain information supplied by the mutual fund sponsors of the site.
- *Programming.* An example is "Expectations", an area for parents about to have, or who have just had babies. AOL provides the content (a chat forum, advice from doctors, mothers, etc.) and invites relevant marketers – diaper companies, toy makers – to display a banner linking to a corporate Web site.
- *Directories.* Downtown AOL, for example, is a small business directory in which firms can be listed for a few hundred dollars a month.

TYPES OF BUSINESS MODELS IN ELECTRONIC COMMERCE

Over the past seven years, Internet pioneers such as Amazon.com, Yahoo!, America Online and FreeMarkets, blazed new trails and created new business models. These models are defined along a continuum from creators and producers to distributors and customers. Traditionally, this continuum has been defined as a value chain. Each participant in the chain performs a specific, well-defined role. It receives inputs from those downstream in the chain, adds value, and delivers output to the next participant. In emerging Internet markets, this orderly sequence of value-creating activities, transactions and relationships, may no longer apply. Participants in an e-business marketplace may assume more than one role and often relate through a complex series of independent transactions and relationships that are best modeled as a value web. But, before complicating the picture, it is helpful to analyze these models using the familiar value chain.

Creators, the first role in the value chain, develop new ideas, products or services, and refine existing ones. These individuals may be inside your company, inside someone else's company, or free-lancers. *Producers* package the work of creators into products, services and, most importantly, solutions that meet a specific customer or market need. They may sell and maintain the product or may share that role with others in an industry or – within Internet markets – even with those outside traditional industry boundaries. *Distributors* enable buyers and sellers to connect, communicate, and transact business. These distributors may connect suppliers to business customers, forming what is called a supply chain, or they may connect producers to customers, forming what is called a demand chain. *Customers* may be either individual customers or businesses that are willing to pay for a product, service or solution. When selling to business customers, individual consumers – the actual end users – are often located inside the customer firm. This often creates a two-stage adoption cycle – first the businesses must decide to purchase a product or service and then individuals must decide to use it. In considering these roles, it is important to note that the process begins and ends with people, an important feature for Internet commerce, considering technology's ability to personalize experiences.

Before defining individual business models, a final industry characteristic bears mentioning. The point in an industry where maximum economies of scale and scope are created determines whether market power favors the supply side (most often producers) or the demand side (most often powerful customers or distributors). In the Industrial Age, the key technologies that enabled participants to achieve market power were production technologies. As a result, Industrial Age industries consolidated around a few large producers. In the Internet Age, the key technologies that enable participants to achieve market power are distribution, communication, and information technologies. As a result, in emerging Internet markets, we see power shifting to customers and distributors.

The new e-business models emerging on the Internet may play one or more of four generic roles. In addition they can be grouped into two categories. First, are businesses being built and launched on the Internet. The most powerful of these digital business models are arising in distribution channels that link:

- businesses-to-consumers (B2C), for example, Amazon.com and LandsEnd.com,

- consumers-to-consumers (C2C), for example, eBay,
- consumers-to-businesses (C2B), for example, Priceline.com,
- businesses-to-businesses (B2B), for example, FreeMarkets, Grainger.com and Chemdex.

The second major category of e-business models comprises businesses that provide the digital infrastructure upon which digital businesses are built. Models in this category include:

- computer and network equipment providers, for example, IBM, Hewlett-Packard, Cisco Systems and Lucent,
- software firms, for example, Microsoft and Oracle,
- custom suppliers, for example, Dell, Viant and Sapient.

Interestingly, in these infrastructure provider industries, we have seen less of a tendency than was seen with digital businesses – especially customer-driven digital businesses – for power to shift to distributors. Instead, powerful technology infrastructure providers such as Cisco, Microsoft and Dell, have used the Internet to connect directly with customers. In most cases, these infrastructure producers have added new Internet distribution channels that enable direct customer interactions and relationships, while still maintaining traditional channels, including existing direct sales forces and indirect distribution channels such as retailers, wholesalers and value-added resellers.

Why have high-tech producers maintained – and even increased – their power within e-business markets while non-high-tech producers across a number of industries have ceded significant control to emerging Internet distributors and portals? Many believe that the ability to distribute the software component of high-tech products directly over the Internet helped producers maintain strong connections to their customers. In addition, technology-savvy high-tech customers may have been more ready to do business online directly with producers. As attention shifts from business-to-consumer to business-to-business markets, it is commonly believed that producers will exert significant effort to ensure that e-business channel players do not gain the upper hand.

Until recently, there was a distinct separation between companies that produced and sold technical infrastructure and the businesses that used this technology to support business strategy and design. Toady, that distinction is blurring as the Internet penetrates the very core of how firms do business. IBM, Microsoft and Intuit, no longer just sell technology products; these companies are now content aggregators, portals and media companies. At the same time, non-high-tech businesses are becoming technology infrastructure providers. David Pottruck, CEO of Charles Schwab, says: "Charles Schwab is a technology company that just happens to be in the brokerage business. If we are going to be successful, technology is going to have to be built into our DNA".

E-businesses are built artfully combining a variety of business models. These businesses are then linked with others in a business community. By incorporating multiple business models that generate separate revenue streams off the same infrastructure, a firm can more efficiently utilize resources and create additional value. This is necessary for success given the slim margins that accompany much Internet commerce. A firm can also protect itself from the uncertainty associated with rapidly changing technology and unstable business and regulatory environments. By then linking the web of business models inside a firm with its business community composed of a much larger web of business models, a company can leverage the resources of the community to further enhance value delivered to all members. Because it provides a common infrastructure for sharing information and coordinating business transactions, the Internet dramatically increases the ability to create value webs.

Some of the revenue categories for the various e-business models are listed below:

- Commerce Revenues
  - *Product Sales*. Sell or license physical or information-based products.
  - *Commission, Service or Transaction Fees*. Charge a fee for services provided; can be a set fee of a percentage of the cost of a product or service.
- Content Revenues
  - *Subscription Fees*. Charge for receipt of updated information on a particular topic or a broad range of topics for a specified period of time (e.g, annual).
  - *Registration or Event Fees*. Charge a fee for attendance at an online event, workshop or course.
- Community Revenues
  - *Advertising and Slotting Fees*. Collect a fee for hosting a banner advertisement or special promotion.
  - *Affiliate Fees*. Collect a fee for an exclusive or non-exclusive partnership relationship.
  - *Referral Fees*. Collect a fee for each time a visitor clicks through from your site to another company's site.
  - *Membership Fees*. Charge a fee to belong to a private group or service.
- Infrastructure Revenues
  - *Software / Hardware Sales*. Sell or license a technology product.
  - *Installation and Integration Fees*. Charge either a set or variable fee for services provided.
  - *Maintenance & Update Fees*. Charge a fee for software/hardware maintenance and updates.
  - *Hosting fees*. Charge a fee for hosting a software application, Web site, data center, or network.
  - *Access Fees*. Charge a fee for providing access to a network and/or to an Internet service

Some of the cost categories for the various e-business models are listed below:

- *People & Partners*. Cost to acquire, develop and retain skills and expertise needed to execute strategy; includes employees and partners.
- *Advertising, Marketing, Sales*. Cost of offline and online advertising, marketing and sales.
- *Business Development*. Cost of designing and launching new businesses, developing alliances, and acquiring partners.
- *Materials and Supplies*. Cost of physical materials used in production of products and delivery of services; includes general purpose and specialized supplies and components.
- *Specialized Equipment (does not include IT)*. Cost of equipment – especially capital equipment – used in design, production, delivery and distribution.

- *Research & Development.* Cost of designing and developing digital business products and services; may overlap with IT infrastructure costs.
- *Physical Facilities and Infrastructure.* Cost of corporate and regional headquarters, sales offices, factories, warehouses, distribution centers, retail stores, service centers, etc.
- *Information Technology Infrastructure.*
  - [] Cost of computers and equipment (e.g., printers, data storage devices).
  - [] Cost to operate and maintain data centers.
  - [] Cost to design, develop, implement and maintain software.
  - [] Cost of voice, data, and video network equipment (e.g., physical cables, routers).
  - [] Cost to operate and maintain networks.

Model & Examples	Model Differentiators				Likely Revenues	Likely Costs
	Control Inventory	Sell Online	Price Set Online	Physical Product/ Service		
Retailer Amazon.com LandsEnd.com Walmart.com	Yes	Yes	No	Yes	Product/ service sales	Advertising & marketing; physical facilities, inventory & customer service; R&D; IT infrastructure
Marketplace E-Loan QuickenInsurance	Possibly	Yes	No	No	Transaction fees; service fees; Commissions	Advertising & marketing; R&D; IT infrastructure
Aggregator / Intermediary InsWeb AutoWeb.com Individual.com	No	No	No	Possibly	Referral fees; Advertising & marketing fees	Advertising & marketing; R&D; IT infrastructure
Exchange Amazon.com (B2C) Ebay (C2C) PriceLine (C2B) FreeMarkets (B2B)	Possibly	Possibly	Yes	Possibly	Depends on model	Advertising & marketing; Staff support for auctions (especially B2B) inventory & logistics; R&D; Technical infrastructure

Table 8-3: Distributor E-Business Models

Model & Examples	Model Differentiators			Likely Revenues	Likely Costs
	Gateway Access	Deep Content & Solutions	Price Affinity Group Focus		
Horizontal Portals AOL.com Yahoo.com iWon.com Virgin.com	Yes	Through partnerships with vertical & affinity portals	Possibly	Advertising, affiliation & sorting fees; Possibly subscription or access fees	Advertising, marketing & sales; Content & information asset management; R&D; IT infrastructure
Vertical Portals Quicken.com Healtheon/WebMD	Limited	Yes	No	Transaction fees; Commissions; Advertising, affiliation & slotting fees	Advertising, marketing & sales; Content & information asset management; R&D; IT infrastructure
Affinity Portals Women.com Women's Financial Network	Possibly	Within affinity group	Yes	Referral fees; Advertising, affiliation & slotting fees	Advertising, marketing & sales; Content & information asset management; R&D; IT infrastructure

Table 8-4: Portal E-Business Models

Model & Examples	Model Differentiators			Likely Revenues	Likely Costs
	Sell / Serve Online	Sell / Serve Offline	Level of Customization		
Manufacturers Ford.com GE.com Medtronic.com	Yes	Yes	Low to Moderate	Product sales; Service fees	Advertising, marketing & sales; Content & information asset management; R&D; IT infrastructure
Service Providers American Express eCoverage.com American Airlines	Yes	Possibly	Moderate to High	Commission, service, or transaction fees	Advertising, marketing & sales; Content & information asset management; R&D; IT infrastructure
Educators Ecollege.com Harvard Business School Pensare.com	Yes	Possibly	Moderate to High	Registration or event fee; Subscription fee; Hosting fee	Content & information asset management; R&D; IT infrastructure
Advisors Ernst & Young[12] Knowledge Universe[13] Mainspring.com	Yes	Usually	Moderate to High	Subscription fee; Registration or event fee; Membership fee, Commission, transaction or service fee	Content & information asset management; R&D; IT infrastructure
Information & News Services Financial Times[14] Forrester WSJ.com	Yes	Possibly	Moderate to High	Subscription fee; registration or Commission, transaction or service fee	Advertising, marketing & sales; Content & information asset management; R&D; IT infrastructure
Custom Suppliers Boeing Dell McGraw Hill	Yes	Yes	High	Product sales; Service fees	Advertising, marketing & sales; Content & information asset management; R&D; IT infrastructure

Table 8-5: Producer E-Business Models

---

[12] http://ww.cy.com
[13] http://www.knowledgeeu.com
[14] http://www.ft.com

Model & Examples	Model Differentiators				Likely Revenues	Likely Costs
	Control Inventory	Sell Online	Price Set Online	Physical Product/ Service		
Infrastructure Retailers CompUSA.com Staples.com	Yes	Yes	Not Usually	Yes	Product / service sales	Advertising & marketing; Physical facilities, inventory & customer service; R&D; IT infrastructure
Infrastructure Marketplaces IngramMicro.com TechData.com	Usually	Yes	May enable some bidding	Yes	Transaction fees; Service fees; Commission	Advertising & marketing; R&D; IT infrastructure
Infrastructure Exchanges Egghead/ Onsale.com[15]	Possibly	Possibly	Yes	Yes	Depends on model	Advertising & marketing; Staff support for auctions; Inventory and logistics; R&D; Technical infrastructure

Table 8-6: Infrastructure Distributor E-Business Models

---

[15] http://www.egghead.com

Model & Examples	Model Differentiators			Likely Revenues	Likely Costs
	Gateway Access & Hosting	Deep Commerce, Community Solutions	Hosting Services		
Horizontal Infrastructure Portals AOL.com AT&T.com USWeb / CKS[16]	Yes	Through partnerships with non-infrastructure portals and ASPs	Yes	Access fees; Commission, service, or transaction fees; Subscription fees; Hosting fees	R&D; IT infrastructure; Advertising, marketing and sales
Vertical Infrastructure Portals (Application Service Providers – ASPs) Oracle Business Online Sales.com Ventro.com	Usually	Yes	Usually	Licensing fees; Service & transaction fees; Maintenance & Update fees; Hosting fees	R&D; IT infrastructure; Advertising, marketing and sales; Content and information asset management

Table 8-7: Infrastructure Portal E-Business Models

---

[16] http://www.usweb.com

Model & Examples	Model Differentiators			Likely Revenues	Likely Costs
	Sell / Serve Online	Sell / Serve Offline	Level of Customization		
Equipment / Component Manufacturers IBM Compaq Cisco Lucent	Yes	Yes	Low to Moderate	Product license or sales; Installation & integration fees; Maintenance, update & service fees	R&D; Advertising, marketing and sales; Production; Physical facilities & infrastructure; Equipment & supplies; IT infrastructure
Software Firms Ariba Microsoft Oracle Siebel SilkNet / kana	Yes	Yes	Moderate to High	Product license or sales; Installation & integration fees; Maintenance, update & service fees	R&D; Advertising, marketing and sales; Production; Physical facilities & infrastructure; Specialized equipment, materials & supplies; IT infrastructure
Infrastructure Services Firms Agency.com Doubleclick Federal Express Webvan	Yes	Yes	High	Commission, service or transaction fee; Hosting fee	Content and information asset management; R&D; IT infrastructure
Custom Suppliers – Hardware MicroAge	Yes	Usually	High	Product/service sales; Licensing fee; Installation & integration fees; Maintenance, update & service fees	R&D; Production; Physical facilities & infrastructure; Equipment & supplies; IT infrastructure; Content and information asset management;
Custom Suppliers – Software Andersen Consulting Sapient Viant	Sometimes	Yes	High	Service & consulting fees; System integration fees	Service delivery expenses; Design & programming expenses; Content and information asset management; Business development

Table 8-8: Infrastructure Producer E-Business Models

Analyzing E-Business Models

Building a new Internet business is not for the faint-hearted. You have to deal with ambiguity on a daily basis, and you need to internally confront yourself and ask: Can I can be operational? Can I be functional in a business where I am not sure what is going to happen tomorrow? You may open up a newspaper and find that a new competitor has sprung up with $100 million in capital to spend. You may find that regulators have come in and locked up a whole section of the business. The most important criteria for success is tolerance for ambiguity.

Business models must be continuously evaluated to adapt to changes in the market, the competitive environment, the business itself, and technology. Thus, to build robust e-businesses, executives must understand the range of generic business models available to them. The following steps can be used to profile the e-business models currently used and those that could potentially be used in your business.

Step 1: Discuss the following issues at a high level across multiple parts of your organization and business community.

- What percentage of our customers do business with us offline, online, or both?
- What business models do we currently use and which ones are we planning to adopt?
- What revenue models are currently in place?
- What cost models are currently in place?
- What are the strengths of our business models?
- Where do opportunities exist to improve our existing business models?
- What new business models might we use in the future?
- What additional sources of revenue might we generate?
- How can we improve our margins?

Step 2: Analyze your current business models and identify potential new models that could be employed. Use the following series of questions to assess your company's business model profile and to identify priorities for improving and adding business models in the future.

- Are we using the right business models to accomplish our strategy?
- Is the mix of revenue generating and non-revenue generating models appropriate? If a model does not generate revenues, would it make sense to evolve the model? If so, how?
- For revenue-generating business models, which revenue models have the largest potential opportunity, and have we dedicated sufficient resources and attention to these models?
- What cost categories can be reduced to improve margins and profitability?
- Are there ways we could increase the value of our tangible and intangible assets?
- Are there models that we don't currently use that could be added to create a more robust and sustainable business?

- What business models do others in our industry use?
- What business models do best-in-class businesses outside of our industry use?
- What models do our customers believe we should use?
- What models do industry experts suggest?
- What models do our suppliers and strategic partners recommend?
- What are the key weaknesses of our current e-business?
- How might we improve our current business model profile?
- What models might we add to our profile to make our business more sustainable and economically viable?
- What opportunities should we pursue to:
    - Enhance our existing business?
    - Expand into new markets and / or add new products or services?
    - Extend our business by incorporating new lines of business or new business models?
    - Exit an existing business, market, product line, or business model?

Key Insights

Anyone who has ever talked to a customer or a focus group knows that they rarely tell you exactly what they want. Instead, breakaway business innovations demand that executives listen closely and then invent. But that is just the beginning. Once the new invention is introduced, success is determined by the ability to continue to listen closely and then adapt quickly – not just to the customer, but also to every member of the business community. As we study the evolution of e-business models of early Internet pioneers, such as Amazon.com and Charles Schwab, we clearly see this cycle of listening, inventing, and then adapting to the experiences and expectations of customers and the business community. And, in most instances, e-businesses that have pulled ahead of the pack have been those that successfully integrated the best of traditional and new-age business models, enabling customers and the business community to move seamlessly between the online and offline worlds. Some of the key insights we can derive are:

- The best designs integrate familiar ways of doing things with value-added enhancements; however, customers and members of your business community may not be able to tell you the familiar experiences they want to keep and the new value-added enhancements they are willing to pay for. Listen, invent, listen more, and then adapt based on what you learn.
- Attention must be paid to both transactional efficiency and a personalized, engaging customer experience.
- The best experiences enable a smooth transition between the online and offline worlds for customers and all members of the business community.
- As e-businesses adapt to the needs of the customer and the requirements of the business community, early "click and order" e-business models are evolving into "click and mortar" models.
- Survival and success demands that executives learn to evolve their businesses in Internet time.

- Business model evolution is a continual process of learning and adaptation that must be integrated within a firm's daily operations – not left to chance.

Initially, business strategists believed that the impact of the Internet and associated technologies would result in disintermediation. Instead, in many industries, power is shifting to the channel. Powerful new business-to-consumer (B2C) and business-to-business (B2B) portals are controlling access to online channels. But the game may not be over yet. In many industries, established suppliers and manufacturers have begun to respond – creating their own portal or partnering with others in their industry. In the high-tech industry, hardware and software firms such as Cisco, IBM, Dell, Oracle, and Microsoft are either bypassing the channel and going direct, or they are forming their own digital infrastructure portals; these infrastructure portals may be horizontal, providing gateway access (for example, Internet Service Providers), or they may be vertical destinations (for example, Application Service Providers). It is still unclear which models will dominate in the future. Some of the key insights we can derive are:

- Horizontal and vertical portals are emerging as dominant sources of power.
- Focused distributors that do not allow customers and the business community to transact business online are losing power.
- To capture customer and channel attention, producers must be best-in-class – the # 1 or # 2 most well-respected brand.
- Infrastructure producers – hardware and software providers – staked their Internet claim early and have established powerful positions, selling direct to customers.
- The distinct separation between digital infrastructure providers and the digital businesses that are being launched on the infrastructure is beginning to blur; horizontal and vertical business portals are merging with horizontal and vertical infrastructure portals.
- Vertically integrated producers are launching producer portals.
- Coalitions of suppliers are forming business-to-business portals.

Many of the most powerful e-businesses are anything but simple and focused. In fact, the most successful e-businesses have been built artfully combining a variety of old and new business models. As models are added, flexibility increases and the ability to respond to unforeseen events and conditions improves. The value webs within the firm are then linked to the value web – or webs – that make up the company's business community. These complex webs of interconnections and relationships enable firms to work together to increase value for all members of the community. Value webs create a robust and flexible business community that unites members in a dynamic and complex set of transactions and interactions through which value is created and exchanged. Some of the key insights we can derive are:

- E-businesses are built combining old and new models that provide multiple revenue streams.
- E-businesses evolve through four mechanisms: enhancing, expanding, extending and exiting.
- The orderly, sequential transactions and relationships among participants in an industry value chain are being replaced by a more complex web of transactions and relationships among members of a business community.

185

- Successful e-businesses are able to create and nurture strong, flexible and resilient value webs that work together to benefit every member of the community.
- Vertical integration through ownership and virtual integration through partnerships is back in vogue. But, unlike the vertically integrated conglomerates of the first half of the 20th century that managed complexity by minimizing it, e-business conglomerates of the 21st century use sophisticated digital business designs to embrace complexity and manage it directly.

THE RISE OF SYNDICATION

There is no question that the Internet is overturning the old rules about competition and strategy. But what are the new rules? Many of them can be found in the concept of syndication, a way of doing business that has its origins in the entertainment world but is now expanding to define the structure of e-business. As companies enter syndication networks, they will need to rethink their products, relationships, and even their core capabilities.

Syndication involves the sale of the same good to many customers, who then integrate it with other offerings and redistribute it. The fixed physical assets and slow-moving information of the industrial economy made it difficult, if not impossible, to create the kind of fluid networks that are essential to syndication. But with the rise of the information economy, that is changing. Flexible business networks are not only becoming possible, they are becoming essential. As a result, syndication is moving from the periphery of business to its center. It is emerging as the fundamental organizing principle for e-business. Although few of the leading Internet companies use the term syndication to describe what they do, it often lies at the heart of their business models.

On the Web, unlike in the physical world, syndication is not limited to the distribution of content. Commerce can also be syndicated. One company can, for example, syndicate a shopping-cart ordering and payment system to many Internet retailers. Another company can syndicate a logistics platform. Another can syndicate fraud detection and credit-scoring algorithms. Another can syndicate human resource processes. Businesses themselves, in other words, can be created out of syndicated components. The much discussed virtual company can become a reality.

Syndication is a radically different way of structuring business than anything that has come before. It requires entrepreneurs and executives to rethink their strategies and reshape their organizations, to change the way they interact with customers and partner with other entities, and to pioneer new models for collecting revenues and earning profits. Those that best understand the dynamics of syndication – that are able to position themselves in the most lucrative nodes of syndication networks – will be the ones that thrive in the Internet era.

Why Syndication Suits The Web

Syndication has traditionally been rare in the business world for three reasons. First, syndication works only with information goods. Because information is never "consumed", infinite numbers of people can use the same information. That is not the case with physical products. As long as most of the business world was engaged in the production, transport and sale of physical goods, syndication could exist only on the margins of the economy. Second, syndication requires modularity. While a syndicated good can have considerable value in and of itself, it does not normally constitute an entire product; it is a piece of a greater whole. In the old physical economy, modularity was rare. The boundaries between products, supply chains, and companies tended to be clearly demarcated and impermeable. Third, syndication requires many independent distribution points. There is little to be gained by creating different combinations and configurations of content if there is only one distributor, or if every distributor is controlled by a content creator.

With the Internet, information goods, modularity and fragmented distribution become not only possible but essential. Everything that moves on the Internet takes the form of information. The hyperlinked architecture of the Web is modular by nature. And because anyone can start a Web site, there are literally millions of different distribution points for users. In such an environment, syndication becomes inescapable.

The Three Syndication Roles

Traditionally, companies have connected with one another in simple, linear chains, running from raw material producers to manufacturers to distributors to retailers. In syndication, the connections between companies proliferate. The network replaces the chain as the organizing model for business relationships. Within a syndication network, there are three roles that businesses can play. *Originators* create original content. *Syndicators* package that content for distribution, often integrating it with content from other originators. *Distributors* deliver the content to customers. A company can play one role in a syndication network, or it can play two or three roles simultaneously. It can also shift from one role to another over time.

Players	Role	Traditional Examples	Web Examples
Originators	Create original content	Dreamworks Charles Schulz Oprah Winfrey	Inktomi Quote.com Motley Fool
Syndicators	Package content and manage relationships between originators and distributors	King World United Features	iSyndicate LinkShare Motley Fool
Distributors	Deliver content to consumer	New York Times CBS CNN	Women.com Yahoo! Motley Fool
Consumers	View or use content; create revenue through fees, purchases, or viewing advertisements		

Table 8-9: The Structure of Syndication

Originators. The Internet broadens the originator category in two ways. It expands the scope of original content that can be syndicated, and it makes it easier for

187

any company or individual to disseminate that content globally. Anything that can exist as information – from products and services to business processes and brands – can be syndicated. A good example of an Internet originator if Inktomi, a start-up that created a powerful Internet search engine.

Syndicators. By bringing together content from a variety of sources and making it available through standard formats and contracts, syndicators free distributors from having to find and negotiate with dozens of different originators to gather the content they want. In other words, syndicators are a form of infomediary, collecting and packaging digital information in a way that adds value to it

Distributors. Distributors are the customer-facing businesses. They use syndication to lower their costs for acquiring content and to expand the value they provide to consumers. E*Trade is one example of a distributor.

Syndication Versus Outsourcing

On the surface, syndication looks a lot like outsourcing. They both involve the use of outsiders to supply a business asset or function. But syndication holds two large advantages over traditional outsourcing. First, because syndication deals with information rather than physical resources, a company can syndicate the same goods or services to an almost infinite number of partners without incurring much additional cost. The second advantage is that online syndication can be automated and standardized in a way that physical outsourcing can't. An important feature of syndication relationships is that business rules, such as usage rights and payment terms, can be passed between companies along with the syndicated asset or service – both take the form of digital code. Moreover, because the Internet is an open system, the rules can be coded in standard formats that can be shared by any company. That allows syndication networks to be created, expanded, and optimized far more quickly than is possible in the physical world.

Syndication provides choices far beyond those that companies had with outsourcing, but the existence of those choices makes a coherent strategy all the more important. Companies should look for relationships that offer the greatest speed and flexibility, but they should also carefully identify the business terms they consider most important. Should you pay an up-front fee for a syndicated search service for your site, or would it make more sense to receive the service for free but let the provider run a banner advertisement? The flexibility of the Internet architecture and the limitless creativity of Internet entrepreneurs means that every company will face a multitude of complex choices in structuring relationships.

Syndication Strategy

Internet syndication opens up endless opportunities for entrepreneurs, and it provides enormous freedom to all companies. It enables businesses to choose where they wish to concentrate their efforts and to piggyback a myriad of other businesses that can handle the remaining elements of a complete end-to-end service. Unlike outsourcing, it does not restrict flexibility. Syndication relationships can change rapidly and companies can quickly shift between different roles. But because syndication networks are so complex, they also present a host of challenges. Fortunately, however, the content flows, the business rules, and the revenue streams can largely be managed by software.

The bigger challenge lies at the strategic level. Given the unpredictable and ever-changing flows of revenues, profits and competition on the Web, companies need to choose their place in a syndication network with care, and they need to be adept at reconfiguring their roles and relationships at a moment's notice. The syndicated world of the Web is radically different from the traditional business world, where assets tend to be fixed and roles and relationships stable. To thrive in a syndication network, executives first have to shed many of their old assumptions about business strategy.

	Traditional Business	**Syndication**
Structure of Relationships	Linear supply-and-demand chains	Loose, weblike networks
Corporate Roles	Fixed	Continually shifting
Value Added	Dominated by physical distribution	Dominated by information manipulation
Strategic Focus	Control scarce resources	Leverage abundance
Role of Corporate Capabilities	Sources of advantage to protect	Products to sell
Role of Outsourcing	Gain efficiency	Assemble virtual corporations

Table 8-10: Traditional Business vs. Syndication

In setting strategy, companies have always sought to organize their markets so as to place themselves in the sweet spot of the value chain – the place where most of the profits reside. Traditionally, the way to do that has been to seize upon or create scarcities. Control over a scarce resource is always more valuable than control over a commodity. The Internet, however, replaces scarcity with abundance. Information can be replicated an unlimited number of times. It can be reassembled and recombined in infinite combinations. There are no limits on shelf space on the Internet, every store is accessible to every shopper, the lanes of supply and distribution are wide open, and even the tiniest new company can achieve enormous scale in almost no time. Because the constraints of physical inventory and location don't apply, creating and maintaining scarcities isn't an option.

Instead, successful strategies must be designed to benefit from abundance. Companies need to seek out and occupy the most valuable niches in syndication networks – which turn out to be those that maximize the number and strength of the company's connections to other companies and to customers. And because those connections are always changing, even the most successful businesses will rarely be able to stay put for long.

Rethinking Core Capabilities

In a syndicated world, core capabilities are no longer secrets to protect – they are assets to buy and sell. In an economy of scarcity, core capabilities are sources of proprietary advantage. In an economy of abundance, they are your best product. If you try to sequester them, you may gain a short-term competitive edge, but your competitors will soon catch up. If you syndicate them, you can turn those competitors into customers.

In some cases, the syndicated assets themselves may be valuable enough to generate big revenues. But even if they aren't, the other benefits of syndication can be significant. Companies can use syndication to broaden their distribution in an efficient manner. Syndication can also bring companies data about customer usage patterns. And it can generate leads and reinforce brands. All of these are benefits that companies have traditionally sought to derive by dominating their markets and by exercising exclusive control over information. But with competitive advantages increasingly difficult to lock in – thanks to the leveling power of the information economy – syndication provides a superior route to the same benefits.

The New Shape of Business

Beyond its impact on individual companies' strategies and relationships, syndication promises to change the nature of business. As organizations begin to be constructed out of components syndicated from many other organizations, the result will be a mesh of relationships with no beginning, end or center. Companies may look the same as before to their customers, but behind the scenes they will be in constant flux, melding with one another in everchanging networks. The shift won't happen overnight, and of course there will always be functions and goods that don't lend themselves to syndication. But in those areas where syndication takes hold, companies will become less important than the networks that contain them.

Indeed, individual companies will routinely originate, syndicate, or distribute information without even being aware of all the others participating in the network. A particular originator may, for example, have a relationship with only one syndicator, but through that relationship it will be able to benefit from the contributions of hundreds or even thousands of other companies. While every participant will retain some measure of control – choosing which syndication partners to have direct relationships with and deciding which business rules to incorporate into its syndicated transactions – no participant will control the overall network. Like any complex, highly adaptive system, a well-functioning syndication network will be self-organizing, constantly optimizing its behavior in response to an unending stream of information about the transactions taking place among its members.

Syndication may not be a new model, but it takes on a new life thanks to the Internet. Virtually any organization can benefit from syndication, often in several different ways if it is willing to view itself as part of a larger, interconnected world rather than seeking exclusive control at every turn. The tools and intermediaries that facilitate syndication relationships will become more sophisticated over time. Already, though, there are many syndication networks in place and many examples of successful syndication strategies. As the Internet economy continues to grow in importance, syndication will grow along with it as the underlying structure of business.

Chapter 9

Electronic Commerce Strategy and Implementation

COMPETING IN CYBERSPACE

In the first generation of electronic commerce, retail space on the Internet was claimed by whoever got there first with enough resources to create a credible business. It took speed, a willingness to experiment, and a lot of cybersavvy. Companies that had performed brilliantly in traditional settings seemed totally lost. Achieving profits during this phase was deemed unnecessary by cheering investors. The stock market has voted a higher valuation for Amazon.com than for the entire traditional book retailing and publishing industries combined, even though Amazon has yet to turn a profit. In private, some e-commerce entrepreneurs confess perplexity as to how they ever will make a profit. They have, of necessity, focused far more on growth. Strategy is subordinated to tactics, which are subordinated to experimentation.

But that phase is ending. The traditional incumbents are getting serious, and the Internet stock bubble is losing some buoyancy. We are entering the second generation of electronic commerce. The key players – branded-goods suppliers, physical retailers, electronic retailers and pure navigators – will shift their attention from claiming territory to defending or capturing it. They will be forced to focus on competitive advantage and on strategies to achieve it.

Navigation As A Separate Business

In the familiar world of physical commerce, consumers rely on product suppliers and retailers to help them navigate among their choices. Those businesses, in turn, exploit the consumers' search costs to build competitive advantage. They create navigational tools – everything from branding and advertising to relationship building and merchandising – to help consumers short-circuit the complexities of a comprehensive search and find products they are willing to buy. Indeed, in most consumer businesses, far more profitability derives from influencing navigation – by means of a strong brand identity, say – than from manufacturing or distributing the physical product itself.

On the Internet, by contrast, millions of people exchange massive amounts of information directly, quickly, and for free. Consumers can search much more comprehensively and at negligible cost. Navigation and selection occur independently of physical warehousing and distribution. Product suppliers can sell directly to customers. Electronic retailers can focus on navigation and outsource fulfillment. And "pure" navigators, like the Yahoo! search engine and Quicken software, can organize information, helping people make sense of it without being party to the transaction at all.

The importance of this shift cannot be over-emphasized. Navigation is the battlefield on which competitive advantage will be won or lost. At stake is much of the profit potential of most consumer-products suppliers and retailing businesses. For navigation is a business with enormous potential scope. The services navigators provide will correspond only coincidentally to any physically defined business or industry.

Navigation has three dimensions: reach, richness and affiliation. It is along these dimensions that the struggle for competitive advantage will take place. *Reach* is about access and connection. It means, how many customers a business can access or how many products it can offer to those customers. Reach is the most visible difference between electronic and physical businesses, and it has been the primary competitive differentiation for e-businesses thus far. *Richness* is the depth and detail of the information that the business can give the customer, as well as the depth and detail of information it collects about the customer. Electronic businesses haven't yet learned to compete seriously on the richness dimension. But richness holds enormous potential for building close relationships with customers in a future dominated by e-commerce.

Traditional businesses have always had to make a trade-off between richness and reach. Doing both – getting highly detailed, customized information to and from a massive audience – was prohibitively expensive. E-commerce businesses can exploit the dramatic displacement of the trade-off permitted by electronic connectivity and information standards. For very little money, an e-business can provide a wide base of customers (reach) with access to a broad range of products (reach) and detailed, complete information about each product (richness). It can also collect huge amounts of information about each customer (richness) and use it to sell more products and services.

The same technological forces that blow up the trade-off between richness and reach also open up a third competitive dimension - *affiliation,* or whose interests the business represents. Until now, affiliation hasn't been a serious competitive factor in physical commerce because, in general, no company ever devised a way to make money by taking the consumers' side. However, it's a natural progression for pure navigators to affiliate with customers; they aren't selling anything except, possibly, information – and therein could lie a huge competitive advantage. E-retailers with navigational functions are also shifting their affiliation toward customers. Traditional manufacturers and retailers must find ways to fight, co-opt, or imitate their e-commerce competitor's affiliation strategies.

Competing On Reach

Before the advent of e-commerce, retail superstores competed brilliantly on reach by offering convenient locations and broad selection. But theirs is a format constrained by physical limitations. The largest physical Barnes & Noble bookstore in the United States still carries only 200,000 titles. Amazon.com offers 4.5 million volumes and is "located" on some 25 million computer screens. This orders-of-magnitude jump in reach is possible precisely because the navigation function (catalog) is separated from the physical function (inventory). Unconstrained by physical limitations, reach explodes. That explosion extends beyond conventionally defined industry boundaries. If consumers value comprehensive search capabilities, then the smart navigator will span across the search domain that consumers prefer. The first navigator to do so will capture an advantage. Dell sells more than computers. Amazon has rapidly moved beyond books.

For insurgents – for e-retailers in particular – this raises the terrifying prospect of unstable business boundaries. CDNow carved out a dominant, reach-based position in the CD sales category, only to lose it in just a few months to Amazon. CDs are not a domain within which consumers meaningfully define reach. The erosion of category boundaries will continue, as electronic retailers encroach on one another's territories and probe the true boundaries of consumer search domains.

The explosion of reach on the Internet also raises an acute dilemma for product suppliers. At first blush, it looks like a godsend – a chance to break free from the stranglehold of the retailer and build direct relationships with the final consumer. But any attempt to do so is by definition a navigational vehicle offering the consumer limited product reach. This might be offset by other factors, but if product suppliers offer navigation to only their own offerings, they put themselves at an inherent disadvantage. Stuck in a mind-set that confuses navigation with marketing, they may forgo competing in the emerging navigation business.

For many supplier businesses, that is just fine: they do not wish to be in the navigation business, and they welcome an explosion of information channels by which consumers can find their products and services. Small publishers consider Amazon to be a blessing. But for many large suppliers, the navigation function is precisely where their differentiation and competitive advantage lay. To lose control of navigation would be to lose ownership of a primary source of competitive differentiation. But how can they keep it?

The knee-jerk reaction of product suppliers is to try to keep the new navigators from achieving critical mass. Consumer-product suppliers, after all, are the ultimate source of information on product features, price and availability. If sellers don't let Yahoo! or Quicken parse their product lists and compare them with those of their competitors, then Yahoo! and Quicken will be confined to their current roles of glorified phone directory and checkbook.

There are two problems with that defensive strategy. The first is that technically it is difficult to stop a navigator from parsing information that's available electronically. If customers can go to the Web site, so can navigators. Obviously, the seller can stop this game, if only by refusing to operate a Web site. But therein lies the second and more fundamental issue: it is not obvious that it is in any single seller's interest to do so. A navigator is still a source of incremental business to a seller. Unless the selling business is highly concentrated, it is unlikely that the navigator's ability to achieve critical mass will depend on the availability of data from any one source. Therefore, while denying data to the navigator may be in the interest of all sellers *collectively*, it is not in the interest of any one seller *individually*.

So if critical mass cannot ultimately be denied, then the old players have to match the reach of the new. Product suppliers that want to communicate with the consumer directly must do whatever it takes to achieve the reach that consumers value. That may mean entering into joint ventures with competitors to achieve critical mass. It may mean navigating to other companies' products and services.

Physical retailers may have to take a similar approach. Most treat their Web presence as a means of driving traffic to their physical locations. Treating electronic retailing as a serious business in its own right – indeed as both the greatest threat and opportunity that they face – forces them to act quite differently. They have to define their product mix as the e-retailers do, not as the physical constraints of their bricks-and-mortar stores forced them to. This may necessitate acquisitions and joint ventures. They need to fulfill orders in whatever way is most efficient for the electronic business – separating, if necessary, from their traditional warehousing infrastructure. They have to exploit synergies with the physical retail business, but only where that helps the electronic business to compete. Above all, they have to think of e-commerce as a business in its own right and not compromise its success in an effort to protect the traditional physical model. They must *expect* the new business to cannibalize the old.

Of all the incumbent retailers, catalog companies are best positioned to make the shift. Their lines of business are already defined around brand identities and search domains that make sense to consumers. They revise their offerings continuously through sophisticated data-mining techniques. Their fulfillment systems are designed for remote delivery. It is not surprising that the pre-Internet retailers that have most successfully managed the transition to electronic commerce are Land's End and Victoria's Secret.

But other incumbents will find managing the transition to the Web much more difficult. Product suppliers and physical retailers still see the Internet as an arena for marketing and promotion: a new channel for doing old things. If they persist in that view, they will handicap themselves against new competitors – whether e-retailers or pure navigators – that see e-commerce as a business in its own right and pursue reach single-mindedly.

Competing On Affiliation

E-commerce businesses are already tilting their affiliation away from suppliers toward the consumer. Net-savvy consumers are forcing them to. Affiliation is shifting, in ways that even the electronic retailers cannot control. This change in affiliation is partially a manifestation of Internet culture and the greater transparency under which everyone operates. But it is also a consequence of the blowup of the trade-off between richness and reach. The pure navigator is poised to exploit the affiliation dimension. Lipper and Motley Fool are in a better position for navigating to mutual fund investments than Fidelity precisely because they are *not* in the business of selling funds. Pure navigators can serve as "meta-navigators", using technologies that compare multiple electronic retailers.

The player in the worst position to exploit affiliation is the product supplier, because by definition the supplier has an interest in the transaction that is different from the consumer's. One response is to exploit that way the navigational businesses evolve beyond product categories. Offer a navigation service that solves consumer problems instead of merely pushing products. Add in objective data and decision-support software about content unrelated to your own business. Provide objective information about products and services in the consumer's search domain that you do *not* sell. Perhaps provide comprehensive but not necessarily comparable data on your own products and those of direct competitors, but slightly bias the presentation through the ordering and emphasis of alternatives.

Competing On Richness

When competing on reach and affiliation, traditional players have to struggle to keep abreast of electronic retailers and pure navigators. But they have natural advantages when it comes to richness. Traditional retailers can exploit their detailed information about customers. Suppliers can use extensive product information to their advantage. Doing so will most certainly involve revisiting how they think about branding.

Rich Customer Information

Retailers have always been well positioned to collect and use information about their customers, but the Internet greatly enhances their ability to do so. The Web offers an unparalleled opportunity for cheap and infinitely discriminating customization of offers, products, and advertisements. Data-mining techniques can be applied to browsing behavior as well as to purchasing history and demographics.

The great advantage of the physical retailers is the rich data that they collect from *other* sources. Web-derived information, even when thoroughly mined, is actually a surprisingly thin database compared with those developed by grocery stores or credit card companies. However, by putting the two kinds of information together and using the Web as a means of customizing on the fly, businesses have the potential to build powerful relationships and strong competitive advantage.

Two factors limit strategies based on rich consumer information. The first is privacy constraints, which require that consumers be informed of, and agree to, any exchange of data. The second factor is consumers' option to search and organize information for themselves. These two factors do limit the power of rich customer information, but, within those limits, electronic and physical retailers have an effective weapon. No single player is likely to have the ideal database, and digital information can be bought or sold, so alliances and markets for swapping information will probably begin to form. The originators and primary aggregators of such information, whether they are grocery stores, portals, credit agencies, or the consumers themselves, will extract most of the value.

Rich Product Information

It is generally difficult for manufacturers to use rich customer information competitively because retailers are more directly connected to customers. But manufacturers have distinct advantages when it comes to rich product information. As a low-cost way to build a channel of communication that circumvents the retailers, the strategy has powerful potential.

Rich product information is a powerful but uncertain weapon for the product supplier. Wherever consumers welcome evangelism, enthusiasm and a strong connotative context, rich product information strategies can be effective. But when detachment, objectivity and comprehensiveness matter more, that approach may prove counterproductive. Hot news and breathless excitement about mortgages or groceries will impress nobody.

Brands

Manufacturers use branding all the time, of course, to communicate rich, product-specific information to their consumers. But there are two different types of brands, and one is better suited to e-commerce than the other. Some companies attempt to convey facts or beliefs about product attributes through branding. Other manufacturers use branding to communicate an experience: feelings, associations and memories. Rich information channels have very different effects on brand-as-belief and on brand-as-experience. To the extent that a brand is a matter of belief, the brand message is fundamentally a *navigator* message. Because an objective navigator could provide those messages, the brand-as-belief competes with the navigator. Brand-as-experience is a different story. The broadband, interactive, customized environment enhances the brand, and it also enhances the product and the experience of owning it.

Where brands are already defined in terms of experience rather than belief, the evolving medium will strength them. Brands that have elements of both (as most do) must play up their experiential aspects. Rich, product-centered information, supporting a brand defined as experience, is the product supplier's counter to the superior reach and affiliation of retailers and navigators.

The Incumbent's Dilemma

The logic of reach, affiliation and richness poses a profound organizational dilemma for incumbent product suppliers and retailers. They have to recognize that their value chain is being deconstructed. Aspects of navigation are no longer functions; they are becoming businesses. And if incumbents choose to compete in any of those emerging businesses, they must do so by building reach, affiliation and richness, and redefining strategy and scope as the business evolves beyond its physically defined origins. They can do all this if they mentally break down the current business into its components, understand the evolution of new business models from the outside-in, and free their new-business managers from any obligation to prop up the old. Indeed, the new businesses will quite properly compete against the old, buy from or ally with traditional competitors, and take risks that may prove to be costly errors. Every aspect of organization, incentive and operating style will change.

This is an enormous challenge to an established organization. Its competencies, procedures, and power structures stand in the way. The only answer, many incumbents have found, is to separate the new venture as much as possible from the established organization, perhaps even to spin it out. If the aim is to compete on reach or affiliation, that is probably the only answer. But richness is the incumbent's greatest strength. How can an incumbent achieve the autonomy, motivation and freshness of an Internet start-up and simultaneously exploit its uniquely rich customer information and product information? That may require a far more threatening corporate transformation – the kind of reinvention that Schwab undertook when it halved its brokerage fees, committed to navigation as its business definition, and started selling its competitors' products. But Schwab has a history of reinventing itself. For many incumbents, their first attempt to reinvent themselves may also be their last.

Strategic Guidelines For Various E-Commerce Players

Guidelines for the Pure Navigators

- Never take your business definition for granted. You must compete with other navigators on richness and reach within a search domain whose boundaries are constantly moving.

- Recognize that close affiliation with consumers is a major competitive advantage for you. It is part of your Web identity. Cultivate it. Do not compromise consumer interests for your own short-term gain. Never do anything you would not want all your users to know, because within a few days, they will.

- Build richness fast. When the incumbent suppliers get serious, that is where they will attack.

Guidelines for the Electronic Retailers

- Define your business in terms of a coherent consumer search domain, not an irrelevant physical category.

- Be very skeptical of exclusives with product suppliers. The sacrifice of reach and consumer affiliation is likely to cost you more in competitive advantage than the gain in margin is worth.

- Beware of physical retailers: they often have better consumer information and better logistics. Their only handicap is an inability to think differently. That could change.

Guidelines for the Incumbent Product Manufacturers

- Adding richness – especially product-specific richness – is the most powerful way for you to compete. Concentrate on enhancing brand-as-experience.

- Mentally deconstruct your own business. Look at its organizational components as businesses in their own right. Develop independent strategies for them. Create an organization that takes those strategies seriously.

- Reach for you is a two-edged sword: it might enable you to escape the stranglehold of your retailers, but it simultaneously exposes you to new navigators whose potential reach is far greater than yours.

- Look seriously at alliances to address the affiliation and reach problems: a group of suppliers may be able to create a navigator that is more comprehensive and credible than any of its members.

Guidelines for the Incumbent Physical Retailers

- You have been competing on the reach game through overwhelming selection and mastery of logistics. But that is all economics of physical things. The new reach game is about information. If you play it seriously, it will force you to redefine your business.

- You are going to be attacked, so do it yourself before somebody does it to you. And understand the multiplicative effects that even slight revenue erosion can have on the profitability of a high-fixed-cost physical business. You will need to make those fixed costs variable.

- You ought to win in the new world of e-commerce. You start with reach, a high measure of consumer affiliation, physical distribution, rich consumer data, options for multichannel marketing, brands, and many of the right merchandising skills. You just have to be willing to compete against yourself.

- Know that your operating managers, if left to themselves, will never make the necessary changes. The threat to their core business is simply too great. Create a separate entity and give its managers the authority to exploit the assets of the traditional business. Synergy must be a one-way street, from the old business to the new.

THE NEW ECONOMICS OF INFORMATION

A fundamental shift in the economics of information is underway. Millions of people at home and at work are communicating electronically using universal, open standards. This explosion in connectivity is the latest – and for business strategists, the most important – wave in the information revolution. Over the past decade, managers have focused on adapting their operating processes to new information technologies. Dramatic as these operating changes have been, a more profound transformation in the business landscape lies ahead. Executives – and not just those in high-tech or information companies – will be forced to rethink the strategic fundamentals of their businesses. Over the next decade, the new economics of information will precipitate changes in the structure of entire industries and in the ways companies compete.

In many businesses not widely considered information businesses, information actually represents a large percentage of the cost structure. About one-third of the cost of health care in the United States – some $300 billion – is the cost of capturing, storing and processing such information as patients' records, physicians' notes, test results and insurance claims. More fundamentally, information is the glue that holds together the structure of all businesses. A company's value chain consists of all the activities it performs to design, produce, market, deliver and support its product. The value chains of companies that supply and buy from one another collectively make up an industry's value chain, its particular configuration of competitors, suppliers, distribution channels and customers.

When we think about a value chain, we tend to visualize a linear flow of physical activities. But the value chain also includes all the information that flows within a company and between a company and its suppliers, its distributors, and its existing or potential customers. Supplier relationships, brand identity, process coordination, customer loyalty, employee loyalty and switching costs all depend on various kinds of information.

When managers talk about the value of customer relationships, for example, what they really mean is the proprietary information that they have about their customers and that their customers have about the company and its products. Brands, after all, are nothing but the information – real or imagined, intellectual or emotional – that consumers have in their heads about a product. And the tools used to build brands – advertising, promotion and even shelf space – are themselves information or ways of delivering information. Similarly, information defines supplier relationships. Having a relationship means that two companies have established certain channels of communication built around personal acquaintance, mutual understanding, shared standards, electronic data interchange (EDI) systems, or synchronized production systems.

In any buyer-seller relationship, information can determine the relative bargaining power of the players. Auto dealers, for example, know the best local prices for a given model. Customers – unless they invest a lot of time shopping around – generally do not. Much of the dealer's margin depends on that asymmetry of information.

Not only does information define and constrain the relationship among the various players in a value chain, but in many businesses, it also forms the basis for competitive advantage – even when the cost of that information is trivial and the product or service is thoroughly physical. To cite some of the best-known examples, American Airlines for a long time used its control of the SABRE reservation system to achieve higher levels of capacity utilization than its competitors. Wal-Mart has exploited its EDI links with suppliers to increase its inventory turnover dramatically. And Nike has masterfully employed advertising, endorsements and the micro-segmentation of its market to transform sneakers into high-priced fashion goods. All three companies compete as much on information as they do on their physical product.

In many ways, then, information and the mechanisms for delivering it stabilize corporate and industry structures and underlie competitive advantage. But the informational components of value are so deeply embedded in the physical value chain, that, in some cases, we are just beginning to acknowledge their separate existence. When information is carried by things – by a salesperson or by a piece of direct mail, for example – it goes where the things go and no further. It is constrained to follow the linear flow of the physical value chain. But once everyone is connected electronically, information can travel by itself. The traditional link between the flow of product-related information and the flow of the product itself, between the economics of information and the economics of things, can be broken. What is truly revolutionary about the explosion in connectivity is the possibility it offers to unbundle information from its physical carrier.

The Trade-Off Between Richness And Reach

To the extent that information is embedded in physical modes of delivery, its economics are governed by a basic law: the trade-off between richness and reach. *Reach* simply means the number of people, at home or at work, exchanging information. *Richness* is defined by three aspects of the information itself. The first is *bandwidth*, or the amount of information that can be moved from sender to receiver in a given time. The second aspect is the degree to which the information can be *customized*. The third aspect is *interactivity*.

In general, the communication of rich information has required proximity and dedicated channels whose costs or physical constraints have limited the size of the audience to which the information could be sent. Conversely, the communication of information to a large audience has required compromises in bandwidth, customization and interactivity. This pervasive trade-off has shaped how companies communicate, collaborate and conduct transactions internally and with customers, suppliers and distributors. A company's marketing mix is determined by apportioning resources according to this trade-off. A company can embed its message in an advertisement, a piece of customized direct mail, or a personal sales pitch – alternatives increasing in richness but diminishing in reach.

The rapid emergence of universal technical standards for communication, allowing everybody to communicate with everybody else at essentially zero cost, is a sea change. And it is as much the agreement on standards as the technology itself that is making this change possible. The important principle here is that the same technical standards underlie the *Internet* which connects everyone, *extranets* which connect companies to one another, and *intranets* which connect individuals within companies. Those emerging open standards and the explosion in the number of people and organizations connected by networks are freeing information from the channels that have been required to exchange it, making those channels unnecessary or uneconomical. Although the standards may not be ideal for any individual application, users are finding that they are good enough for most purposes today. And they are improving rapidly. Over time, organizations and individuals will be able to extend their reach by many orders of magnitude, often with a negligible sacrifice of richness.

The Deconstruction Of The Value Chain

The changing economics of information threaten to undermine established value chains in many sectors of the economy, requiring virtually every company to rethink its strategy – not incrementally, but fundamentally. What will happen, for instance, to category killers such as Toys "R" Us and Home Depot when a search engine on the Internet gives consumers more choice than any store? What will be the point of having a supplier relationship with General Electric when it posts its purchasing requirements on an Internet bulletin board and entertains bids from anybody inclined to respond?

The value chains of scores of industries will become ripe for unbundling. The logic is most compelling – and therefore likely to strike soonest – in information businesses where the cost of physical distribution is high: newspapers, ticket sales, insurance, financial information, scientific publishing, software and encyclopedias. But in any business whose physical value chain has been compromised for the sake of delivering information, there is an opportunity to unbundle the two, creating a separate information business and allowing (or compelling) the physical business to be streamlined. All it will take to deconstruct a business is a competitor that focuses on the vulnerable sliver of information in its value chain.

Implications For Competitive Advantage

Deconstructing a vertically integrated value chain does more than transform the structure of a business or an industry – it alters the sources of competitive advantage. The new economics of information therefore not only present threats to established businesses but also represent a new set of opportunities. Every industry will shift according to its own dynamics, and those shifts will occur at different speeds and with varying intensity. No single set of predictions can be applied across the board, but some fundamental strategic implications of the changing economics of information can be drawn.

Existing value chains will fragment into multiple businesses, each of which will have its own sources of competitive advantage. When individual functions having different economies of scale or scope are bundled together, the result is a compromise of each – an averaging of the effects. When the bundles of functions are free to re-form as separate businesses, however, each can exploit its own sources of competitive advantage to the fullest.

Some new businesses will benefit from network economies of scale, which can give rise to monopolies. In a networked market, the greater the number of people connected, the greater the value of being connected, thus creating network economies of scale. This self-reinforcing dynamic builds powerful monopolies. Businesses that broker information, make markets, or set standards, are all taking advantage of this dynamic. The implication: the first company to achieve critical mass will often be an outright winner and eliminate competing firms from the marketplace.

As value chains fragment and reconfigure, new opportunities will arise for purely physical businesses. In many businesses today, the efficiency of the physical value chain is compromised for the purpose of delivering information. The new economics of information will create opportunities to rationalize the physical value chain, often leading to businesses whose physically based sources of competitive advantage will be more sustainable.

When a company focuses on different activities, the value proposition underlying its brand identity will change. Because a brand reflects its company's value chain, deconstruction will require new brand strategies.

New branding opportunities will emerge for third parties that neither produce a product nor deliver a primary service. Navigator or agent brands have been around for a long time. The Zagat guide to restaurants and *Consumer Reports* are two obvious examples. The dramatic proliferation of networked markets increases the need for such navigators and other facilitating agents, such as those that guarantee a product's performance or assume risk. Thus there will be many new opportunities to develop brands.

Bargaining power will shift as a result of a radical reduction in the ability to monopolize the control of information. Market power often comes from controlling a choke point in an information channel and extracting tolls from those dependent on the flow of information through it. For example, sellers to retail customers today use their control over the information available to those customers to minimize comparison shopping and maximize cross-selling. But when richness and reach extend to the point where such channels are unnecessary, that game will stop. Any choke point could then be circumvented. Buyers will know their alternatives as well as the seller does. Some new intermediaries – organizers of virtual markets – may even evolve into aggregators of buying power, playing suppliers off against one another for the benefit of the purchasers they represent.

Customers' switching costs will drop, and companies will have to develop new ways of generating customer loyalty. Common standards for exchanging and processing information and the growing number of individuals accessing networks will drastically reduce switching costs. For example, proprietary EDI systems lock companies into supply relationships. But extranets linking companies with their suppliers using the Internet's standard protocols make switching almost costless.

Incumbents could easily become victims of their obsolete physical infrastructures and their own psychology. Assets that traditionally offered competitive advantages and served as barriers to entry will become liabilities. The most vulnerable companies are those currently providing information that could be delivered more effectively and inexpensively electronically – for example, the physical components of sales and distribution systems, such as branches, shops and sales forces. The loss of even a small portion of customers to new distribution channels or the migration of a high-margin product to the electronic domain can throw a business with high fixed costs into a downward spiral.

It may be easy to grasp this point intellectually, but it is much harder for managers to act on its implications. In many businesses, the assets in question are integral to a company's core competence. It is not easy psychologically to withdraw from assets so central to a company's identity. It is not easy strategically to downsize assets that have high fixed costs when so many customers still prefer the current business model. It is not easy financially to cannibalize current profits. And it is certainly not easy to squeeze the profits of distributors to whom one is tied by long-standing customer relationships or by franchise laws.

Newcomers suffer from none of these inhibitions. They are unconstrained by management traditions, organizational structures, customer relationships or fixed assets. Executives must mentally deconstruct their own businesses. If they don't, someone else will.

IMPLEMENTING AN ELECTRONIC COMMERCE STRATEGY

The impact of the Internet is obvious in business-to-consumer transactions: witness the proliferation of Web sites for facilitating sales and services across a broad range of offerings. But the real revolution is happening in business-to-business value chains as companies restructure their operations with trading partners. The Internet has become more than a simple and effective way to exchange e-mail and documents; it is emerging as a critical backbone of commerce. And, it is happening at a faster pace than many thought possible and with which few feel comfortable. Although most managers are cognizant of impending changes, the business landscape is fuzzy and fast-changing. We are navigating in uncharted waters. Vision, governance, resources, infrastructure and alignment are the stepping stones to a successful Web strategy. Building on your current operations, experimenting with new approaches, and creating new business models all play a part.

How should companies develop effective strategies in such a situation? Four interrelated issues are useful in orchestrating conversations about the electronic commerce agenda. Effective strategizing for the electronic commerce business operation requires the management team to consider these issues together, not in isolation. Consistent answers to these five questions indicate an effective strategy for the e-commerce business operation. The relevant questions are:

1. What is your strategic vision for the e-commerce operations?
2. How do you govern the e-commerce operations?
3. How do you allocate key resources for the e-commerce operations?
4. What is your operating infrastructure for the e-commerce operations?
5. Is your management team aligned for the e-commerce agenda?

Strategic Vision for the Electronic Commerce Operations

Articulating a strategic vision for e-commerce business in precise terms is futile; the Internet is evolving at such a dizzying pace that it is nearly impossible to work towards a specific end-state. It is more useful to approach the issue of strategic vision for e-commerce operations as a continuous cycle involving building on current business models and creating future business models through selective experimentation. The aim is to balance refining the current business rules with creating new business rules for the e-commerce agenda. A business strategy that fails to recognize the Internet is destined to fail. Past success is no guarantee of future success, and calendar-driven strategic planning is giving way to strategic experimentation and rapid adaptation. The challenge is to pursue experiments that not only augment current business models, but also create new business models and rules of competition.

Build on Your Current Business Models

For every corporation, the Internet – at a minimum – offers opportunities for reducing operating cost levels and/or enhancing services delivered to customers. Every company should identify ways to leverage the Internet for restructuring the cost base. The Internet exposes the inherent weaknesses of high-cost competitors – whether they are big or small. The cost of Web-based transactions is an order-of-magnitude lower than traditional means of transactions, and is decreasing at a faster rate. The cost of an Internet-based banking transaction is about one-fiftieth of the cost of a human-teller transaction. Companies not pursuing cost-based advantages through the Web will be left behind in the massive sea-change under way.

The e-commerce operations allow for enhanced services. Today, customers expect logistics companies to make their inventory chain visible. Placing content on Web sites is a powerful differentiator. Customers can now get critical information at their convenience. Indeed customers expect timely updates (delivery schedules, product updates, account information), product enhancements (patches for software glitches), rapid resolution of problems not found in the Frequently Asked Questions list through e-mail and remote-monitoring capabilities, as well as personalized interactions through customized navigation paths on company Web sites.

Create New Business Models

The power of the Web lies in the creation of new business models. New business models are those that offer, on a sustained basis, an order-of-magnitude increase in value propositions to customers compared to companies with traditional business models. In doing so, these new models disturb the status quo and create new rules of business. Traditional companies cannot easily match the value propositions offered by these new business models without substantially altering their margin structures. They also find it difficult to go beyond incrementally refining the current rules to create radically different rules. However, an important part of the strategic thinking for every company is to develop scenarios of new business models – even though they might challenge the status quo and cannibalize current revenue and margin streams.

Experiment with Scenarios

Companies need to abandon calendar-driven models of strategy perfected under predictable conditions of the Industrial Age. They should embrace the philosophy of experimentation since the shape of the future business models is not obvious. The strategic challenge is to spearhead experiments to assess probable future states and migrate operations to the desired state. Establishing the vision and rationale for these experiments – including the mandate to proactively cannibalize current business models – is a critical hallmark of leadership for the e-commerce world. Coordinated experimentation is required to develop the building blocks for success in the e-commerce arena.

Selective strategic experimentation is the sine qua non of strategy formation for the e-commerce world. However, a major danger is that these experiments could be seen as standalone tangential projects decoupled from the mainstream operations. It is important that they be seen as building blocks for migrating and transforming the corporation to the e-commerce world. Strategic experiments – when properly conceived and executed – can reveal powerful new ways to succeed in the e-commerce world, where history offers little guidance.

Governing the Electronic Commerce Business

The challenge of how best to govern the e-commerce operations is daunting. Managers must attract and retain key management talent. They are intrigued by the differential market valuation of e-commerce operations and are struggling with the requirement to give adequate management time and attention to the e-commerce strategy and operations. At the same time, they find that the e-commerce operations differ from their traditional operations and find it difficult to reconcile them.

Two major categories of decisions influence the governance mode: operational decisions (production, sourcing, logistics, marketing, and human resources) and financial decisions (investment logic, funding sources and performance criteria). The governance of e-commerce business is best seen as a trade-off between these two categories: how firms differentiate and integrate operational and financial decisions. The basic governance choices can be arrayed along the diagonal as a continuum from subsidiary (spin-off) at one end and seamless integration at the other end.

When faced with the fast-paced changes unleashed by the Internet, managers may benefit from differentiating the operations and decoupling the financial arrangements. This governance mode makes sense under the following conditions:

1. The company is willing to explore new business models apart from the constraints of current operations.
2. The subsidiary or spin-off can be created without being constrained by current technology and legacy operations.
3. The company bestows the subsidiary with the freedom to form alliances, raise capital and attract new talent.

At the other end of the continuum, operational and financial decisions of the e-commerce operations are intermingled with the traditional business domain. In some cases, differentiation of the e-commerce operations may be inappropriate, because it would dilute the level of management attention needed to ensure success. The e-commerce operations are seamlessly integrated as the traditional company morphs to become an e-commerce company. This seamless governance mode makes sense under the following conditions:

1. There is no meaningful way to separate digital and physical operations without creating confusion in the minds of customers.
2. Senior management is committed to embracing the opportunities and challenges of the Internet to redefine the value proposition as well as aggressively react to competitive moves.
3. The entire organization can be mobilized to migrate to the e-commerce world.

Different companies rightfully choose different governance models depending on their views of the centrality of the e-commerce operations. Governing in the e-commerce world depends on a dynamic interplay between the two decisions on this continuum. It can be understood through two transition paths. One is to leverage financial instruments and the discipline of financial markets, whereas the other is to restructure relationships – both internally and with alliances and partnerships.

The financial leverage transition path allows companies to exploit two popular mechanisms: (1) issuing separate stock through an initial public offering (IPO) of the e-commerce operations, and (2) infusion of external venture capital funds. These initiatives reflect an important strategic consideration: the financial markets bring external discipline to governance that is critical under fast-changing conditions. An alternative to the use of tracking stocks is to pursue private placement through venture capitalists. This is an interim position before taking the e-commerce operations public. Indeed, the question of whether to infuse external venture capital to spearhead the e-commerce operations is a key strategic issue facing every company today.

The relationship leverage transition path focuses on organizational arrangements to bring the governance issue into sharper focus. Raising the organizational level of attention to the e-commerce operations is an essential step in crafting a coherent strategy, because multiple conflicting decisions must be coordinated across traditional and e-commerce spaces. The transition to the e-commerce world is not limited to internal restructuring, but also involves alliances and partnerships.

Clearly, these two transition paths are complementary ways to position along the governance continuum. This is not a static decision since a mode of governance is only appropriate for a given context, and the context is fast-changing in the Internet world. Recognizing the complementary roles of both financial and organizational instruments in this e-commerce world is key. Clearly, the governance of the e-commerce operations for every corporation is a critical management issue that could either unleash or constrain the hidden value of core assets in this time of profound transformation.

More than understanding the potential challenges and opportunities posed by the Internet, the biggest stumbling block for an effective strategy will be lack of attention to the governance issue. In Internet time, mistimed and ill-prepared strategic moves can be costly. Pursue financial and relationship leverage paths to continually fine-tune the governance position along the continuum between subsidiary and seamless integration.

Allocating Resources for the Electronic Commerce Business

Closely related to governance is the allocation of resources: how best to assemble and deploy the key resources for succeeding in the e-commerce world. The e-commerce operations is a war for talent. It is a war for three types of resources – human, technological, and financial. It is a war because traditional companies need these critical resources to migrate their operations to the Internet, and new entrants seeking to establish their superiority in the new world also need them. The new Internet startups are attracting young talent away from established industries. Four different but interlinked approaches are required for assembling and deploying the required resources. Effective strategies for the e-commerce world are based on the pattern and timing of resource deployment. The overall logic of resource allocation for the e-commerce world is different from the predictable models of the physical world. Assemble resources from multiple sources and manage them on a dynamic basis.

Placing Strategic Bets

Here, the company commits internal resources to differentiate its e-commerce operations from those of competitors. These resources may be financial, technological or human. The leaders in the traditional world, such as General Electric, NBC, CNN, Pearson, Wal-mart, Citicorp and Kraft Foods, are making significant strategic bets in e-commerce experiments. From a human-resource point of view, the real challenge is to stem the brain drain away from the traditional established companies towards the e-commerce startups. Companies such as General Electric, IBM and British Telecom have lost senior managers to Web startups. What are the key human resources required to run the e-commerce operations, and what changes in incentives are required to make this happen? Articulating these strategic bets is absolutely critical

Strategic bets should be placed on a set of probable opportunities instead of predictable ones. When investments in the e-commerce world are viewed as real options, companies can potentially invest in a broader range of opportunities than otherwise.

Instead of fully funding a smaller set of relatively predictable projects, the aim should be to acquire a set of options with rights to acquire and leverage certain capabilities, should they prove successful.

Learning How to Leverage Your Alliances

Differentiated capabilities can be created through alliances and partnerships. The e-commerce operations are by definition networked and call for assembling complementary strategic capabilities through relationships. More than ever before, it is the pattern of strategic alliances and relationships that indicates strategic strength in the e-commerce world. These alliances are not limited to the players in the physical world linking up with e-commerce players. Even first-generation e-commerce companies, such as Amazon, Priceline and eBay, are steadily evolving and refining their alliance structures to redefine their business models. These alliances will reflect more joint profit sharing rather than fee-for-service. Consulting companies that are building digital businesses will move away from fee-for-service toward equities and risk-reward sharing. This trend will continue at a faster pace.

The e-commerce operations are network-centric. Hence, they call for strategic approaches that are not anchored on resources inside the firm but fundamentally involve resources acquired and leveraged in a network of relationships. They call for strategies to be seen as a portfolio of capabilities that are acquired and deployed through a portfolio of relationships. This is a far cry from strategy seen as primarily resource deployments inside the firm. Positioning and navigating in a complex network of resources is a hallmark of differentiation for companies like Amazon, Yahoo, America Online and Microsoft.

Outsourcing Electronic Commerce Operations and Maintaining Operational Parity

There are areas of the e-commerce operations in which activities like web hosting, back-end processing, and order fulfillment can be conducted outside the firm. More than in the traditional world, e-commerce operations (by virtue of their networked infrastructure) allow for complementary players to be easily linked. Companies increasingly find it easier to rely on standard services from established players like IBM, Hewlett-Packard, Oracle, Microsoft, EDS and AT&T so that they can build their operations on a robust and stable platform. Given the rate of change in technology and the impressive cost-performance shifts, it is more important to rely on best-in-class providers rather than create these operations inside the company.

Whether or not you outsource, your information technology support operations must achieve competitive parity. Resources should be allocated on the basis of predictable models and supported by techniques such as activity-based costing. The aim is to ruthlessly achieve the lowest operating costs for the required level of functionality, as well as to evaluate possible risks and rewards of outsourcing.

Setting up the Operating Infrastructure for the Electronic Commerce Business

The next major requirement is to design the operational infrastructure. It is important to understand the characteristics of the infrastructure that provide value for customers – the features that draw customers to the e-commerce world and encourage them to continue to use the Internet as a primary way of using products and services. Digital infrastructure should be designed and deployed to enhance customer value propositions. Design the infrastructure so that e-commerce operations make it easier for customers to do business without sacrificing customer trust about reliability, security and privacy. Straddle physical and digital spaces with relevant linkages to partners and alliances to offer a seamless and effective way for conducting the business. It is useful to look at the operating infrastructure as four building blocks that reflect an integrated physical-digital platform.

Attaining Superior Functionality

Do customers find their online experience supported by the appropriate functionality? Better quality images, audio clips, and 3-D rendering have enhanced the power of the Web to be realistic. As technology evolves, we will see far greater functionality – especially as wireless application protocols (WAPs) become commonplace and wireless devices like cellular telephones and personal digital assistants (PDAs) are connected to the Internet. Changing functionality will make e-commerce operations appealing to a broad range of companies and customers.

Offering Personalized Interactions

Can we make each customer feel unique on the Internet? The appeal of the Internet lies in its personalization potential. Customers want to be connected to other customers and appreciate personal business-to-customer linkages. The challenge is to encourage each visitor to establish a Web-based personal identity without invading privacy. Amazon.com shot into prominence early with its personalized recommendations. Now, many consumer sites incorporate personalization of some kind.

Streamlining Transactions

The power of the infrastructure lies in its simplicity and efficiency. Increasingly, the winners will be differentiated by their ability to execute streamlined transactions. Amazon pioneered and patented one-click settings – an important differentiator in its bid to establish supremacy. Dell allowed its customers to see the status of their custom-built machine at every stage of the cycle. Streamlined operations require a reliable infrastructure. Reliability plays a key role in enhancing customer confidence. As more devices connect to the Internet and as more functionality is processed through the Internet, reliability will emerge as a major catalyst for Internet-based business and a key differentiator for individual companies.

Ensuring Privacy

The idea behind pragmatic privacy is to convince customers that their privacy will be safeguarded and used only for the purpose of delivering superior value to them. Privacy emerges as a major inhibitor because customers are still not comfortable with electronic transactions. Credit-card companies have played an important role in offering the same level of protection on the Web as in the physical space, and the browser software companies (Microsoft, Netscape) have incorporated critical safety features into their latest software. Security is more about consumer perception than technical features or products per se. Privacy is closely related to security. Customers become concerned about privacy on the Internet, due in part to the proliferation of software cookies that help Web sites learn about visitors. These products are supplied by DoubleClick[1] and Firefly Passport[2]. Being forthright with customers about privacy will go a long way in enhancing the use of the Internet.

Aligning the Management Team for the Electronic Commerce Agenda

Who leads the corporation to the e-commerce world? Is this an opportunity for the senior information technology manager to earn the right to become a member of top management? Or is it the marketing manager who articulates how the customer value propositions can be redefined? Articulating the roles of key members of the management team is central in shaping the strategy of the e-commerce operations. Many companies treat their e-commerce operations as a project. Some see this as an extension of technology-led business initiatives. The e-commerce operations require a pattern of leadership alignment that differs greatly from other business transformation activities. The e-commerce world is about value creation. It involves strategic challenges of business creation, important governance issues of organizational structure, new avenues of financing, and changes in operating infrastructure, external relationships, and patterns of resource deployment.

It is crucial to emphasize the importance of senior management alignment in mobilizing the organization to recognize and respond to the e-commerce world. If the management team is not in sync, it is easy for the e-commerce agenda to be hijacked by one or two members reflecting a partisan, parochial perspective. Every company needs a champion to get started, but it needs more than one champion to succeed. It is encouraging to see many leading companies already embracing the e-commerce world. It is more than merely grafting the Web as part of business strategy. It is a serious challenge with profound opportunities and threats to the status quo.

Succeeding in the Electronic Commerce World

New companies with an Internet focus have grabbed the headlines. Employees and stockholders of these startups have reaped the benefits of new wealth. As new devices emerge and become part of the critical backbone for e-commerce applications,

---

[1] http://www.doubleclick.com
[2] http://www.firefly.net

every company will need to develop a strategy for the e-commerce world. Ultimately, business strategy will be e-commerce strategy.

We are in the midst of major shifts. Traditional logic, so fundamental to the industrial revolution, is challenged every day by the possibilities of the e-commerce world. Well-understood sources of value creation through tangible, physical assets are being replaced by newfound sources through digital assets and networks of relationships. Every market – from agriculture to automobiles to financial services, entertainment and healthcare – is affected by interactive technology. New entrants are crafting powerful new business models and rewriting the rules of competition. Established companies urgently need to embrace the e-commerce agenda; failing this, they will be left behind. They need to blend their traditional and e-commerce operations while confronting the challenge of brain drain as their top talent jumps ship for other e-commerce operations. The game is far from over, and we will see powerful transformations as companies embrace the Internet and craft innovative strategies that successfully blend physical and digital infrastructures. It is up to managers to take the necessary actions to align their visions to the e-commerce world. While it is too early to declare the leading corporations of the Industrial Age to be the dinosaurs of the digital era, clearly they face daunting challenges.

STRATEGIES FOR STARTING E-BUSINESSES

Established companies stand the best chance of getting a jump on e-commerce if they look outside their ranks – for both venture capital and the scaling-up experience of incubators and professional-services firms. In fast venturing, innovating companies tap into the specific knowledge and experience of equity partners (usually venture capitalists or banks) and operational partners (sometimes incubators, sometimes professional-services firms, such as consulting companies, systems integrators and Web portals) to get a project to market and scaled up fast.

Speed is a widely acknowledged necessity in the Internet economy, but many current approaches to starting a new venture are just not rapid enough. Several strategic thinkers believe that to create the novel products and services mandated by the Internet economy, companies should establish pockets of creative thinking under their own aegis and launch new ventures from the inside out. Although internal venturing might be feasible in a few cases, the strategy is too difficult and too slow for most companies. By the time an organization incorporates Silicon Valley into its traditional structure and is ready to reap the benefits of a fluid exchange of ideas, capital and talent, the Internet economy has moved on.

Today most companies are likely to confront competitor innovations that undermine their area of competence. Disruptive technologies may change the definition of the company's products, customers, channels and competitors. Responding to disruptive innovations often requires entirely new business models, skills and systems. And if the company wants to fight back by establishing a presence on the Internet with its own status-quo-disrupting idea, it can be sure that the same innovation already figures in the dreams of at least 10 potential competitors.

Electronic commerce forces innovation to move at lightning speed. Fast venturing can be considered as taking three to six months from idea to launch of an operating venture. New ventures such as goodhome.com, Epinions.com and Accompany.com, which established substantial market positions in just twelve weeks, leave old models of business planning, financing and implementation in the dust. Of the top ten brands on the Internet, nine were first movers, and although being first to market may not guarantee success, being late is costly. Moreover, today's information products attract customers, and the existence of customers attracts more customers, so companies benefit from positive network effects. Sustaining first-mover advantages requires continuous innovation and operations that ramp up quickly to meet customer expectations. Fast-venturing partners can make that happen.

The secret of fast venturing lies in its ability to expand the knowledge and capabilities of internal resources by drawing on the experience of outsiders. Standard new-venture approaches use outside financing expertise only: fast venturing also calls on partners for operational expertise. So how does it work? First, the entrepreneur or traditional company doing the venturing sets up a distinct equity structure for the new company; next, it finances the venture with equity participation from venture capitalists or other financial partners; and finally, it plugs the new venture into a network of operational partners who help build the business quickly by designing and implementing strategies and organizational processes and systems to access markets at scale. A likely scenario is that traditional brick-and-mortar companies will increasingly execute their dot-com strategies through fast venturing and dot-com startups will increasingly tap incubators or venture networks.

Fast venturing is a promising new model for launching new ventures. Along with strategic investments and internal venturing, it should be part of the arsenal of strategies used to achieve growth. Managers are best off starting with a clean sheet – working to bring the best assets, ideas, and resources of the Internet economy to unlock the value of existing assets through partnership and alignment with others in the company's emerging business environment. To succeed in the Internet economy, a dynamic environment of fast innovation and value creation, there is no time to lose. Companies should fast venture and partner to propel their new business faster and farther.

Internal Corporate Venturing and Investment

Internal corporate ventures are semi-autonomous structures set up by companies wishing to enter areas where the company's typical processes for introducing new products do not apply. Such initiatives focus of creating new businesses and entering new markets to diversify and grow. Internal corporate venture returns look much less secure than those of more independent ventures. Corporate ventures require a longer nurturing period before commercialization and take nearly twice as long to reap a profit compared to entrepreneurial start-ups.

Getting the green light for an internal venture typically requires approval cycles that sacrifice swiftness for a certainty rarely attainable in today's fast-moving markets. Human-resource allocation, annual budgeting, and political power struggles all conspire to limit a company's ability to innovate. Traditional companies are good at value creation and delivery systems for current customers and markets. They find it difficult, however, to create new systems to address the need of uncertain and small markets. Companies have also found it hard to establish the balance between managerial autonomy and financial control in internal corporate ventures. Internal corporate ventures risk devoting too many resources for uncertain outcomes. Successful intrapreneuring companies – that is, companies that grow internally through radical innovation of products or business models – are few and far between. As difficult as it is to create true innovation, it is harder still for the innovator in an established company to internally venture in the dot-com space at the speed of industry-changing new entrants.

Strategic investments provide another way for companies to participate in the opportunities created by a disruptive innovation. Many traditional companies have a venture-capital arm. Like internal corporate venturing, they have had mixed success. Unlike traditional venture capital funds, many of these funds have a broader strategic objective than just maximizing returns – say, expanding the company's markets. Furthermore, salary caps of fund managers in traditional companies make it difficult to acquire the best talent except in companies with substantial growth.

The Fast-Venturing Model

Fast venturing involves a network of partners, each contributing different skills and specialized resources to the three stages of the fast-venture process: illumination, investigation and implementation. The strategy of fast venturing – the quick migration from illumination to investigation to implementation – transforms the promise of an e-business into the reality of a sustainable operation. And the partnership can extend beyond the liquidity event. Innovators and equity partners often keep working together to increase the value of their investments: innovators and operational partners may collaborate on further growth objectives post-initial public offering.

Illumination

At the core of a new venture is an idea that creates a compelling value proposition. Playing a critical role in the Internet economy are venture capitalists acting as equity partners. The venture capitalists have fine-tuned their ability to winnow ideas, while identifying and refining the business models most likely to succeed. Venture capitalists can provide guidance for developing a business concept, helping managers integrate related innovations and selecting the right managers for the new venture. Venture capitalist partners can provide not only capital, but ideas and access to skilled personnel to support fast venturing.

Operational partners, whether they are professional-services firms or Web portals such as VerticalNet and Lycos, Excite or Yahoo are also becoming critical at this stage of fast venturing because they aggregate many buyers. Operational partners can provide deep expertise about potential channels, customers, and markets. Because venturing in the Internet economy is increasingly critical for companies' growth, operational partners, such as Bain & Co, Andersen Consulting and McKinsey & Co., have also created venture capital funds to serve as equity partners. Working together, equity partners and operational partners evaluate the feasibility of new business models and markets, suggest other partners, and provide financing to mitigate business-model and financial risks.

During the illumination stage, the innovators play the following roles:
- Develop concept and ideas.

During the illumination stage, the equity partners play the following roles:
- Filter ideas.
- Refine ideas.

During the illumination stage, the operational partners play the following roles:
- Refine ideas.
- Develop new business models.

Investigation

Investigation, the testing-and-refinement stage, is critical but increasingly compressed as ventures move ever more swiftly from illumination to implementation. Equity and operational partners are helpful. They have the experience and the industry contacts to develop, tailor and test new business models. They can help create action plans to manage proof-of-concept activities – quick market tests to see if the product will fly. Consulting firms with systems-integration and development expertise are especially well prepared to design and test prototypes of business models – a key capability now that pilot testing is growing more and more critical to new ventures. Entrepreneurs rarely get the business model correct on the first pass, and pilot testing lets them refine their offerings and better match customer needs. Incubators dedicated to e-businesses also do pilot testing of new concepts.

In the refinement phase, professional-services firms develop sales and marketing plans. Professional-services firms with broad reach can promote new ideas across domestic industries; those with global reach can facilitate business development in international markets. Outsourcing those functions to operational partners reduces the time to market and frees the always short-handed entrepreneurial team to focus on refining the product, addressing customer needs, competitive responses and financing, and creating the organization.

Finding talented people to build the company is also critical. With the Internet economy expanding rapidly, the people and skills needed to lead the transition to a full-scale operation are in ever-shorter supply. Fast-venture partners can use their vast networks of contacts to locate people with the attitude, values and work ethic necessary to build a business from scratch. For established companies looking internally for fast-venturing talent, the objectivity of outside partners is a plus. Outside partners' contacts are also helpful in finding deeper functional or industry talent to lend credibility and capability.

During the investigation stage, the innovators play the following roles:
- Identify leadership team.
- Acquire critical know-how.
- Develop proof of concept.
- Secure investment for growth.

During the investigation stage, the equity partners play the following roles:
- Secure capital.
- Offer advice and network.
- Evaluate proof of concept.
- Approve leadership team.

During the investigation stage, the operational partners play the following roles:

- Develop global prototype.
- Provide talent (financial, technical, legal, strategy, operations).
- Share best practices and industry knowledge.
- Provide access to industry partners.
- Promote concept across industries.

Implementation

The challenges of executing strategies and rapidly scaling up can sink a new venture. Poor execution drives customers away and swiftly destroys the brand image. A once-promising business model becomes someone else's successful implementation. Established professional-service firms – experienced with supply-and-demand management, procurement, distribution and fulfillment, customer-relationship management, enterprise systems, and organizational and change management – can help companies maintain quality during the scale-up phase.

A critical capability that requires fast scaling is order fulfillment. Indeed, consistently reliable order fulfillment, a major source of competitive advantage among retailers, remains one of the most vexing challenges facing e-businesses. Professional-services firms help companies develop the necessary building blocks. They help them decide, for example, where to put warehouses, how to design warehouse processes, how to connect to logistics providers such as FedEx or UPS and how to handle fulfillment. They can design and set up a network of third-party firms to handle such links of the value chain as distribution or customer service. The outsourcing arrangements free new-venture leadership teams to focus on core competencies.

During the implementation stage, the innovators play the following roles:
- Provide stewardship.
- Establish marketplace presence.
- Focus on marketing and sales.

During the implementation stage, the equity partners play the following roles:
- Reduce involvement post liquidity event (initial public offering or acquisition).

During the implementation stage, the operational partners play the following roles:
- Provide global breadth and depth of talent and experience.
- Provide services including:
  - E-fulfillment and supply-chain management
  - Organizational design and change management
  - Customer-relationship management
  - Human resources.

Incubators in Action

Commercial e-business incubators have taken wing. Corporations (such as Panasonic and IBM), consulting firms (such as Anderson Consulting, Bain & Co. and McKinsey & Co.) and venture capitalists (such as Softbank) have developed what are sometimes called accelerators, launch centers, or incubators. Incubators offer a venture more managerial attention than most venture capitalists. Incubators generally take from

5% to 50% of equity ownership. The e-commerce ideas that an incubator helps develop may earn it handsome returns after a successful initial public offering. Incubators relieve innovators of administrative drag, which absorbs an estimated 40% of the entrepreneur's time, and they fast-cycle business concepts to the marketplace.

How do incubators differentiate themselves? Superficially, incubators offer what appears to be a fairly uniform value proposition to entrepreneurial start-ups and incumbents: seed capital, office infrastructure, business insight, and access to markets and partners. All incubators strive to take months off the new-venture-creation process. Yet incubators differ – sometime substantially – on details, including management control, monthly fees, specialization, aggregation of proffered services, depth and breadth of functional expertise, developmental stage at which the incubator prefers to become involved, length of stay and the funding and ownership structure.

Fast Venturing in Practice

There's no one-size-fits-all road map to launching a fast-venture relationship, nor is there an established protocol for selecting the network of partners. Moreover, choosing a lead partner will depend on two factors: existing informal relationships and reputations and the innovator's stage of business development. On one hand, a start-up with an existing management team and a wholly developed concept might be served best by initially partnering with an operational player to develop operational capabilities and scaling. On the other hand, an incubator as lead partner works well for early-stage start-ups, when the proof of concept and proof of management are evolving. In addition to speed to market, innovators seek six key benefits from the fast-venturing arrangement:

- Refinement of strategic intent
- Access to specialty skills
- Access to markets and contacts
- Access to talent
- A focusing of managerial attention
- Building scaled, operational capabilities

Why Should Traditional Companies Fast Venture?

Why should traditional companies use equity and operational partners when starting a new venture? The answer lies in the need for speed in the Internet economy. Traditional strategies such as internal corporate venturing show a mixed track record and are often too slow to capitalize on innovations. Today, we find both start-up and incumbent innovators are increasingly willing to relinquish some degree of operational and financial control to get to markets and scale up quickly.

Fast venturing realizes speed by having fewer organizational constraints than traditional internal corporate ventures and through access to the new concepts, capital, capabilities and channels that partners provide. By establishing a separate equity structure and organization, fast venturing allows an initiative to be liberated from the company's traditional hierarchy and rules, which often restrict the use of internal or external resources. Left alone to make decisions, new-venture teams are motivated by financial gain and the opportunity for personal satisfaction, rather than by career advancement or company politics; they answer only to market forces and their boards. Internal corporate initiatives often suffer because managers have little personal stake in the outcome. Fast venturing is different. Nothing so concentrates a manager's mind as the prospect of an initial public offering in three months. Beyond execution capabilities, operational partners provide access to channels and customers. Partner access to channels and customers is helpful to start-ups as well.

When Should Traditional Companies Fast Venture?

In deciding whether to fast venture, a company must first consider whether the innovation propelling the new venture is a sustaining or disruptive one – and how much organizational change in scale and scope it will require. If disruptive, the scale and scope of change will probably be substantial. The company will need to access new customer segments through new channels – with new products implemented through new capabilities. Senior managers will have to decide if the company has the resources of capital and capabilities to support the scaling of the new venture or if it needs to access such resources through equity and operational partners. They must also critically evaluate their organization's track record of launching new products and services and must decide to what extent their company's market position, capabilities, and organizational policies and culture will support alternative venturing strategies.

If the innovation is primarily a sustaining innovation with limited requirements for organizational change, the company may be able to realize value through internal development without having to share equity with venture capitalists and other investors. Alternatively, if the expected scale and scope of changes are large and the company has a poor track record of realizing value from innovations through internal corporate venturing, a fast-venturing partnership may be advisable.

Managers in traditional companies are being torn in two directions today. They must maintain and improve the performance of existing businesses while simultaneously launching entirely new ventures for growth. It is difficult to allocate sufficient attention to both tasks. In order to be responsive to changing competitors and markets, a separate organization with a management team focused on the new venture is likely to increase chances of success. Furthermore, operational and equity partners provide expanded levels of the attention resources needed in different stages of growth. As the scale and scope of change increase, companies are compelled to adopt a fast-venture strategy.

Questions to Test Your New-Venture Orientation

The more you answer no to these questions, the more you need outside partners.

Innovation

- Has your business unit launched more products and services than the industry average?
- Is the time to market of a new idea less than 12 months?

Capital

- Does your company have a fund to support new ventures?
- Can investments over $1 million skip the annual financial budgeting process?
- Can financing of new initiatives bypass traditional annual budgets?

Talent

- Do you have the skills and expertise within your organization to develop an e-business?
- Are the best and brightest employees available to work on a new venture?
- Does your company share rewards with employees?
- Would the company be willing to share the wealth generated from an e-business with its creators and developers?

Market Position

- Are you a dominant market leader in your competitive segment?
- Are shareholder expectations currently being met? Is the company under scrutiny?

Organization and Culture

- Are long-range strategic and business plans standard operating procedure?
- Are new ideas embraced within the organization?
- Does the organization have room for failure? Are leaders pummeled for market failure?
- Do you have fewer than four layers from top to bottom in your organization?

How Should Traditional Companies Fast Venture?

Fast venturing is a promising new model, but it is not without risk. Venture capitalists, professional-services firms and traditional businesses are only beginning to learn how to do fast venturing, and mistakes are inevitable. Five sets of decisions are critical to fast-venturing success.

Defining the Critical Requirements

At the outset of a new venture, one innovator's needs will differ from another's. Innovators must determine the critical constraints to their aspirations: access to ideas, capital, capabilities or customers. They must then consider what lead partner would be most appropriate in helping them strengthen their areas of weakness.

Selecting Partners and Committing to Fast Venturing

Next, innovators must select the lead partner who will help them launch their new ventures. They need to select equity and operational partners whose networks can create the greatest value and who have track records that demonstrate success with speed. Track records, however, are not sufficient. To avoid downstream problems, careful diligence about culture is essential. In addition, both innovators and partners must demonstrate commitment to fast venturing by establishing a separate equity structure with an option for an initial public offering. Without this equity structure, it is highly unlikely that top-tier venture capitalists or other equity partners will participate. If innovators insist on restrictive covenants or limitations on new alliances, they are likely to undermine the interest of the better equity partners. Traditional company innovators must be ready to accept that the new venture can cannibalize the traditional company offerings and must be committed to allowing the new venture to compete fiercely, fairly, and with agility in the marketplace.

Clarifying Roles, Responsibilities, and Incentives

Perhaps the most critical set of decisions that will shape the operation of the new venture relates to aligning the goals of venture partners and structuring the roles, responsibilities, and organization of the fast venture. Stock options are vital for attracting and retaining talent and for ensuring employee commitment to the success of the new venture. An established company that wants to align the interests of its internal staff with the new venture can use stock options for that purpose as well.

A new venture that is sponsored by a traditional company must have substantial autonomy. Clarity about how the roles of people in the new venture differ from the roles of people in the traditional company is essential for speed. Defining the differing roles and responsibilities of managers and partners is especially critical. Moreover, for a fast venture to be truly fast, it must have commitment from executives or board members with key decision-making and resource-allocation authority.

Selecting Strong, Independent Leadership

For any new venture, strong, independent leadership is key to developing the distinctive culture and operations required for speed to market.

Making Optimum Use of Partners at Every Stage

New ventures are uncertain, and the business models that succeed may not be the ones defined at the outset of the fast venture. To adapt to changing markets and effectively realize value from partnerships with equity and operational partners, the new-venture management should put in place processes to leverage partner assets at each stage: illumination, investigation and implementation. Building explicit processes to involve partners in each stage of the fast venture is important for realizing the value of the partnership.

The Emergence of Incubators and Venture Networks

Fast venturing is rewriting the rules of competition for professional-services firms and providers of venture capital. Today, capital is hardly a constraint for creating new Internet businesses, and rivalry among venture-capital firms in increasingly intense. The demand for winning ideas and the capacity to implement a new business venture at speed are today's constraints. For professional-services firms, value and growth in the Internet economy is migrating away from traditional clients toward new ventures. Both venture-capital firms and professional-services firms are investing in fast venturing and are providing more specialized infrastructures. Specifically, they are investing in incubators and venture networks – one-stop shops for launching or scaling up new ventures and for accessing critical resources, whether new concepts, capital, capabilities or channels to customers.

Incubators can provide multiple ventures with shared infrastructure and support, strategic guidance and shared services (legal advice, accounting, graphic design, advertising and public relations) as well as office space at a common location. Some offer systems capabilities and organizational-development assistance. In gathering innovators under one roof, they give members an inspiring setting and the sustaining energy of being around like-minded people exuding creativity, motivation and purpose. The resulting social capital leads to sharing of approaches, models, tactics, competitive information, contacts, and ways to avoid mis-steps. The learning accelerates progress. A 1999 National Business Incubator Association study found that 87% of U.S. incubator graduates remain viable after three years – as contrasted with most new businesses, which have an overall success rate of 20%.

Idealab! emerged early to support e-commerce initiatives as both incubator and venture capitalist. The need for speed to market has prompted traditional venture-capital firms to create incubators too. Softbank, for instance, created the HotBank incubator. Management consultants and traditional corporations are forming incubators as well. Bain & Co. opened its London-based BainLab in late 1999 to support three start-ups and one established company moving into e-commerce. McKinsey and Scient have created extra-fast accelerators and Andersen Consulting has created dot-com launch centers.

But incubators by themselves are unlikely to be sufficient in the race to scale up fast. Both venture capitalists and professional-services firms are recognizing the need to bring a broader array of resources to new ventures, such as access to channels and customers, and technologies and services beyond those available in the incubator (such as specialized tools for customer-relationship management). Leading firms are looking at the relationships they have with business-to-business channels and business-to-customer portals, and then organizing their contacts into venture networks that can give new ventures a one-stop shop.

The CMGI model typifies a new-venture network. The firms in which CMGI has holdings are encouraged to trade ideas and services with one another. CMGI Solutions, for example, can help launch e-businesses; CMGI@Ventures provides venture capital; and nearly 60 other CMGI companies support fast venturing with content, channels to customers, technology assistance, or business-to-business and business-to-customer e-commerce capabilities. Nearly every company in the CMGI portfolio has multiple strategic relationships with other companies in that portfolio.

Major consulting firms are not standing still either. In the business-to-business marketplace, where relationship selling is more prevalent, they are leveraging their extensive relationships to create their own value networks. Similarly, companies such as Microsoft and Cisco are poised to develop their extensive value networks into powerful venture networks.

Such networks can and do propel new ventures to market at scale and speed, but they face certain risks. Holding companies such as CMGI confront the regulatory risk of being classified as mutual funds. Or networks may run the risk that expansion will cause member companies to lose focus and work at cross purposes. Nevertheless, smaller venture-capital firms investing in Internet businesses will have to partner with others or scale up to provide the full array of resources in venture networks.

Both full-service incubators and emerging venture networks are increasingly formalizing the processes of fast venturing. In the future, traditional company managers and entrepreneurs will be tapping into such networks more than ever. But they will have to carefully evaluate and select partners. Some venture networks will tightly couple capital, channels, capabilities and concepts into a one-size-fits-all process. Others will be more flexible and will feature an equity and operational partner that has relationships with multiple alternative partners. As incubators and venture networks proliferate, Internet innovators will no longer have to hatch companies in garages. Nor will traditional companies have to undertake new ventures through internal corporate ventures that struggle with internal politics. Innovators that plug into fast-venture networks will gain the best access to ideas, capital, channels, and execution capabilities and will most likely win the lion's share of new value creation in the Internet economy.

Building A Company On Internet Time

Start-ups everywhere have a common problem: How do you scale a company faster than companies have ever scaled before? The power and potential of the Internet have led to incredible opportunities to create companies. However, the biggest challenge is to build an organization that can match the opportunity. Far too many start-ups crash and burn, despite a promising start.

There are four key principles which start-ups can apply:

- Create a compelling living vision of products, technologies, and markets that is tightly linked to action.
- Hire and acquire managerial experience, in addition to technical expertise.
- Build the internal resources for a big company, while organizing like a small one.
- Build external relationships to compensate for limited internal resources.

By developing a clear roadmap that is linked to products, the organization will be able to navigate the uncertainty that plagues many entrepreneurs. By hiring and acquiring experience, the organization can be kept aligned. By pushing systems one step ahead of needs, the organization can be kept under control. Finally, by heavily leveraging external resources, the organization can take full advantage of almost everything the Internet has to offer.

Principle 1: Create a Compelling, Living Vision of Products, Technologies and Markets That Is Tightly Linked to Action

Most great companies start with a very simple, powerful vision of their industries and the potential for their firms.Yet no one can have perfect foresight in their visions of the world. Mistakes are made all the time. The key question is whether the people and the organization can capitalize on the right observations and make quick adjustments when managers discover that they are on the wrong path.

Principle 2: Hire and Acquire Managerial Experience, in Addition to Technical Expertise

Start-ups are generally alive with young, hungry entrepreneurs who drive their companies to the market through sheer willpower, youthful energy and new, creative ideas. That youthfulness also helps to explain why most start-ups fail: exuberance can only get you so far. To mitigate the risk of failure, organizations can take the following steps:

- *Hire People Who Can Hit the Ground Running.* Hiring aggressive self-starters with industry experience will allow the company to save on training and orientation.
- *Acquire the Talent, Expertise and Experience You Cannot Hire.*
- *Experience is a Double-Edged Sword.* Deep experience in a young company has a darker side. For one thing, the people who are great for scaling the organization are not always the right people to grow a successful, ongoing venture. If you hire experienced, senior people into a company and they all have large egos, you have got to do something to get those egos to work together and to function together. When the company is small enough, it is okay because cooperation isn't going to be helpful anyway. However, later on, it will be necessary to get the executive group to work together as a team.

Principle 3: Build the Internal Resources for a Big Company, While Organizing Like a Small One

Most start-up companies scale their systems to meet their current needs. In fact, they usually allow their systems to lag behind their growth. One of the biggest traps for an entrepreneur is to build an organizational structure in advance of sales, profits, and stable cash flow. Far too often, wildly optimistic sales projections do not materialize, the company gets overextended, and everything comes to a crashing halt. So most companies build systems as they need them and replace those systems as they grow. However, this approach can be dangerous when you are competing on Internet time. When you grow at 50 percent per year, you may be able to adapt your systems; when you are growing at 50 percent per quarter, you can grow so fast that you are out of touch.

The trick is to know when to bring on the bureaucrats. There is a stage in a company's life where it's fine to be loosely controlled. There's another stage where you have to get more and more serious. What you don't want to do is get too serious too soon. That stifles a lot of things.

Manage growth through decentralization and small teams. Another challenge is maintaining the intensity, innovation and flexibility of a small start-up, while simultaneously acting like a billion-dollar company. The solution is to continuously decentralize, breaking the structure into smaller and smaller teams, with some of them in a matrix with functional groups. The idea is to operate like a big company, with big-company control systems, but maintain flexibility and creativity as the organization scales by creating lots of small teams.

Principle 4: Build External Relationships to Compensate for Limited Internal Resources

It is difficult to keep up with the demands of Internet time without outside help. Ultimate success depends critically upon a wide variety of external resources and relationships. It is essential to exploit the Internet and other external resources to create a virtual workforce – people outside the organization who are working on the company's behalf. This can be achieved in the following ways:

- *Create a Virtual Marketing Organization.* The biggest problem for any firm, especially a firm initially targeting a consumer market, is how to get recognized. You can create a virtual marketing organization by leveraging external resources, namely, the press and the Web.
- *Create a Virtual Development Organization.* Many organizations post a beta version of their software on the Internet. By downloading the beta version, trying it out, and filing their complaints, customers serve, sometimes unwittingly, as a virtual quality assurance team.
- *Create a Virtual Financing Organization.* Start-ups can finance all their acquisitions with stock. The problem with a virtual finance department is that management sometimes feels like it is playing with other people's money, rather than its own.
- *Leverage Partners to Build a Platform.*

Lessons Learned

When scaling a company on Internet time, don't depend on the revolution coming tomorrow. Overestimating the pace of change is the greatest risk for visionary companies. Revolutions do not happen overnight in information technology, even when the technology is the Internet. Early adopters become excited by new technologies and often assume that the rest of the world will follow their lead. There are roughly 500 million operating personal computers in the world today, and it takes a long time to change the behavior of 500 million users.

The last two revolutions in information technology are good examples. We had a revolution in the mainframe segment when IBM introduced the System 360 in the 1960s. That revolution took more than two decades to unfold. Steve Jobs started the personal computer revolution in 1977. This revolution took over a decade and a half to bring about fundamental changes in user behavior. Not until the late 1980s did minicomputer and mainframe customers and vendors begin to feel the heat. The Internet revolution is undoubtedly moving much faster than any previous revolution, but it will probably be five to ten years before the impact diffuses more fully to the mass market. If you believe the revolution is coming tomorrow, you can fall into several traps. One trap is that you create a strategy to take all products into all markets. A second trap of prematurely proclaiming the revolution is to do rocket science to accelerate solutions and solve hard technical problems.

Scaling a company on Internet time demands good strategic planning. Start-ups inevitably have to compete with more mature companies with more systematic approaches to strategy. No matter how fast a company is scaling its operations, it usually needs to build partnerships that are a two-way street. All too often, companies focus on what partners can do in the short term, instead of building relationships that will generate greater value over time.

Chapter 10

Electronic Commerce and Public Policy

Ever since the Internet burst into the public realm, it has held aloft the promise of a commercial revolution. The promise is of a radical new world of business – a friction-free arena where millions of buyers and sellers complete their transactions cheaply, instantaneously and anonymously. Cut free from layers of middlemen, companies will be able to sell their products directly to their customers; consumers will be able to customize products, interact with the companies that supply them, and conduct business from the comfort of their own homes. By bringing companies and customers together, the Internet thus promises to widen markets, increase efficiencies and lower costs. Those are radical promises, and on their strength, thousands of companies have joined a massive scramble to cyberspace.

For many of those companies, however, the Internet has yet to deliver on its promises. Although doing business in cyberspace may be novel and exhilarating, it can also be frustrating, confusing, and even unprofitable. Whereas for some companies online commerce is a natural outgrowth of their business, for others – particularly in information-intensive industries such as software, publishing and financial services – moving into cyberspace is a difficult endeavor. The problems these companies face have little to do with a lack of technology or imagination. They stem instead from a lack of rules. Why, in the midst of such a critical transformation should managers pause to consider anything as mundane as rules? The answer is that rules are critical to commerce. Without the order that rules create, business cannot be conducted.

At the moment, there are few rules in cyberspace. The legal status of electronic copyright is still vague, as are the legal and practical issues surrounding online exchange and "electronic cash". There is also limited authority to enforce rules on the Internet and little capacity to punish those who violate the norms of online conduct. Although these problems have been well documented, they persist nevertheless. And until they are solved, cyberspace will remain a land of opportunities, but also one of tremendous risks. This simply means that companies need to think carefully before making any headlong leaps into cyberspace. Rather than just posting pages on the Web, for instance, companies may want to move more selectively, clustering themselves into online communities where rules prevail and commerce can proceed.

These sorts of online communities will create a very different form of electronic commerce from the one envisioned today by many Internet proponents. The communities will not be open to all, they will increasingly charge customers for their services, and they will not permit information to flow across seamless borders. They will change the current spirit of the Internet and bring order and management to the Internet's unruly tangle. By writing the rules for commercial transactions, online communities will also shift the balance of power between business and government in favor of business. That evolution will occur not because of the power of particular companies, or because business is opposed by nature to an open Internet or a free flow of information. Rather, commerce will move toward online communities simply because companies need a basic infrastructure of rules to survive.

This vision of electronic commerce is a less radical one than that embraced by many Internet proponents. But it takes into account the realities facing most companies today. The commercial promise of the Internet is still vast, but it does not lie in the unmanaged reaches of cyberspace. Nor does it come solely from the Internet's technical ability to facilitate transactions and reduce costs. Instead, the promise lies in the ability of companies to form well-defined communities that will protect their property and promote their own interests. It lies in the potential of other companies to construct these communities, to intermediate their commerce, and to guard their members. The commercial promise of the Internet, in short, requires rules for its fulfillment. And the companies that stand to reap the greatest profits in cyberspace are the pioneers who will write, support and enforce the new rules of electronic commerce.

THE RULES OF EXCHANGE

When the Internet was first developed in the 1960s, it was governed by clear codes of conduct and working norms of behavior. Developed by a community of like-minded scientists, the rules were rarely written down or explicit, but they did not have to be, because surfers on the Internet could easily observe them. Despite its outward image as an untamed realm of hackers, the early Internet was in fact a rule-bound, orderly community. The rules, however, evolved to serve the interests of a particular community – researchers in academia and in the U.S. Department of Defense, who had no desire to profit from their online activities. For roughly 20 years, that community flourished. But in the early 1990s, the community's rules and values were suddenly attacked by hordes of new users who had scrambled online.

The entrance of the new users did more than just increase the sheer number of people connected to the Internet; it led to a fundamental change in the Internet's culture. Arriving online largely through commercial services and Internet access providers, these new users were riding a wave of privatization that began with the emergence of commercial service providers in 1989 and continued when the Internet was officially opened to commercial ventures in 1990. The newcomers had little interest in the research questions that had previously bound Internet users together. They were also largely unfamiliar with many of the Internet's protocols. Cyberspace for the newcomers was simply an adventure – an opportunity to meet people, gather information, and perhaps recreate some sense of small-town intimacy and immediacy. But many newcomers also came to cyberspace for profit, to explore the potential of the Internet, and to stake a claim in a technology that promised to revolutionize the nature of transactions. As a result, the Internet's new business district – the dot com domain – quickly swelled to become the largest sector on the Internet.

Dramatic levels of growth and a radical shift in the Internet's population of users make necessary a new set of online rules. Yet because the Internet lacks any central authority or organizing structure, rules are emerging piecemeal, pulled and prodded by the often conflicting interests of business, governmental agencies and traditional Internet users. In general, the governmental agencies and traditional Internet users have been more explicit than businesses in describing how they want rules to evolve. The U.S. government, for example, has focused largely on safeguarding defense-related access and regulating access to pornography. Traditional users have lobbied vociferously for open communications, universal access, and a ban on government intervention of any sort. The business community, by contrast, has been relatively quiet. Rather than thinking abstractly about rules, most companies have concentrated on the more immediate tasks of getting online and staking a claim in cyberspace.

That focus is shortsighted because it overlooks the greatest potential for companies on the Internet: the opportunity not only to master the game of electronic commerce but also to create the rules of the game. In particular, companies can influence the creation of rules in three distinct areas: intellectual property rights, means of exchange, and enforcement.

Intellectual Property Rights

All economic systems are based fundamentally on a shared understanding of property rights. Developed over decades or even centuries, property rights clarify the basis of ownership and exchange. They provide a consistent way of defining who owns what and how possession can be transferred from one owner to another. Property rights reduce the costs of exchange by clarifying ownership and providing a means for punishing thieves; thus they define not only possession but also theft.

The connection between property rights and commerce applies with full force to the Internet. The advent of electronic commerce does not eliminate business's basic need for an infrastructure to clarify ownership and allow owners to reap economic rewards. But at the moment, online property rights are imprecisely defined; the Internet remains a virtual free-for-all where information is seen as a public good and ownership is up for grabs. Understandably, then, companies that deal in the business of information are approaching the Internet with caution. The Recording Industry Association of America, for instance, held back because it was worried that its products might be changed or misrepresented online.

There is one fairly easy way to solve the problem of property rights on the Internet: the creation of law by central governments. In cyberspace, that law would probably come from an extension of existing copyright law. Because copyright provides for the commercialization of intangible products – intellectual property – the extension of copyright law into cyberspace would seem to make sense. By guaranteeing the rights of intellectual property owners, copyright law should allow information-based companies to move more confidently onto the Internet.

There are some problems with this scenario. First, copyright is already one of the most intricate and esoteric areas of law. Courts vary widely in their interpretation of existing statutes and even in their understanding of a given law's intent. The extension of those laws into the new realm of electronic commerce is almost sure to create ambiguity and uncertainty, leaving courts and litigants to fumble toward new definitions of private property and intellectual property rights. Second, because the laws are national, they will have little influence on the Internet's international transactions. Finally, even if the laws were applied at the global level (and there is some talk of doing so under the new World

Trade Organization), they still would not provide the means for businesses to determine if their information has been altered or copied in cyberspace.

Meanwhile, the door is open for private companies to move directly into the rule-making business. Although companies cannot write the rules of intellectual property rights, they can establish rule-bound areas of the Internet – "virtual communities" in which rules are enforced. In those areas, companies can perform the functions that governments are not yet capable of fulfilling. For a fee, or by contract, they can protect the rights of online intellectual property.

Means of Exchange

Rules for commercial transactions constitute a second area ripe for private intervention. In most economic systems, currency of one form or another is used as payment in transactions. Typically, currency is issued by a central government that retains a monopoly over its creation and backs it with fractional reserves of precious metals or other countries' currencies. Even when the currency is not directly backed by a tangible asset, a government's management of its supply can create value based on confidence (that the government will always accept it as a store of value) and scarcity (because there is never quite enough to go around).

In contrast to the rules of intellectual property rights, which must change significantly to meet the demands of electronic commerce, the existing rules governing currency could probably function quite well for electronic exchange. Even in cyberspace, consumers can order goods priced in dollars, charge them to a credit card, and let banks intermediate the financial transaction. There is nothing intrinsic about the Internet that demands new means of exchange. There are no technical obstacles to routing and recording even non-traditional transactions through established routes; nor are there demands for new levels of financial oversight or regulation. Instead, the impetus for change stems from the instantaneous and intangible nature of electronic transactions.

Technologically, the creation of electronic money depends on the issuance of an anonymous electronic note. An institution would sell electronic money to its customers, coding the E-cash onto a wallet-sized card or transmitting it directly to another electronic merchant. It would debit the disbursed E-cash, plus a small transaction fee, from customers' regular bank accounts. For this process to work, the electronic transfers must remain anonymous and secure, and transaction fees must be kept low. In the past, similar requirements were met by agencies of a central government. Governments printed currency, allowed it to circulate anonymously, punished those who stole or copied it, and covered their expenses through taxation. On the Internet, however, there is no central authority to establish the means of exchange. And national governments have little interest in tackling the problem, because E-cash raises a host of troubling law enforcement questions. For example, would E-cash expand the possibilities for tax evasion and money laundering. If E-cash proliferates, many aspects of economic activity are likely to escape the scrutiny of government agencies; thus they have little incentive to play any role in its creation.

For private companies, by contrast, the incentives are vast. First, there is the cost-cutting potential of electronic payment. Banks in particular have a considerable interest in cutting the costs of intermediate transactions and moving directly to electronic payment systems. Several institutions, such as Citibank and Wells Fargo, already employ proprietary software systems that allow customers to do their banking online. As banks and other financial-service institutions increasingly compete on the basis of transactions rather than on the basis of relationships, these payment systems will become critical to their success.

But the real breakthrough will come when electronic payment systems are pushed into the broader reaches of cyberspace. Eventually, the value of E-cash, like the value of any currency, will be determined by the market's demand for it. For demand to increase, the currency will have to be widely accepted. In the past, governments ensured this acceptance simply by proclaiming their currency legal tender. In the future, the game will be inherently more competitive. Companies that establish the most accessible and secure means of exchange will capture the market of all those seeking to conduct electronic transactions. And success in this game will breed more success, because a currency's acceptance by some users will increase its attractiveness to others.

Not surprisingly then, the race to develop the means of secure electronic exchange has become one of the most spirited competitions in cyberspace, with startups such as DigiCash and CyberCash taking on established players such as Visa and MasterCard. To some extent, it is a race of technology: Winning will entail the refinement of encryption algorithms – which scramble electronic signals and allow access through mathematically encoded digital signatures – as well as the development of secure "electronic wallets". The race, however, is also about rules, because technology alone cannot support a full-fledged system of electronic exchange. If payment systems are to proliferate on the Internet, some trusted entity will have to oversee and regulate their use. Historically, governments have served in that role, but private companies will have to do so on the Internet. Financial institutions, with their combination of trusted brand-name and risk-management experience, are particularly well suited for this role. In any case, the entity managing an exchange system would also need to bundle its means of exchange with rules of security and enforcement.

Security and Enforcement

Security and enforcement pose the most obvious problems for electronic commerce. They also create the most tantalizing opportunities for new business development. Before any E-cash changes hands, and indeed before any real financial transaction occurs online, the parties to an exchange must have confidence that their transaction is secure. That is, they must know that the buyers or sellers are really who they claim to be, that the information being exchanged cannot be stolen or altered enroute, and that the payment being offered is real.

These levels of security do not yet broadly exist on the Internet. Instead, as information travels on the network, it passes through many computers and is thus exposed to a host of possible points of interception. Although the Electronic Communications Privacy Act of 1986 specifically forbids eavesdropping on electronic transmissions, laws of that kind are extraordinarily difficult to enforce because no policing agency controls the points of access. This basic lack of control is a major impediment to the growth of electronic commerce.

The need to guarantee information integrity presents a second security problem. Once information is put online, it is possible for a hacker to alter the information electronically. Just as the nature of the Internet makes it difficult to detect the theft of information, its current structure also makes it virtually impossible to trace tampering. Anyone can operate online under a false name. As the Internet grows, security problems are likely to increase.

Usually break-ins, such as tampering, fraud and theft, are considered to be within the purview of governmental agencies. But on the Internet, governments have not yet defined precisely what constitutes theft, nor have they established the institutions to trace or apprehend thieves. So the field is wide open to private development. The most obvious opportunity lies with the technologies of electronic security. Theoretically, cutting-edge technologies such as encryption and firewalls can solve security problems by fully protecting online transmissions. Firewalls protect a company's internal network from outside users by establishing physical filters between networks. At the moment, the leader in digital security software is RSA Data Security, which has already licensed its encryption algorithms to major Internet players such as IBM and Netscape. Other companies, such as Verisign and Microsoft, have also joined the race.

Meanwhile, there is another race going on, a race less obvious in some respects but ultimately more important. The development of secure technologies is absolutely critical to the expansion of electronic commerce, but it is not sufficient. To facilitate the expansion of electronic commerce, even the most sophisticated technologies will have to be embedded in broader, more secure networks. And those networks, along with their security systems, will have to be managed by some trusted intermediary. Enter again private companies, making rules and managing virtual communities.

Online communities are necessary because individual security precautions have only a limited value on the Internet. Value lies, instead, in a wider, protected community of users, who can communicate among themselves confidentially and thus confidently. The value of the community is created by the entities that run and manage it. They are the ones who determine its size, choose its members, implement security provisions and punish violators.

COMMUNITIES AND COMMERCE

For online communities to form, content providers need to feel confident about whom they are dealing with, how their material is being used, and how they are receiving payment. What they need, in short, is an entity to transform the anonymity and anarchy of the Internet into a market with identifiable customers and recordable transactions. That entity would manage a corner of the Internet where explicit rules would prevail.

Early forms of management entities already exist in such Internet service providers as UUNet, PSINet and Bolt Beranek & Newman. But the services they make available are still minimal, limited largely to granting their users a means of access to the Internet and some tools for navigating it. What these service providers could offer are the value-added services associated with rules and rule making. They could, for instance, provide secure transaction services, limit access to certain groups, or cluster their users into communities linked by similar interests or needs. Such communities already exist online in the form of chat groups and bulletin boards. But their rapid proliferation has undermined some of the Internet's early sense of community and begun to raise concerns among some users about the risks of association with unknown, untraceable parties. Some users, especially old-time hackers and technophiles, will probably want to remain in the vast, anonymous realm of the open Web. But others will probably prefer to exchange the adventure of cyberspace for a more regulated and predictable community. Service providers can fill this need by creating customized, managed communities in cyberspace and setting their own standards for online exchange.

To set and maintain those standards, service providers will need to employ many of the technologies described earlier. They will need, for example, an accurate means of tracking who is online and what those people are doing. That way, any content provider can learn who is making use of its product and, more important, can be paid for its sales to those users. Armed with the appropriate tracking and billing technologies, the service provider would perform the crucial functions of intermediation: It would track customers, bill them, and pay content providers. It would also guarantee that violators of the rules would be punished, most likely by expulsion from the community.

While the shift toward communities of commerce is most evident in consumer-oriented services, the logic of communities extends even further than that. The vision of walls and guards and tracked activities is diametrically opposed to the open market and universal access approved of by most Internet proponents. It is also seemingly at odds with the democracy that mass electronic communication is though to foster. But although private communities may well undermine the broad goals of an open, egalitarian society, managed virtual communities do not restrict the prospects for free, open communication. They merely divide the realms of activity, just as most people divide their own activities into public and private spheres. Moreover, by establishing limited, ordered communities, service providers have the potential to increase dramatically the number of people who venture online. For despite the terrific growth in Internet use, many people still find cyberspace too noisy, too anarchic and too cumbersome for their purposes. By restricting the online options, fine-tuning the offerings to match a select group of users, and offering some means of recourse in case of fraud or abuse, service providers can develop the kinds of managed communities that will draw new users online and increase the productivity of those already there.

Most important, though, service providers can create an environment conducive to commerce. As long as the Internet remains an open, unregulated space, companies from information-intensive industries such as publishing, software and financial services are unlikely to shift large segments of their business online. They may advertise or encourage chat groups to discuss their products, but will be reluctant to sell their products directly through cyberspace. To make the final leap, they – and presumably all content providers – need systems of intellectual property rights and exchange, as well as a means of enforcement. Individual companies or entrepreneurs are likely to develop the technological means for implementing rules – encryption, firewalls, tracking systems, and so on – but only if they have some prospect of reaping the benefits from their investment or innovation. Service providers can facilitate the development of a market by purchasing or licensing the technologies from their creators and then using them to create a commercial space that would bring together buyers, sellers, browsers and advertisers in a regulated, orderly community.

In the long run, the Internet will not transform business into a friction-free realm in which millions of anonymous buyers and sellers meet for one-shot instantaneous transactions. Nor will the Internet remain unregulated and uncensored. Portions of the Internet may stay that way, but they will not be busy with commerce. Rather, commerce will migrate to areas where rules prevail and responsibility can be assigned. Some of those areas probably will appear unorganized, and transactions within them will take place faster and more cheaply than in the physical world. But increased speed and reduced costs will not lead to the disappearance of rules, communities or intermediaries. On the contrary, the real move to electronic commerce will demand several layers of intermediaries to form new communities and support new rules. Electronic commerce requires those changes, which will also provide companies with the greatest opportunity for profit. In cyberspace, the real power will lie with those who make the rules.

THE ARCHITECTURE OF CONTROL

We have many choices to make regarding the very nature, or architecture of cyberspace. It is far cheaper to architect privacy protections in now rather than retrofit them later. The Internet is not a predetermined environment with immutable rules of behavior. The character of cyberspace is still up for grabs, and different user environments yield widely different experiences. The early Internet did not track the type of data being sent, making it impossible for anyone to filter materials. Today's Internet, however, allows extensive use of data labels. Therefore blocking messages is much easier. We can design cyberspace to permit or prohibit anonymity and to include or exclude kinds of speech. The choice is ours.

Let us examine how some current online environments treat constitutional values. America Online, for example, appears to facilitate free speech by permitting multiple pseudonyms, which make anonymity a snap. But AOL managers can easily trace "anonymous" messages. Also, AOL limits its "public spaces" to chat rooms that can hold no more than 23 people at once. Only the managers of AOL can broadcast messages to all members. To a considerable degree, then, AOL controls speech, security and privacy in its domain. Similarly, eBay controls the security of its community and the type of information made available about its members through its "Feedback Forum".

These are choices by private companies. People who don't like them can take their business elsewhere. The architecture of the entire Internet is being shaped by commercial forces. Online commerce will not fully develop until a suitable architecture is established. The changes that make commerce possible are also changes that will make regulation easy – by both government and commercial interests. Architecture that helps companies collect information and then guides different consumers to different sites also opens' everyone to abuse from unscrupulous companies and overzealous police investigators. The nature of cyberspace may flip. Instead of promoting free and open exchange, it may end up controlling our lives in ways we have never imagined.

The digital revolution has spawned a series of potential laws and regulations that pose novel trade-offs between law enforcement, commercial progress and individual liberty. This is not surprising. From the telegraph to the telephone, from radio to satellite television, new technologies have always required new laws and further interpretation of the constitution. Because cyberspace is likely to become a pervasive part of everyday life, similar legal decisions may have a profound impact. But law alone does not determine how technology is actually used. Market competition will have a lot to do with how well our rights to intellectual property, free speech and privacy are protected.

How Markets Can Promote Fair Use

A popular belief holds that the digitization of information poses a grave threat to the publishing and entertainment industries. The Internet seems to be a vast, out-of-control copying machine, churning out an unlimited number of perfect copies to all takers, regardless of copyright. Intellectual property rights have traditionally balanced the interests of the producers, who should be rewarded for their creative efforts, with those of society, which benefits from the easy and widespread dissemination of ideas. Courts have effectively limited producers' copyrights by holding that individuals may freely make a few copies of publications for personal use. But the main impetus of this fair-use policy has always been technological – publishers weren't about to stake out photocopy machines to prevent unauthorized copying. Soon, however, it may cost publishers next to nothing to charge a fee each time an electronic file is viewed, printed or copied to another device – if we allow cyberspace to evolve that way.

Even with reliable encryption, savvy Internet publishers are likely to promote, not hinder, the widespread dissemination of their ideas. Precisely because cyberspace makes distribution so cheap, it encourages the liberal use of free samples as a way to stimulate interest. Copyright holders may well find it in their own interest to encourage a certain amount of free use, whether or not the law or practicality mandates it.

Making Cyberspace Safe For Free Speech

So far, cyberspace has been an extraordinary boon to free speech, arguably the greatest leap ever in the ability of individuals to disseminate their ideas. It is now almost impossible for governments to exercise prior restraint on publication – controversial material can appear on the Internet before the lawyers can even get to the courthouse. In fact, speech has become so free today that we are suffocating from information overload. What we really need right now are services that screen, edit and certify the accuracy of all that information available online – which is why the Internet is a great opportunity, not a threat, to publishers with established reputations.

It is likely that Internet surfers will be allowed to filter, or block, speech they dislike. Filtering seems unobjectionable when done by the individual user or parent. But it can be a powerful tool of censorship when applied upstream by an Internet service provider, portal or employer – especially if users are unaware that it is happening. Rules need to be put in place that require organizations to disclose their information filtering policies. Internet service providers and other companies will be much less likely to censor if their customers and employees know what they are doing.

Protecting Individual Privacy

Free speech and intellectual property rights are big issues, especially for the entertainment and publishing industries. But every company doing business on the

Internet needs to think about privacy. The use of customer information is at the heart of virtually all business-to-consumer e-commerce strategies. The architecture of cyberspace will allow business and government to take away what little privacy we have left. As consumers use the Internet for more and more purchases, vendors will have access to increasingly rich profiles of shopping and buying patterns. How would you feel if everything you read, every Web site you visited, every file you downloaded, every message you sent or received, and every purchase you made were recorded in a database available to all comers for a moderate fee? Most of us would rise up in arms to prevent such an invasion of privacy. The judicial system needs to be ready to reinterpret privacy rights in the context of cyberspace.

Individuals' rights to privacy in e-commerce certainly are in flux, and we face myriad social and legal decisions in this sphere. Already the Federal Trade Commission and independent privacy advocates are looking closely at the practices of DoubleClick, a company that tracks individual consumers as they surf the Web and sells the clickstream data. As employers compile and share increasingly detailed profiles of job applicants, people are beginning to fear that the personal information they disclose when they apply for a job will be available to all future employers. Will consumers and employees leave it to business to set reasonable privacy policies or will they turn to the political and judicial processes to restrict the use of personal data?

Companies, left to themselves, will probably not respect the privacy of individuals. Companies will not bear the social cost of lost privacy, so they will have little incentive to respect privacy concerns as they set privacy rules in cyberspace. But in competing for customers, they will actually have a great deal of incentive to respect privacy. A look at this issue with the tools of economics and business strategy, not law, offers some reassurance.

Take a look at a Web site about one of the more sensitive areas of life. BabyCenter.com provides information and offers goods to expectant and new parents. After registering with BabyCenter.com and providing some personal details, parents receive newsletters customized for the different stages of pregnancy and child rearing. Necessarily, BabyCenter has access to considerable information about its users. This information is central to the value it offers. The main effect is simply to make the market work more smoothly: products are matched to people, and interests to people, in a way that is better targeted and less intrusive than what we have today. Many parents would oppose having information about their pregnancies and their babies widely known. What protection do they have? BabyCenter is a member of the Truste program and follows Truste's privacy principles. Truste is an independent, non-profit organization whose mission is to build users' trust and confidence in the Internet by promoting the principles of disclosure and informed consent.

This is the market in action, working to offer enhanced services to consumers without compromising their privacy, using reputable third parties as needed. This system of consumer "notice and choice", favored by the U.S. Commerce Department and the Federal Trade Commission, is a classic market-based solution. It defines the property rights (you own information about yourself), permits the trading of some of those rights (you can give up some of those rights in exchange for money, information, or other goods), and establishes a way to enforce those rights (by punishing those who misuse or fail to protect personal data).

Most companies operating in cyberspace are likely to abide by this system, but there will be a few bad apples. Some companies will retain the right to sell consumer information or will simply violate their stated policies against selling without consent. Lax security may allow employees or partners to steal information. The market eventually punishes deviants, but often that doesn't restore the public's trust in the industry, so new regulations follow and law enforcement is tightened.

All consumer e-commerce companies must understand that their success depends upon building public trust, and thus it is critical to state their privacy policies clearly, adhere to them carefully, and pay close attention to the security of private information collected. A combination of voluntary alliances and mandatory rules seems likely. Some of the infrastructure for privacy is already in place. In addition to third parties like Truste, the World Wide Web Consortium has created a platform on which users can express their preferences for privacy and negotiate the use of data about themselves. Law and markets may work together to protect our rights.

Once Congress gets involved, the result may be crude rules that substantially reduce companies' ability to add value for customers. A better approach is to endow individuals with the rights to their own personal information (property rights), require companies to clearly state and abide by their privacy policies (disclosure and enforcement), and permit individuals to relinquish control over their personal information in exchange for money, goods or services (freedom to trade).

Chapter 11

Infrastructure for Electronic Commerce

ARCHITECTURE OF THE INTERNET

The Internet and the World Wide Web are changing the way that organizations and individuals work, communicate and obtain information. It is clear that the technology is different in some important ways from its predecessors.

Characteristics of Internet Technology

Internet technology possesses characteristics that distinguish it from other information technologies. These characteristics make the technology easy to use, extremely powerful, and economically attractive. Some of the important characteristics of Internet technology are:

- *The Internet is based on open standards and protocols*. Because the Internet comprises many different computer networks and many different systems, a common language standard must be used for interconnection. TCP/IP (Transmission Control Protocol/Internet Protocol) is the adopted common language of the Internet. TCP/IP standards define how computers send and receive data packets. The standard was developed for the ARPANET project of the U.S. Department of Defense using public funds and, therefore, exists as a public resource. The fact that TCP/IP is a free resource helps make the Internet largely independent from reliance on proprietary solutions that are developed and marketed by private companies. Insistence on open standards and solutions has become part of the ethos of the Internet's community of administrators and developers.

  The reliance on open technologies facilitates economic efficiencies that could not be realized using older technologies. Historically, technologies from different companies did not work easily together. Choosing a computer hardware or software vendor locked the purchaser into that company's offerings even in areas where its products were not the best. Computer companies embraced this strategy of locking in clients to proprietary architectures. The Internet has changed the game somewhat by making open technology a priority. Companies that once would have resisted modifying their products to work with others' products must do it routinely or risk market censure. For users of the technology, this means more product and vendor choices. It also means systems that have not worked well together can be consolidated around the common TCP/IP standard, thus saving the costs of operating and maintaining redundant networks and systems.

236

- *The Internet is asynchronous.* Communication of information via the Internet does not rely on dedicated, bi-directional connections between sender and receiver. Rather, packets are sent toward their destination without any prior coordination between the sender and the receiver. E-mail messages are addressed and delivered over the Internet much as physical mail is sent via a postal service. As with postal mail, a recipient has a mailbox where mail can accumulate until it is accessed. Unlike regular mail though, e-mail messages can be sent around the globe almost simultaneously.
- *The Internet has inherent latency.* The computers that make up the Internet are connected by links of varying bandwidth or size. As packets carry information along different paths toward a common destination, some packets flow quickly through wide links while others move more slowly through narrow links. Packets that together comprise a single message do not arrive at the destination at the same time. Thus, there is variable wait time between the time a message is sent and the time that the last packet in the message arrives at the destination. Because traffic volume is somewhat unpredictable, wait time can be difficult to predict.

The bandwidth of a communication link is the maximum rate at which information can be transmitted along the link. The smallest unit of information handled by computers is called a "bit". Bandwidth is measured in bits per second, or bps. Bandwidth capacity is usually referenced in one of three contexts: kbps or kilobits per second (thousands of bits per second), mbps or megabits per second (millions of bits per second) and gbps or gigabits per second (billions of bits per second).

Communication Technology	Bandwidth	Type of User
Modem	56 kbps	Individuals and small businesses
Integrated Services Digital Network (ISDN)	128 kbps – 1.544 mbps	Individuals and small businesses
Ethernet LAN	10 mbps – 100 mbps	Most medium to large businesses and organizations
Leased Lines (T1 and T3)	1.544 mbps, 45 mbps	Government, universities, and large corporations
Asynchronous Transfer Mode (ATM) and Gigabit Ethernet	155 mbps – 25.6 gbps	Government, universities, and large corporations

Table 11-1: Technology Bandwidths and Common Users

- *The Internet is distributed.* There is no central traffic control point within the Internet. There is also no central authority which oversees or governs the development or administration of the system, except for one that assigns TCP/IP addresses. As a result, individuals and organizations are responsible for managing and maintaining their own Internet facilities in a way that does not hinder the operation of the network as a whole.

237

- *The Internet is scalable.* Because Internet communication is intelligently routed along multiple paths, adding to the Internet is as simple as connecting to a machine already connected. Just as the Internet is not significantly affected when a link is removed (packets simply get routed a different way), it is also not significantly affected when another link is added. Additional links can be added in parallel with overworked links to provide more paths along which packets can be routed. Furthermore, Internet technology allows relatively easy reorganization of sub-networks. If a network segment has become overloaded, the network can be split up into more manageable sub-networks. Because of the scalability and openness of Internet technology, it has become very pervasive in a short period of time. Information providers are racing to make their networks speak the same TCP/IP language. There has rarely in history been a comparable race to make information accessible via the same widespread medium.
- *Internet technology is inherently attractive to a broad cross-section of people.* Unlike many technologies that have been implemented in the past, Internet services (especially e-mail and the World Wide Web) have been demanded by prospective users with substantial vehemence. While user acceptance has always been a concern of those who implement new technologies, there is a real sense in which Internet services were accepted as soon as they appeared. People want to use this technology. They use it at home as well as at work, and they carry their expertise from home use with them into work.

Evolution of System Architectures

The large-scale computer networks of today are relatively new features of the computing landscape. Today's network-centric world evolved from earlier centralized and client-server computing paradigms.

The Mainframe Computing Era: 1960s – 1970s

Computers have been used by people and organizations to manage and disseminate information since the 1950s. Until the 1980s, a centralized computing architecture was prevalent, based on a central mainframe computer and terminals. The mainframe provided computational and storage capabilities, while terminals were used as simple input/output devices. It was not until organizations began to share information and services among mainframes that computer networks were developed. Early networking technologies were proprietary and relatively simple, since they needed to handle traffic between a small number of large mainframe computers.

Distributed and Client-Server Computing: 1980s

With the introduction of the personal computer (PC) in 1981, individuals could suddenly install significant computing power on their own desktops. Much of the processing and data storage that had occurred on a central mainframe could, therefore, be distributed throughout the organization. Coordination of this much more distributed processing necessitated the development of much more sophisticated and robust networking technologies.

The client-server computing model was the eventual result of distributing computer processing. Client-server divides the work done on computing facilities. Client programs are installed on the user's local workstation (usually a PC) and allow the user to interact over a network with back-end computers, also called servers. User interface and some processing duties are handled by the local workstation. Tasks requiring more power or access to information stored elsewhere are sent across the network to powerful servers, which send back results when they are finished. Sharing processing in this way can more efficiently distribute work, eliminate bottlenecks, and improve performance.

Network Computing: 1990s - present

Network computing is a refinement of client-server. To consolidate and reduce the costs of managing the client-server environment, network computing dictates moving data storage and processing capabilities to the back-end servers, which leaves clients operating mostly as standardized input/output devices. Networked clients are usually personal computers with powerful graphical, audio and video interface capabilities. Because processing is handled primarily on servers, changes that would have previously required physically visiting each client machine can be distributed automatically from a central point. On the back-end, the addition of more computing power by adding extra servers has proven to be significantly cheaper than attempting the same upgrades using traditional mainframes.

A Local Area Network (LAN) is a relatively small computer network that tends to use one type of transmission medium and covers an area that is usually within a building. A Wide Area Network (WAN) links LANs to form a larger network. A router defines the boundary between LAN and WAN. A Metropolitan Area Network (MAN) is a hybrid term sometimes used to refer to a WAN that is geographically contained within a city.

The Internet and The World Wide Web

The Internet is the network upon which the service known as the World Wide Web runs. The Internet also supports a wide variety of non-Web services. Electronic mail (E-mail) allows individuals to send and receive electronic messages. File Transfer Protocol (FTP) supports copying a file from one Internet location to another. Telnet enables remote access of an Internet connected computer.

The World Wide Web is the assemblage of content documents in browser-accessible formats dispersed throughout the Internet. These documents contain text, data, and sometimes embedded graphics, video and audio. They are identified by addresses known as Uniform Resource Locators (URLs). Hyperlinks on document pages connect documents to other documents. Clicking on a hyperlink transfers the user to a different document. That different document can be any other document on the network, regardless of where in the world it might be physically stored. The tangled and complex nature of these hyperlink connections amounts to a "Web" of information connections – hence the name.

Web content is the substantive material that is stored on the Internet and gives this medium its energy and life. Content is created using standard presentation languages, the most prevalent of which is the Hypertext Markup Language (HTML). Using text editors or more sophisticated authoring tools, content designers lay out pages in a browser-readable format.

Maneuvering around the Web to access information is often called browsing or surfing the Web. Browser software, installed on a user's workstation, employs a graphical user interface (GUI) to guide the user so that content files can be located and accessed quickly. The browser is essentially a navigational tool used to access and display files. Currently the leading browser software packages are Netscape Navigator and Microsoft Internet Explorer. Users can locate files by typing in the URL, or they can use search engines to look up information by keyword or combinations of keywords. Search engines such as Yahoo and Excite are Web sites where a user can stop and ask for directions.

Internet Security

Security is a primary concern for most people who are considering business uses of the Internet. The same open standards and protocols that make the Internet a powerful communication medium also create a need for systems that govern who has access to what. Unlike mainframe-era systems to which access was denied unless explicitly enabled, Internet access is enabled unless explicitly denied. Further, information exchanged on the Internet can be passively intercepted. In some situations, Internet links can be the entry point for hackers who intend harm to an organization's computer systems. While these threats are real, security measures related to memory protection, encryption, and runtime verification are used to eliminate these dangers and ensure protection of the computer system.

Internet commerce is a common use of the Internet. One of the inhibiting factors in this area has been the concern users have had over transmitting sensitive credit information on the Internet. Banks and merchants are also concerned with this issue since traditional credit card losses cost these companies about $1.5 billion a year. As a result, Visa and Mastercard have developed the Secure Electronic Transaction (SET) protocol. This technology will use sophisticated encryption techniques, as well as digital certificates to ensure that information can be sent safely across the Internet.

Encryption uses mathematical algorithms to alter information so that it is unrecognizable to electronic eavesdroppers or other unauthorized individuals. An encrypted document looks nothing like the original and cannot be interpreted without a digital key that both the user and sender possess for the purpose of decryption.

Digital certificates work in conjunction with encryption techniques to enhance security. This process uses a trusted third party to assure the identity of an individual who transmits information. In order to obtain a digital certificate, the user must first generate an encrypted key and provide this to the issuing authority. Once the legal status of the organization and the contact names associated with the key have been verified, a certificate is issued which is installed on the user's Web server. This digital certificate is then used to assure others of the user's authenticity and that the connection is secure.

While encryption and digital certificates are designed to protect transmissions sent across a network from eavesdropping, a firewall is a system used to prevent unauthorized access to an organization's internal systems. The firewall effectively blocks message traffic along certain paths, or allows it only after authentication. A firewall is commonly placed between the company's private internal network and the public Internet. The idea is to provide services and access for members of the organization while at the same time making it impossible for unauthorized users to access the private network from outside the company.

The Internet is a collection of communication and information management technologies that enables a very flexible, yet powerful approach to sharing and communicating information. Two types of networks provide this connectivity – the backbone network, which provides high-speed communication over long distances, and connecting networks, which run at slower speeds and connect an organization's internal network to the backbone. For the most part, the backbone networks provide reliable, high-speed communication. But getting your message to the backbone, and from the backbone to its destination, is much less reliable and can be much slower. Because information you wish to access, or the person with whom you wish to communicate, can reside anywhere within the vast web of networks, and there is no central point of control, you never know whether your message will reach its destination in a reliable and timely manner, or whether you will be able to access that critical piece of information.

In addition to reliability issues, many have appropriately expressed concern about the security of the Internet. Maintaining security and integrity of information across interorganizational boundaries is always a challenge. On the Internet, however, it is a nightmare. The Internet grew in an uncontrolled manner. Anyone in almost any country can connect to the Internet with a PC, a modem, a network address and a connection to an Internet server. The level of security on the Internet depends on how the system is used and whether there are any direct links between the Internet and your company's information system.

Managers who contemplate conducting electronic commerce across the Internet must assume that anybody in the world might attempt to break into their internal networks, and plan accordingly. Table 11-2 summarizes the security features necessary for conducting electronic commerce. Managers need to secure internal corporate networks from unwanted outsiders by using firewalls. Firewalls are electronic barriers created with dedicated hardware and software systems that screen network traffic and validate the flow of information between internal and external networks. Companies generally designate one or more separate computers as Internet servers and carefully barricade their internal systems behind a firewall.

Problem	Business Concern	Technology Solution
Authorization	Does a user have permission to access a specific computer or collection of information?	User name and password, or other kinds of access control mechanisms.
Authentication	Is the user truly whom he/she purports to be?	Special purpose hardware and software system generates random number which user then matches to authenticate identity.
Integrity	Did the person sending a message actually send it? Can the receiver be sure that the message has not been changed?	Digital signature.
Privacy	Is my conversation (or business transaction) private? Is anyone eavesdropping or spying?	Public / private key encryption algorithms.
Fraud/Theft	Is anyone stealing from me?	Log, audit, systems management policies and procedures.
Sabotage	Can anyone enter my system and destroy or alter information?	Firewalls.

Table 11-2: Internet Security Issues

In addition to firewalls, passwords can screen prospective users and ensure that only those on an approved list can enter your network. Of course, this requires additional administrative overhead and is somewhat antithetical to the idea behind electronic commerce. The benefits of opening an electronic store, for example, are greatly reduced if you must restrict access to those you already know. Furthermore, while passwords can be encrypted, they may still be easily intercepted in a networked computing environment populated with technologically sophisticated users.

In some situations, a company may wish to require individuals to validate that they are who they say they are. One approach to authenticating network users combines special hardware and software. Authorized users, able to connect to a specific server, or to pass through a company firewall, receive a special handheld device about the size of a credit card. This device contains an encryption algorithm. When an authorized user tries to connect to another company's computer, he or she receives a five-digit randomly-generated number as an authentication challenge. The user enters the number into the device, receives another five-digit number, and then replies with this number as the key to the challenge. If the remote system is satisfied with the response, the user can access the server.

Another thorny problem with electronic commerce is protecting the privacy of personal information. For example, one company created an internal Web application to enable information sharing among internal employees. Despite the fact that the server was behind a firewall, and that password entry was required, the company found that an intruder had been able to break in and steal highly confidential information. Electronic financial transactions are also of great concern. Some firms are using digital signatures and encryption keys to authenticate financial transaction data. The search continues for a foolproof form of electronic currency so that buyers and sellers can transact business easily over the Internet.

The online world of electronic commerce also raises many issues about information privacy. When we buy a published book, we assume that copyright protections and intellectual property rights have been addressed by the author and the publisher. Each book is bound to ensure that all portions of the book are considered and protected as a whole. By contrast, in on online world, information is transmitted in small bits and pieces that can be reconstructed by many different users in different forms. Copyright laws have yet to accommodate this, and maintaining intellectual property and privacy rights becomes a logistic nightmare. While digital signatures, firewalls, encryption algorithms, and passwords can help to protect our rights, they are not sufficient. Current security, privacy and information integrity procedures and practices must be examined, and interorganizational information and communication policies must be established.

Finally, electronic commerce requires interorganizational and management process redesign. New structures and systems to coordinate and control information-enabled relationships must be implemented, and interorganizational change processes must be managed. The dynamic and uncertain nature of the business and technology environments will make it impossible to create iron-clad contracts to define the relationship. Instead, interorganizational authority and control systems need to be designed so that shared values are clearly articulated and interorganizational boundary systems are defined. Real-time, shared information on interorganizational processes and frequent interaction support the development of a more collaborative administrative structure.

Current Issues In Internet Computing

The Need for Speed

The Internet is a voracious consumers of network bandwidth. New technologies that will permit order-of-magnitude higher transmission speeds are, therefore, of great interest in Internet circles. New high-bandwidth technologies are generally implemented first on the heavy traffic paths along the backbone of the Internet, then spread to connect individual machines to the backbone as the costs of the technology come down.

One possibility, called asynchronous transfer mode (ATM) incorporates aspects of circuit switching, where a direct temporary connection is established between two parties. This virtual circuit, established before information is sent, remains in place for the length of time the transmission requires. The main advantage of such dedicated circuits is that they support transfer of information within guaranteed time intervals. Hence ATM can be guaranteed to be fast enough to support real-time applications like video teleconferencing. Proponents contend that with ATM, remote parties can be located faster. In addition, by channeling traffic into defined connections, ATM arguably makes it easier to centrally manage large volumes of traffic on the Internet and provides a way to track and charge users for time online.

Despite these attractions, ATM is being resisted by influential members of the Internet community. Because it relies on synchronous links between sender and receiver, it departs from the routing paradigm that is characteristic of Internet technology. It constitutes a step toward more active management of traffic from a central location. Thus it departs in some degree from the distributed management ideal that is characteristic of Internet technology. Also ATM users may face potential difficulties dialing others who are using different kinds of network services, because of inconsistencies between the ATM addressing scheme and the open standard TCP/IP addressing that prevails on today's Internet.

There is evidence that ATM may be losing ground to Gigabit Ethernet and other technologies that are faster versions of existing Internet-related technologies. The Internet's inherent latency is the main obstacle to be overcome by these rivals. To support real-time video and other time-sensitive applications, enhanced Internet technologies must develop reliable sources for giving time-sensitive messages priority as they traverse a network and for assuring that a transmission path will always be available for high-priority messages. As the speed of these technologies increases, and as they evolve to a point where they can make near guarantees that are close to the guarantees that ATM provides, they may eventually prevail.

High-bandwidth technologies currently being explored for connecting end users to the Internet include ISDN (Integrated Services Digital Network), satellite technologies, broadband cable, ADSL (Asymmetric Digital Subscriber Line) and other variations on wireless and telephone technologies. Each of these technologies has advantages and disadvantages, and each fits most naturally with a subset of the communication challenge.

Personal Computers vs. Network Computers

As information technology becomes more network-centric, ways are being sought to reduce the costs of maintaining computing services. One debate centers on whether personal computers should be replaced by much simpler input/output machines, called network computers, or whether personal computers should simply be modified to be easier and less costly to maintain. In essence, this issue pits a coalition consisting of companies such as Sun Microsystems, Oracle, Netscape and IBM, against others, namely Microsoft and Intel, in a struggle to determine the shape of the computing desktop of the future.

Network computers are designed to run small chunks of functionality sent to them across the network on an "as-needed" basis. Java, a computer language developed by Sun Microsystems, has received much attention as one way of creating this kind of network application. The advantage of Java-based applications is that they are platform-independent – that is, they can run on computers made by any manufacturer and running any underlying computer software. Thus the choice of operating system and hardware platform becomes less important, possibly even irrelevant, and current market leaders (e.g., Microsoft, Intel) could lose some of their power over these markets.

Microsoft has developed a set of technologies that offer Microsoft-specific enhancements of Java capabilities. These Microsoft enhancements are feature-rich and well integrated with other widely deployed Microsoft products. Thus they can leverage the knowledge and work of development communities already familiar with Microsoft tools and environments. Critics of the Microsoft enhancements, however, point out that using Microsoft's enhanced functionality makes software once again dependent on the Microsoft platform, and see the company's introduction of these enhancements as a clever effort to head off the benefits of platform independence initially offered by Java.

IMPLICATIONS FOR MANAGEMENT

We are in a period of upheaval as we shift from an industrial economy to an information economy. Although information technology has evolved over four decades, we are now experiencing a period of radical change as the cumulative impacts of technological, organizational, social and economic adaptations begin to coalesce, giving rise to new business models. In a world in which information crosses the globe in seconds, profound changes are occurring within and between organizations as firms large and small rewrite the rules of commerce.

The power of the Internet as a tool for electronic commerce comes from four key features: global connectivity, shared ownership, flexible information and low cost.

Global connectivity. The network infrastructure that makes up the Internet does not represent a startling advance in technology. In fact, the Internet's technical communications platform is less advanced than many proprietary networks. Instead, a key source of the Internet's power comes from its global connectivity; it connects millons of individuals and thousands of companies all over the world.

Shared ownership. Because it was developed to allow anyone and everyone to connect to it, the Internet provides an open platform for information exchange. No one organization, company, or government agency owns the Internet; it comprises more than 100,000 interconnected yet independently owned and managed networks all over the world. The fact that the Internet is widely viewed as a shared, global communication resource has fostered participation and joint collaboration not usually found on proprietary networks. Still, this same feature causes the Internet to be less reliable and secure, and more difficult to control than a proprietary network.

A flexible platform for information sharing. Organizations and markets are inherently information processing systems. The ability to connect individuals to one another through a physical network is only the first step in expanding information processing capabilities; tools to support communication, and flexible, interactive information management are also required. The Internet's network connections and communication tools – such as electronic mail and electronic bulletin boards – have been around for decades. But the introduction of the World Wide Web and associated Web browsers captured the attention of the business community.

A network infrastructure that is nearly free. The cost savings to be achieved from electronic commerce on the Internet are impressive. Most of the network infrastructure is already in place. The cost to an organization to connect to the Internet – based on the number of users and the speed of the connection – is well below that of a proprietary network service. Once connected, there is no charge for usage. The scale of the Internet and the number of users is so massive that costs are expected to be dramatically lower than if a firm attempted to operate a proprietary network.

The low cost, flexibility, shared ownership, and global connectivity of the Internet dramatically expands the opportunities for electronic commerce.

Mass Customization and Commodity Markets

Today, the bulk of commercial activity on the Internet is customer-focused and transaction-oriented. The ubiquitous shared nature of the Internet as a potential platform for electronic commerce allows customers (and competitors) to easily and thoroughly compare prices and product features. As access to timely market information increases, sustainable advantage through differentiation of products and services is more fleeting. Markets become more "commodity-like", and prices are more dependent on supply and demand. In the absence of restrictions to supply or the emergence of a new breed of channel manager, prices could be expected to fall and consumers will become more powerful.

How can managers deal with a commodity market that simultaneously demands customization? The answer lies in the ability to harness the power of digital information. In the turbulent world of electronic commerce, expect the commercial value of information to increase dramatically. Some properties of digital information influencing its value include:

- *Information can be used to create new products and services or to add value to existing ones*. Physical products or services can be infused with added value by adding information, or new products or services can be created from information collected in the course of doing business.
- *Information is reusable*. Unlike physical products, information can be sold without transferring ownership and used without being consumed.
- *Information is highly customizable*. The same information can be presented in different forms (e.g., text, graphics, video, audio) and in varying levels of detail. It can be combined with information from other sources to communicate different messages and to create new products and services.
- *Information has an inherent "time value"*. As the speed of business accelerates, the time value of information increases.

Despite its technical limitations and chaotic nature, the Internet is a powerful tool for accessing information in digital form and packaging and delivering it easily and cheaply. Managers are finding that the features that differentiate a home page and draw people back are related to the utility and uniqueness of the information that is presented – not the glitzy graphics.

Complex messages can be organized as linked documents, color photos, and audio and video clips that readers can explore, based on their interests, simply by clicking on a word or image. Each time a person stops to read, view or listen to your message, the system can track which items were viewed and how much time was spent in each area. Market surveys are easy to develop and deliver, providing up-to-date data on market interest and the persuasiveness of your message. This data can be transferred automatically to internal sales and marketing databases providing a steady flow of market information. While many managers are hard pressed to estimate the true value of this interactive flow of content-rich information between their firm and the marketplace, the ease of development, low cost, and global market reach have led many to experiment.

Firms that sell their products through direct marketing, for example, L.L. Bean, Spiegel, Sharper Image and Sundance, are making extensive use of the Internet to create electronic catalogues of their products. Some merely replicate the pages of their current paper-based offering; others use the power of the Internet to create a totally new approach to marketing.

In their search to deliver information value to their customers, many IT vendors – such as Apple, AT&T, IBM, Novel, and Microsoft – provide extensive product descriptions, up-to-date technical information on their products, and customer service online. They also attempt to enhance their image as a specialized expert by providing the answers to the most frequently asked technical questions and in-depth technical reports on emerging technologies online.

Information can also be used to signal quality and to induce customers to purchase your existing products. Companies that sell information-based products (for example, newspapers and magazines) have been quick to cash in on the reusability and customizability of information by delivering their products over the Internet – an exceptionally low-cost channel for reaching new markets with a more customizable product. Firms that sell time-dependent, perishable products – hotel room reservations, dinner reservations, airline flight seats, play or concert tickets – are finding a natural home on the Internet.

While most firms use the Internet primarily for marketing or customer service, some are venturing into the more risky area of online shopping. Since the Internet is not yet considered a completely secure place to carry out financial transactions, they may turn to third-party Internet providers – for example, Open Market – to serve as the development company, helping with construction of the stores and ensuring safe, reliable sales transactions within them.

Relationships with suppliers also take on a new look when translated onto the Internet. While many companies use the Internet merely to share information with suppliers, the more adventurous companies are creating virtual auctions in which suppliers bid to obtain a specific contract. The ability to turn supplier relationships into a bidding auction has provided the business concept for several Internet entrepreneurs, who have established themselves as auctioneers in an electronic marketplace.

The Internet still has to resolve problems with reliability and security. If the reliability and security problems are overcome, and if the software required to seamlessly integrate the Internet within a firm's internal information and communication platform is developed, firms will be poised to take advantage of the real power of electronic commerce – the ability to integrate, coordinate and control value chain activities across organizational boundaries.

From Vertical Integration To Value-Chain Linking

Before computer networks emerged, direct ownership was the most economical way to coordinate and control value-chain activities within a firm. The successes in the history of electronic commerce demonstrated how firms could use electronic linkages to integrate, coordinate and control the value chain across organizational boundaries.

As sophisticated networked information systems enable firms to reduce the cost and risk of coordinating and controlling value-chain activities with market participants, the rules for determining which activities to own and which to source from others favors outsourcing. The availability of the Internet as a low-cost, flexible, easy-to-use and widely available platform for electronic commerce continues to fuel this trend. As firms contract out more and more non-core activities, we observe increasing specialization within industries as specialized experts replace vertically integrated generalists.

Can a firm maintain high levels of specialization and differentiation around a core competency, yet also achieve seamless integration with other market participants and end-to-end control of the value chain? This is an interesting paradox that lies at the heart of the future of electronic commerce. Increased specialization leads to increased power within a more limited sphere; still, experts must unite and act as one to deliver products to a more demanding global customer base. Firms will be invited to participate based on their specialized knowledge and skills, but the ability to remain in the game will depend on the ability to participate in the complex interorganizational relationships required to coordinate and control the entire set of value-chain activities. The feature that distinguishes those firms that evolve toward becoming powerful specialists from those that move toward becoming extinct is an ability to become both a high-quality provider of a core activity and, through hybrid relationships that include elements of partnership agreements, contracts and transactions, to share information and integrated processes that enable end-to-end coordination and control of the value chain.

The connectivity, flexibility, and power of the tools available on the Internet provide an excellent platform for delivering interactive real-time information both inside and outside the firm. But taken alone, they are insufficient. The Internet's power must be integrated with the internal databases, networks and transaction processing systems within each firm that unites to deliver value-chain activities.

A New Breed of Channel Manager

Many believe that yesterday's channel manager, such as American Airlines, that controlled both information content and electronic channels through proprietary ownership is a dying breed. The 1990s saw the growth of third-party network service providers offering low-cost, secure, network connections and communications services upon which companies could deliver information-based products.

The Internet extends the concept of shared ownership and low cost of the infrastructure for electronic commerce even further. It represents not one, but many independent networks, linked through common standards and protocols, and made useful through common access to powerful non-proprietary tools for creating, sharing and storing information. Does this mean that the opportunity to control the channel through proprietary ownership is gone? Probably so. Could a new form of channel manager emerge? That is the more interesting question to ponder as established vendors, Internet entrepreneurs and powerful coalitions jockey to gain control over the Internet. Many of the established vendors are hedging their bets by developing the tools and network services required for firms to participate in electronic commerce over both proprietary networks and the Internet.

Telecommunications companies are gearing up to exploit the huge potential market for electronic commerce that most believe will evolve over the next few years. Internet entrepreneurs are also jockeying for position. Hundreds of tiny local firms offer Web page construction services and advice on how to advertise on the Internet. A small number of firms, such as Open Market, Inc., purport to offer end-to-end solutions for doing business on the Internet. These firms are vying for control of the software standards for browsers, secure payment protocols, and other areas that will play a critical enabling role in electronic commerce. Other Internet entrepreneurs, including Spry, Terisa Systems and RSA data Security, are attempting to define Internet security standards by providing software for data encryption, digital signatures and authentication. Since many of these technologies are patented, winners stand to reap hefty licensing fees for their efforts. CyberCash, DigiCash, First Virtual and NetBill are developing secure payment mechanisms.

In addition, new types of channel brokers are emerging on the Internet, and each is trying to reap profits from the online transactions they bring together. The history of electronic commerce suggests that networked information systems that reduce complexity and improve channel coordination and control make it easier for buyers and sellers to interact directly. This reduces the need for channel intermediaries. On the Internet, in the short term, the absence of tools to help structure information and communication provides an excellent opportunity for the emergence of channel brokers. In time, it is expected that much of the value addition provided by the broker can be embedded in software. In the short term, Internet entrepreneurs are rushing in to cash in on this window of opportunity. Two types predominate: information brokers and market brokers. Information brokers are trying to establish themselves as the preferred source for information in various categories ranging from the very broad to the specialized. Many of the traditional information providers are actively pursuing opportunities to serve as Internet information brokers. Market brokers match buyers and sellers.

These three trends – the emergence of mass customization within commodity markets, the rise of specialized experts who must unite to provide seamless value chain integration, and the current power struggles that could result in new forms of channel management – make it important for managers to be aware of the Internet and to be actively involved in decisions concerning its use within their firm. The Internet grew as a playground for hackers and techies. As it migrates toward a serious business tool, it is easy to become a casualty of the transition. Learning to harness its power is a delicate balancing act. The features of the Internet that enhance its value also increase its risk, making senior management oversight much more important. Because it is easy to use and flexible, almost anyone can quickly create a new business application, and information contained in it can be rapidly disseminated worldwide. Global connectivity also means that, practically speaking, there is no such thing as a limited roll-out of information. Once it is on the Internet, it is visible to everyone – all your customers, all your employees, all your investors, all your competitors.

Strategy For Doing Business On The Internet

Firms that take the Internet seriously – as a potential tool for conducting business and as a real security threat – are establishing a senior position or management team to evaluate and guide organizational learning efforts. The senior manager is often within corporate strategy or public relations, and the team may include representation from line businesses, public relations, marketing and legal divisions. Some firms capture new Internet applications on a secure computer that controls employee access to the Internet. The management team evaluates potential applications before they are released on the

Internet to ensure that they convey an appropriate image and enhance the company's strategy. The responsibilities of the team are threefold:

- Identify promising uses for the Internet as a tool for electronic commerce and for communicating and disseminating internal information.
- Stop inappropriate or risky uses of the technology before they can harm the company's competitive, financial, legal, or ethical position.
- Move quickly and decisively, but safely. Electronic commerce strategies and opportunities are unfolding very rapidly. Firms must be vigilant yet cautious.

Electronic commerce can be a boom or bust for your company. Some traditional catalog retailers, such as Dell Computer, now achieve about half their sales from the Internet. Other firms that don't plan correctly find a lot of money wasted on their electronic commerce efforts. Although the Internet provides us with much new jargon and applications, reapplying traditional management strategies to a wired world can help your effort succeed. The key to a successful business is keeping customers happy. In the electronic world, customers still want to be pampered, just in a different manner. Make sure their credit card numbers and other personal data are kept safe and secure. Provide opportunities to gossip and otherwise share information with friends – even if your customers have never met in person. Provide easy access to information about your products so customers can make an informed decision. Execute transactions quickly and in a friendly manner. Treat employees with respect so they may be of greater assistance to customers, and remove disruptive employees. Planning for these issues in advance will help make your transition to electronic commerce more smooth. Just be prepared to adapt.

Enabling Electronic Commerce

Inexpensive and widely available Internet technologies have made electronic commerce a reality. The cost of personal computers and modems has dropped to the point at which they are more affordable to have in the home now than ever before. Approximately 60 percent of U.S. households own computers. At the same time, the population is becoming increasingly computer-literate. Children are introduced to computers at an early age, and most knowledge-based jobs now require some interaction with computers. In the networking area, an increase in competition in the telecommunications industry has also led to decreased costs in Internet access fees. Competition among providers has also led to increases in the number and quality of telephone lines for data transmission.

Much of electronic commerce today is conducted through these Internet technologies, although proprietary electronic data interchange (EDI) networks capture a significant amount of business-to-business electronic commerce. Computers connect to the Internet using TCP/IP (transmission control protocol/Internet protocol) and with the Web as an interface. Once the connectivity is achieved though, there is little value without standards. Open standards, such as TCP/IP, facilitate the acceptance of the Web.

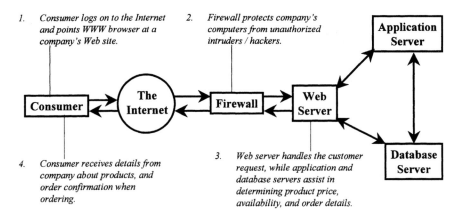

1. *Consumer logs on to the Internet and points WWW browser at a company's Web site.*

2. *Firewall protects company's computers from unauthorized intruders / hackers.*

4. *Consumer receives details from company about products, and order confirmation when ordering.*

3. *Web server handles the customer request, while application and database servers assist in determining product price, availability, and order details.*

Figure 11-1: Model of Electronic Commerce

Conducting electronic commerce with individuals outside a firm requires establishing an electronic presence in the virtual world. This is normally done by creating a Web site, which entails attaching or using a previously attached computer to the Internet to serve Web pages to other computers that request them. These pages contain the information a company wishes to share with others – a corporate history, press releases, product information – as well as an electronic catalog of goods and services for sale. The electronic catalog has many advantages over the print version. It can be updated continuously and instantaneously to reflect current inventories and prices. To maintain transaction accounting, the Web server is attached to the firm's database. Through forms on the Web page, the user enters personal data and any payment information, which is sent to the database, stored, and used as if it were a telephone order placed through a traditional mail-order company.

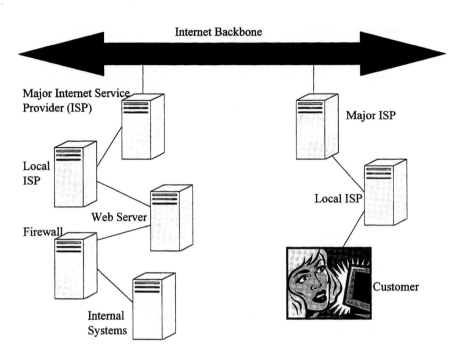

Figure 11-2: Business-to-Consumer Electronic Commerce

INTRANETS

Internet technology and the World Wide Web are rapidly being deployed inside organizations and between partner organizations, replacing older technologies in areas ranging from order processing to electronic data interchange (EDI). These applications operate in the same manner as the Internet, generally possess the same characteristics, and have the same system architecture. The difference is in where they are located and how access within the network is governed.

An intranet is an Internet technology-based network used within the boundaries of an organization. Intranets need not be connected to the public Internet, but most are. Those that are connected to the Internet are protected by firewalls from outside intrusion. An intranet provides a cost-efficient way for an organization to exchange corporate data and files. The most common use of intranets is to electronically publish company documents, such as employee manuals, product catalogs, brochures, 401(k) information or engineering drawings. Documents published in this way can be accessed and used by employees around the office or, depending on the size of the organization, around the world. Intranet publication saves printing costs, aids in communication among team members, and helps reduce cycle times. In some cases, it also helps centralize data and reduce redundancy.

Intranets are also capable of supporting business and technical computing applications that include all of the functionality that can be produced using older technologies. Some organizations plan to move more and more of their transaction-based day-to-day communications to their intranets.

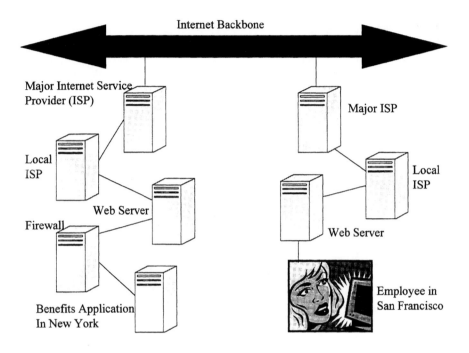

Figure 11-3: Sample Intranet Application

EXTRANETS

An extranet extends an organization's intranet to include outside companies that it interacts with regularly. Use of extranets enables organizations to have direct interaction with suppliers, dealers and customers, while maintaining security through the use of a firewall. Authorized personnel from partner companies can exchange information such as proposals, cost estimates and product specification in a timely manner. This can be accomplished regardless of whether the physical separation between the two locations is across a town or across the country. Aggressive use of extranets in areas such as purchasing have resulted in substantial costs reductions and cycle time improvements.

Eventually, the distinction between intranets, extranets and the Internet may blur. There will be one global network, and everyone will be able to access some places and not other places. Geographically dispersed organizations will work better together. The world will be smaller, in no small part because of the Internet and the World Wide Web technology.

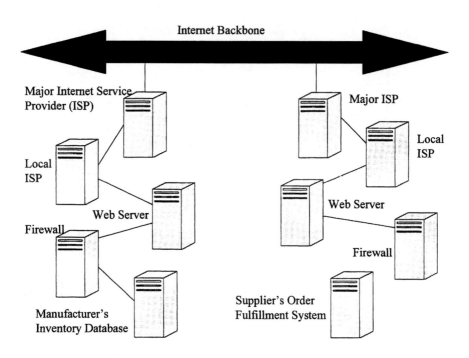

Figure 11-4: Extranets: Business-to-Business Electronic Commerce

Chapter 12

Impact of Electronic Commerce on the Consulting Industry

E-commerce consulting comprises the services consulting firms provide to help conceive and launch an e-commerce business model and integrate it, if necessary, with an existing business. E-commerce consulting is expected to grow explosively in the coming years. Forrester Research estimates that the U.S. market alone will reach $47.7 billion in 2002. E-commerce consulting is destined to grow quickly and become a huge business for those consulting firms willing and able to capitalize on the opportunity. E-commerce consulting is not one but a range of services that includes strategy, implementation and outsourcing. Organizations are expected to spend heavily on the third category of e-commerce services, outsourcing, in addition to strategy and implementation consulting. Outsourcing services include Web hosting, Application Service Providers (ASP's), network management, logistics, fulfillment, call centers and financial transaction processing.

Companies, ranging from industrial giants to start-ups, are embracing the Internet for several reasons:

- To maximize firm value by exploiting the premium placed by the financial markets on e-commerce business models.
- To gain or protect a competitive advantage.
- To reduce costs.
- To increase customer satisfaction.

The prospect of making millions through stock options, the fear of being left behind competitively, the potential to reduce costs substantially, and the opportunity to dramatically increase customer satisfaction is proving to be a fertile ground for start-ups to sprout up, and for traditional companies to plant seeds that grow into e-businesses. That being said, achieving these results is no simple matter. Four challenges confront those driving forward to these goals – figuring out the appropriate solution given the unique circumstances each organization confronts, creating a plan on how to implement the solution, finding resources to do the work, and managing the effort. These are precisely the types of challenges that consulting firms have helped companies solve for years, so companies naturally turn to consulting firms for information, advice and assistance.

The impact of the Internet on the consulting industry has been substantial and is likely to continue during the months and years ahead. In some cases, the technology is accelerating already existing trends such as centralization, reversing others such as increasing leverage ratios, and introducing completely new capabilities, such as finding qualified consultants online. A race is underway to build credible, successful, e-commerce consulting practices requiring massive investments to reposition established firms and grow the new ones. Yet, capturing a slice of the Internet consulting pie is only part of the picture, for the Internet also offers intriguing possibilities for changing how services are bought, sold, and delivered, altering relationships among clients, firms and employees, and speeding the globalization of the consulting industry.

Category	$ billions	Percent of Total
Internet strategy	2.1	4.4 %
Brand strategy	2.9	6.1 %
Business process redesign	2.9	6.1 %
Change management strategy	2.1	4.4 %
Campaign analysis and tracking	0.8	1.7 %
Creative development	2.6	5.4 %
Content management	0.9	1.9 %
User interface design	8.1	12.9%
Application integration	11.3	23.6 %
E-commerce package implementation	3.8	7.9 %
Custom software development	10.3	21.5 %
Total Market	**47.8**	**100.0 %**

Table 12-1: Estimated Detailed Breakdown of the U.S. Electronic Commerce Consulting Market in 2002

Amidst this abundance of opportunity with companies everywhere looking to consultants for help in understanding and adopting e-commerce business models, there is a frantic scramble underway among consulting firms as they seek to gain a strong position in the newly emerging market for e-commerce consulting. On one hand, new entrants such as Scient, Sapient, Viant, Agency.com and Razorfish are rapidly growing and attaining a highly visible presence in this area. Meanwhile, incumbent firms such as Andersen Consulting and McKinsey are overhauling, in some cases dramatically, their long-held business practices and making massive investments to develop credible e-commerce consulting practices. Firms, incumbents and new entrants, can be classified as falling into one of six e-commerce consulting segments. These segments, clusters of similar firms competing with one another, are: business strategy, creative, interactive, infrastructure and integration, Information Technology (IT) staffing, and outsourcing. Of these six segments the newer, Internet-focused consulting firms such as Scient, Viant, Agency.com, and Razorfish, dominate one, interactive. The remaining segments are dominated by incumbent organizations.

- *Business Strategy*: McKinsey, Boston Consulting Group, Bain
- *Creative*: Ogilvy One and Fish
- *Interactive*: Scient, Viant, Agency.com and Razorfish
- *Infrastructure and Integration*: Andersen Consulting, Arthur Andersen, PricewaterhouseCoopers, Deloitte Consulting, EDS / AT Kearney, IBM Consulting, KPMG, Cap Gemini, CSC
- *IT Staffing*: Compuware, Mastech, Infosys, Keane
- *Outsourcing*:
    - Web hosting: Bell South and Digital Nation
    - Application Service Providers: Telecomputing and Corio

- Network Management: AT&T and MCI Worldcom
- Logistics: UPS and Penske
- Fulfillment: Fingerhut
- Call Centers: Network Direct and MCI Worldcom
- Financial Transaction Processing: First Data

While the largest consulting firms, such as Andersen Consulting, PricewaterhouseCoopers and EDS / AT Kearney, will derive the vast majority of their e-commerce consulting revenue from infrastructure and integration – building the robust technical and operation infrastructures to support Web sites and integrating e-business with legacy systems and existing operations – they will also play a significant role in the business strategy and interactive segments. Moreover, due to their sheer size, these firms will provide e-consulting services to most industries and in virtually all regions of the world. Because of their scale, breadth and depth, these firms will be viewed as multi-service or full-service consulting organizations. In contrast will be the tens of thousands of other consulting firms, niche players, whose work will be focused on a much narrower set of services, segments, industries and/or geographic regions.

Many of the firms have expertise and successfully deliver services that fall outside the positioning shown above. By placing a firm such as Boston Consulting Group into the business strategy grouping, Andersen Consulting into infrastructure and integration, Scient into interactive, or Keane into IT staffing, the intent is to represent the primary, predominant, and most widely recognized area of expertise for these firms.

COMPETITION IN ELECTRONIC COMMERCE CONSULTING

The New Entrants

New entrants – Scient, Sapient, Viant, Agency.com and Razorfish – are off to a fast start. Though being founded mostly in the mid-1990's, they have been highly successful both in terms of their rapid growth and high market capitalization. The success of these new firms is the result of several factors. Mostly publicly traded, they have a liquid and, for some, a rapidly appreciating non-cash currency – common stock – that enables them to make acquisitions and acquire talented employees more cheaply, offering stock options in lieu of high salaries and bonuses, than the mostly privately held incumbent consulting firms. Given that compensation is the largest single cost a consulting firm faces, having an advantage here can offer a significant competitive advantage.

In addition, their smaller size and lack of institutional history enables them to integrate disciplines more easily. Also they have a reputation for being more creative - a skill that at most incumbent firms has historically received little attention - and for having deeper knowledge of Internet technologies. And, perhaps most importantly, the new firms grasped the importance of the much faster pace at which things happen in an e-business compared to the traditional business environment, sooner than incumbent firms.

These factors have combined to give the new firms a powerful image in the market for e-commerce consulting. For example, 90% of the Web site developers felt that the Big Five consulting firms do not grasp issues as well as the pure-play Web developers. Yet the advantages of better execution – lower costs, better integration across disciplines, greater creativity, deeper knowledge of Internet technologies and faster delivery of services – is only half of the reason why the new entrants have been so successful to date. The other half has to do with the failure of the incumbents to respond to the e-commerce consulting market as it first began to emerge.

During the mid-1990's, the incumbent technology-oriented consulting firms, such as Andersen Consulting, were in the midst of a period of unprecedented demand and profitability. This was the result of clients procuring complex ERP software, such as SAP's R/3, that took years to install, and could easily cost over $100 million in consulting services to install. Strategy firms too embraced larger-scale projects, such as Booz-Allen's massive reengineering project at Universal Studios and McKinsey's large cost-reduction project at Time-Warner. With such mammoth and highly profitable opportunities abounding, the incumbent firms simply did not want to bother with the much smaller projects usually found in e-commerce. This attitude, common in all major consulting firms at this time, allowed the new entrants to build e-commerce consulting practices, at least initially, without significant competition from their strongest potential competitors, the incumbents.

Incumbents Build Capacity

The incumbents have now awoken to the opportunity of e-commerce consulting and the threat posed by the new entrants. They are employing a number of techniques and making dramatic changes to enhance their e-commerce consulting credibility in the eyes of prospective clients and expand their e-commerce consulting skills. Many of the incumbents have announced plans to make massive investments in their e-commerce consulting services.

Incumbents Change Organizational Practices

The incumbents, aware that a historic opportunity to expand into a new market, e-commerce consulting, may be slipping from their grasp, are taking even more radical actions than simply investing in new marketing campaigns, service development or organizational units. In some cases, they are attempting to change the core principles, practices, and values of their firms.

New Entrants versus Incumbents

As the battle for the e-commerce consulting market intensifies, it remains to be seen who, the incumbent firms or the new entrants, will come to dominate the field. And should it be the incumbents that win, then will it be the business strategy or the technology-oriented firms? The new entrants have benefited from better execution and a lack of competition, at least during the early stages of the development of the e-commerce consulting market. This has allowed them to grow quickly and be perceived as better understanding the Internet and its issues than the incumbent firms. However, though growing at a rapid clip, they remain small compared to the incumbents which places them at a disadvantage when trying to bid or service a large e-commerce consulting project for a global corporation. In addition, their small size and young workforce is often perceived as lacking the insight and experience needed to develop the detailed strategies and approaches appropriate for a company, particularly when it involves industry-specific issues. Indeed, many of the new firms are furiously hiring experienced consultants and managers from the established firms in order to expand, improve their depth of industry knowledge and enhance their project management expertise. Moreover, the days of easy growth for the new entrants are rapidly coming to a close as the consulting giants ramp up their organizations to sell and deliver e-commerce consulting services.

Beyond greater size, deeper industry knowledge and more project-management expertise, the incumbent firms, both business-strategy ones such as McKinsey, and the technology-oriented ones such as Andersen Consulting, have the enormous benefit of large networks of contacts and relationships. Over the years they have built relationships at all levels within major corporations. This network, which some actively use during their selling process, provides them with invaluable inside information and political support – a source of significant competitive advantage when it comes to selling consulting services. And their long track record of successfully delivering results gives them greater credibility with clients than the new entrants whose track record is less extensive.

But the incumbent firms face equally daunting challenges in their race to fight and win in the e-commerce consulting market. Their core offering, business strategy consulting, has, compared to technology oriented consulting, been a slow growth sector for the past ten years. Indeed, some of the largest projects during this period at major business-strategy firms, such as McKinsey and Booz-Allen, have not been in business strategy, rather, in the areas of process improvement and cost reduction. In addition, a trend to shorter-duration strategy projects that hurts profits, has now accelerated due to e-commerce consulting. On an e-commerce consulting project, business-strategy firms are finding that they must dedicate a manager full time to the project because of the speed and intensity of work. Before, a manager could oversee two or three projects concurrently, allowing more junior personnel to perform a greater proportion of the work.

And, as if the challenges of slow growth in core services, shorter-duration projects, and reduced leverage were not enough, the business strategy firms also face an increasing threat from technology oriented consulting firms that offer business strategy services at a discount. They have done so in order to build senior level relationships and to improve their competitive position when it comes time to sell the far more profitable technology implementation services in which they specialize. For the business strategy firms, traditionally unwilling or unable to deliver implementation services, the option of offering discounted strategy services has not been a viable or attractive alternative. At first, the business strategy practices at the large technology focused consulting firms, such as Andersen Consulting and PricewaterhouseCoopers, were viewed as inferior to the services provided by the prestige firms such as Bain, Boston Consulting Group, Booz-Allen, and McKinsey, However, that has started to change, as these units are increasingly successful at winning in head-to-head competitions.

Lastly, the business strategy firms have been viewed as not having a deep understanding of technology issues and lacking the skills and experience to successfully implement technology. Given the central role information technology plays in e-commerce, this places them at a further disadvantage when trying to enter the e-commerce consulting market.

The large, technology-oriented incumbent consulting firms, such as Andersen Consulting and PricewaterhouseCoopers, also face considerable challenges entering the e-commerce consulting arena. During the 1990s, their unprecedented levels of growth and profitability have been powered by multi-year, heavily staffed projects such as those to implement an ERP software package. Pointing toward the declining ERP market, Forrester Research is pessimistic about the prospects of firms such as Andersen Consulting reorienting to deliver e-commerce consulting. Retraining the 65,000 worldwide Andersen Consulting employees to deliver electronic commerce services is a difficult task. The Big Five will ultimately have to blow up their existing operating models and regroup around e-commerce services or perish.

Building Partnerships

Rather than compete head-on, several incumbent and Internet-focused firms are building alliances to leverage each other's strengths. For the Internet firms, such arrangements provide them with access to the contacts, expertise, infrastructure, scale and resources that the incumbent firms already have. The incumbent firms, in turn, gain by enhancing their e-commerce consulting knowledge, skill and credibility through their association with the Internet firms. However, such partnerships are notoriously difficult to manage and make successful for both parties.

Date	Alliance Type	Incumbent firm	Internet firm
March 2000	Joint Venture	Andersen Consulting	Microsoft
March 2000	Joint Venture	Cap Gemini	Cisco
December 1999	Acquisition	Whittman-Hart	USWeb / CKS
November 1999	Alliance	Deloitte Consulting	US Interactive
September 1999	Joint Venture	KPMG	Cisco
August 1999	Alliance	Bain	Mainspring
August 1999	Acquisition	Mitchell Madison	USWeb / CKS
November 1998	Equity stake	McKinsey	Skunk Technologies

Table 12-2: Partnerships and Alliances

The Brain Drain

While everyone, incumbents and new entrants, battles with one another for dominance in e-commerce consulting, there is one problem that impacts them all – people – specifically an acute shortage of experienced e-commerce consultants. In fact, many feel that the battle for e-commerce consulting dominance will be won or lost not in developing and delivering superior services or in creating the best marketing campaign, but rather, in the efforts to recruit qualified personnel. The lack of experienced people is the primary constraint impeding the growth of both the new entrants and incumbent firms. This creates a classic supply and demand problem. The demand for individuals with Internet experience and industry knowledge is high while the supply of them is at an all time low as many individuals leave consulting firms early or bypass them in their careers in favor of working at e-commerce firms commonly referred to as dot-coms. Virtually everyone in the consulting industry is deeply concerned. Many consultants have left Andersen, McKinsey and other firms to take mid-level and senior-level positions at dot-coms.

Similar dynamics existed during the early stages of the ERP software mania in the middle to late 1990s, particularly surrounding individuals with SAP R/3 experience. The consulting industry was able to successfully meet the demand by undertaking large and expensive training programs to create certified consultants. Large firms with extensive professional development and training programs already in place are particularly well positioned to create new armies of technically proficient e-commerce consultants.

However, this approach will only solve part of the problem, for the demand for individuals knowledgeable in e-commerce cuts across all levels, from junior associates to senior executives, and from those possessing hard, technical skills to those with soft skills such as motivating people. The training programs and on-the-job experiences offered by the big consulting firms are quite successful at developing technical skills in low-level and mid-level consultants. But the soft skills and considered business judgment that comes largely through years of experience and personal characteristics, and so much in demand by both dot-coms and consulting firms, are very difficult, if not impossible, to develop quickly through conventional training programs.

Realizing that training programs alone will not solve their acute shortage of e-commerce consultants, consulting firms are also taking numerous steps to stem the tide of those leaving to join dot-coms and to attract new employees to their organizations. The most common techniques are modifying career paths, expanding profit or equity participation, helping launch the business ideas of employees, and/or offering unique benefits.

Growth Prospects, Valuation, and Ownership

Given the comparative strengths and weaknesses of the incumbents and the new entrants, most analysts see each attaining significant market share in the e-commerce consulting space. One research firm predicts that the incumbent firms will win about 75% of the e-commerce consulting market, the remaining 25% going to the new firms. Given the much larger size of the established firms, this translates into a lower relative growth rate compared to the new entrants.

In terms of ownership, private versus public, the growth of e-commerce consulting is proving to be a powerful catalyst for change. Traditionally, consulting firms have been private, either in the form of the partnership (Andersen Consulting) or as a closely held corporation (Boston Consulting Group and McKinsey). However, most of the new entrants (Scient, Sapient, Razorfish, etc.) are public. For the new firms, public ownership has conveyed substantial benefits. It enables them to make acquisitions using stock instead of cash, allows them to access external sources of capital to invest and grow the business, reduces costs by granting employees stock options instead of high salaries, and increases the liquidity and value of ownership stakes. Selling shares to the public allows owners to receive cash immediately instead of, as at a private firm, waiting until a future date, usually when they leave, to be allowed to sell their shares back to the firm. In addition, selling shares to the public typically results in a substantial premium over book value, the way most private firms value their equity. All of these benefits are proving to be a powerful incentive pulling the incumbent, mostly private firms to consider going public.

Another force pushing the incumbents to go public, perhaps the primary one, is the belief among many that the value of these consulting groups is at a maximum. The revenue growth of their traditional (non e-commerce consulting) services has slowed or stopped. They face huge investments in retraining, service development, recruiting, retention and marketing to reposition themselves as legitimate e-commerce consultants. And they face the high risks inherent in undertaking such a profound change. Going public potentially allows the owners of these firms to cash out, often at a premium, at a point when the firms and the market may be at peak value.

Much like other professional service industries, such as investment banking and stock brokerages, the consulting industry may be poised to convert from private to public ownership. Experts on the evolution of capital markets frequently contend that once an industry begins to convert to public ownership, the process becomes irreversible, with all major players ultimately changing over. But this is not a foregone conclusion in the case of the consulting industry, as some industry observers question the sustainability of running a public, professional services firm. Indeed, some consulting firms that have made the transition to public ownership, but whose shares have failed to appreciate or have declined in value, have suffered from morale and turnover problems as a result.

ISSUES IN ELECTRONIC COMMERCE CONSULTING

Beyond the immediate impact that the Internet is having on the consulting industry, the capabilities of the Internet may result in dramatic, long-term changes to the industry. It has the potential to significantly affect how consulting services are bought, sold and delivered, the relationships firms will have with their clients and employees, and the globalization of the industry.

Change in the Consulting Market

The Internet may accelerate changes in the way consulting services are bought, sold, and delivered. Sites such as Expert Marketplace allow prospective clients to search a large number of potential consulting firms, post requests for proposals, or ask the site's staff to recommend someone. Essentially a referral service, it has resulted in some major successes.

One major retailer uses a bidding process on the Internet to select consultants for staff augmentation purposes, that is, finding individuals with specific skills to work with their information technology group or to support a process improvement team. They place their staffing requirements on their Web site, making it accessible to anyone. About 70% of the need is filled by firms submitting proposals or resumes. The remainder is filled by individuals submitting their qualifications. The company currently procures about 60-70% of all consulting services in this fashion. The remaining 30-40%, typically for projects that are more strategic in nature, are still purchased through relationships and a conventional request for proposal process with business-strategy firms such as McKinsey or technology-oriented firms such as Andersen Consulting.

General Electric and General Motors have both announced that they intend to purchase everything via the Internet in the next few years, but to what degree this includes professional services is unclear. Large companies such as these that create a more open and competitive bidding process for professional services could possibly realize substantially lower costs. This has already occurred in two areas of professional services: medical services for employees and outside legal services. In both cases, the rate of cost increases have reduced. But the impact on the quality of the services delivered remains controversial with various studies reaching opposite conclusions.

Aside from buying consulting services, will the Internet be a catalyst changing the way in which consulting services are sold? This is a controversial subject since the selling of professional services depends greatly upon building personal relationships, something many feel cannot be done effectively in an Internet environment. Many feel that the Internet cannot be used to form or maintain relationships because of its limited ability to transmit non-verbal information, and the difficulty in determining the true background and qualifications of those met on the medium. A large number of people believe that the Internet will remain best suited for relatively straightforward transactions - such as buying a CD or car. Complex, customized products, such as consulting services, in their view, cannot be effectively sold on the Internet because of the high degree of interactivity required to configure the proposal, conclude the sale, and complete the work.

Once the project is sold, will the Internet change the way services are delivered? Several large firms are studying this possibility, but are having difficulty reconciling their current approaches with ones that use the Internet. Many consultants feel that a constant physical presence at the client's site is critical to forming strong relationships, delivering high-quality work through the exchange of information that occurs when clients and consultants work side by side, and convincing the client that value is being delivered. Moreover, many consultants and clients do not view dispersed work groups as particularly effective or desirable because of prior bad experiences with such arrangements. But change may nonetheless be on the way. Clients are pushing consultants hard to get work done faster and to better integrate business strategy, technology and implementation. And distributed project teams, replacing a project team that is assembled together at one location, are expected to explode in popularity in the coming years, made possible by a class of Web applications called Enterprise Project Collaboration. Gartner Group estimates that by 2003, 40% of large enterprises will extensively use inter-enterprise project collaboration. Various sites on the Internet – eProject, eGroups, xCollaboration, Centra and Instinctive.com – as well as more traditional groupware products, such as IBM's Notes and Microsoft's Exchange, are quickly developing comprehensive Web applications that help project teams, dispersed or not, complete work faster, with more input and better integration. Relatively simple collaborative and project-management software is even available free on some Web sites.

Aside from using Web applications to help improve the performance of project teams, some firms, usually the established ones, are experimenting with another form of consulting – using the Internet as a pipeline to deliver expert advice to clients. Some view this migration of consulting advice, information and project work to the Internet as inevitable in the years ahead. They speculate that the generation of people that grew up using the Internet is now in college, and about to enter the workforce. They will embrace the Internet in the work environment, speeding its adoption and integration. For these people, comfortable in discussion groups, surfing the Web, holding instant messaging conversations, e-mailing, and the like, working with others over the Internet will seem obvious and natural. As a consultant or as a client, the Internet may become their preferred medium for working and learning.

Change in the Firm-Client Relationship

The Internet is providing customers with more – and better – information about the firms that service them. Consulting has been considered a notoriously inefficient market with limited information about firms available to clients. The information that has been available was not standardized, in large part because the consultants' output was intangible and customized. Contributing to this information asymmetry was the fact that most consulting firms kept client relationships confidential. This limited access to past customers and the products produced for them, perhaps the best indicator of future performance. All these factors combined to make comparisons among consulting firms very difficult.

The Internet could allow greater sharing of information, reducing the information asymmetry. Intermediaries could establish consistent standards for evaluating firms and their consultants. But given the rather chaotic nature of the Internet, finding a qualified intermediary might prove difficult. Moreover, the benefits of doing so may not be sufficient to overcome the inevitable resistance of the consulting industry. And while the customer would benefit from receiving information, sharing information exposes them to risks. Confidential or embarrassing data, opinions or decisions could become public.

Change in the Firm-Employee Relationship

Besides impacting the relationship between consulting firms and clients, the Internet may also hasten changes in the relationship between employees and their firms. Many consultants and clients alike feel that the most important factors determining the outcome of a consulting project are the knowledge, skills and abilities of those delivering the advice. This perception, if it strengthens, portents a shift in power from the firms to the individuals working at them. The Internet may accelerate this shift by making it easier for clients to directly find the most qualified individual to work on a project instead of relying upon the consulting firm acting as an intermediary. Auction-style markets, such as FreeAgent.com, are developing, where individuals post their skills and are then bought by companies and consulting firms to complete a specific project. Such an approach could easily develop into a star system, similar to that seen in professional sports, where people with good track records and relevant experience that is in high demand could command premium compensation by selling their services to the highest bidder.

Trend Toward Centralization and Globalization

The Internet also offers the possibility of removing geographic barriers between consultants and clients enabling dispersed work teams, thus reducing the geographic barriers that have structured the industry. Historically, most consulting firms have been highly decentralized organizations. For many firms, whether a partnership or corporation, the office managing partner or regional director was the most powerful position in a firm. They had almost absolute decision-making authority over everything that happened within their geographic region and were the most senior people in a firm with direct control over staff.

As projects became bigger, clients sought to have fewer but bigger vendors, and various industries have become increasingly global, consulting firms responded by undergoing varying degrees of centralization. The Internet may further accelerate the trend towards centralization by reducing geographic barriers globally. Removing geographic barriers by embracing dispersed work groups can result in substantial cost savings, allowing significant portions of consulting work to be sourced to low-wage countries such as India. Currently, extensive programming occurs there for companies in the U.S. and Europe. One major strategy firm has plans underway to develop research capabilities there too. And the promise of virtual consulting, logging on to a Web site and getting the information and advice you need, is completely independent of geographic constraints from the standpoint of those providing the service and those receiving it. But in developing and using these capabilities in the short term, some U.S. consulting firms are creating more competition for themselves in the longer run. One Indian company, Infosys, started primarily as a contract programming shop, has been so successful that it is now rapidly building a U.S. presence as a full-service consulting firm.

Another example of increased competition for U.S. firms resulting from globalization is the example of a firm based in India that is now building complete Web sites for companies in the U.S. Their location allows them to build sites for a fraction of the cost of their U.S.-based competitors. In the U.S., they have a small staff available to respond to inquiries and sell projects. But the bulk of the design work and all the programming occur in India. Some of their clients remark that the delivery of services is so seamless that it is not apparent to them that they were primarily dealing with individuals located in another country.

The new Internet-focused consulting firms already report hits on their Web sites and inquiries from countries other than the U.S. where they currently have no physical presence. Clearly, the Internet is enabling connections between the solution providers and potential clients that were previously difficult or impossible to make.

Chapter 13

Organizational Design and Change Management in E-Businesses

IMPACT OF ELECTRONIC COMMERCE ON ORGANIZATIONAL DESIGN

The Internet has the power to fundamentally change the way work is done. A temporary, self-managed gathering of diverse individuals engaged in a common task is a model for a new kind of business organization that could form the basis for the Internet economy. The fundamental unit of such an economy is not the corporation, but the individual. Tasks aren't assigned and controlled through a stable chain of management, but rather are carried out autonomously by independent contractors. These electronically connected freelancers join together into fluid and temporary networks to produce and sell goods and services. When the job is done, the network dissolves, and its members become independent agents again, circulating through the economy, seeking the next assignment.

The Internet economy is, in many ways, already upon us. We see it in the evolution of the Internet itself. We see it in the rise of virtual companies, in the rise of outsourcing and telecommuting, and in the proliferation of freelance and temporary workers. Even within large organizations, we see it in the increasing importance of ad hoc project teams, in the rise of "intrapreneurs", and in the formation of independent business units.

All these trends point to the devolution of large, permanent corporations into flexible, temporary networks of individuals. No one can yet say exactly how important or widespread this new form of business organization will become, but judging from current signs, it is not inconceivable that it could define work in the twenty-first century as the industrial organization defined it in the twentieth. If it does, business and society will be changed forever.

The Downsizing of Businesses

Business organizations are, in essence, mechanisms for coordination. They exist to guide the flow of work, materials, ideas and money, and the form they take is strongly affected by the coordination technologies available. Despite all the recent talk of decentralized management, empowered employees and horizontal processes, the large industrial organization continues to dominate the economy today. We remain in the age of multinational megacompanies, and those companies appear to be rushing to merge into ever larger forms.

Yet when we look beneath the surface of all the mergers and acquisitions activity, we see signs of a counterphenomenon: the disintegration of the large corporation. People are leaving big companies and either joining much smaller companies or going into business for themselves as contract workers, freelancers or temps. Twenty-five years ago, one in five U.S. workers was employed by a *Fortune 500* company. Today the ratio has dropped to less than one in ten. While big companies control ever larger flows of cash, they are exerting less and less direct control over actual business activity.

Even within large corporations, traditional command-and-control management is becoming less common. Decisions are increasingly being pushed lower down in organizations. Workers are being rewarded not for efficiently carrying out orders but for figuring out what needs to be done and then doing it. Some large industrial companies, such as Asea Brown Boveri and British Petroleum, have broken themselves up into scores of independent units that transact business with one another almost as if they were separate companies. And in some industries, such as investment banking and consulting, it is often easier to understand the existing organizations not as traditional hierarchies but as confederations of entrepreneurs, united only by a common brand name.

Why is the traditional industrial organization showing evidence of disintegration? The answer lies in the basic economics of organizations. Economists and organizational theorists have long wrestled with the question of why businesses grow large or stay small. Their research suggests that when it is cheaper to conduct transactions internally, within the bounds of a corporation, organizations grow larger, but when it is cheaper to conduct transactions externally, with independent entities in the open market, organizations stay small or shrink. If, for example, the owners of an iron smelter find it less expensive to establish a sales force than to contract with outside agencies to sell their products, they will hire salespeople, and their organization will grow. If they find that outside agencies cost less, they will not hire the salespeople, and their organization will not grow.

The coordination technologies of the industrial era – the telegraph, the telephone, the mainframe computer – made internal transactions not only possible, but also advantageous. Companies were able to manage large organizations centrally, which provided them with economies of scale in manufacturing, marketing, distribution, and other activities. It made economic sense to directly control many different functions and businesses and to hire the legions of administrators and supervisors needed to manage them.

But with the introduction of powerful personal computers and broad electronic networks such as the Internet – the coordination technologies of the twenty-first century – the economic equation changes. Because information can be shared instantly and inexpensively among many people in many locations, the value of centralized decision making and expensive bureaucracies decreases. Individuals can manage themselves, coordinating their efforts through electronic links with other independent parties.

In one sense, the new coordination technologies enable us to return to the preindustrial organizational model of tiny autonomous businesses conducting transactions with one another in a market. But there is one crucial difference: the Internet enables these microbusinesses to tap into the global reservoirs of information, expertise and financing that used to be available only to large companies. The small companies enjoy many of the benefits of the large companies without sacrificing the leanness, flexibility and creativity of the small.

In the future, as communications technologies advance and networks become more efficient, the shift to small, independent, autonomous businesses promises to accelerate. Should that indeed take place, the dominant business organization of the future may not be a stable, permanent corporation but rather an elastic network that may sometimes exist for no more than a day or two. When a project needs to be undertaken, requests for proposals will be transmitted or electronic want ads posted, individuals or small teams will respond, a network will be formed, and new workers will be brought on as their particular skills are needed. Once the project is done, the network will disband. We will enter the age of the temporary company.

A shift to the Internet economy would bring about fundamental changes in virtually every business function, not just in product design. Supply chains would become ad hoc structures, assembled to fit the needs of a particular project and disassembled when the project ended. Manufacturing capacity would be bought and sold in an open market, and independent, specialized manufacturing concerns would undertake small batch orders for a variety of brokers, design shops, and even consumers. Marketing would be performed in some cases by brokers, in other cases by small companies that would own brands and certify the quality of the merchandise sold under them. In still other cases, the ability of consumers to share product information on the Internet would render marketing obsolete; consumers would simply purchase the best offerings. Financing would come less from retained earnings and big equity markets and more from venture capitalists and interested individuals. Small investors might trade shares in ad hoc, project-based enterprises over the Internet. Businesses would be transformed fundamentally. But nowhere would the changes be as great as in the function of management itself.

The Transformation Of Management

In the mid-1990s, when the Internet was just entering the consciousness of most business executives, the press was filled with disaster stories. The Internet, the pundits proclaimed, was about to fall into disarray. Traffic on the World Wide Web was growing too fast. There were too many Web sites, too many people online. Demand was outstripping capacity, and it was only a matter of months before the entire network crashed or froze.

It never happened. The Internet has continued to expand at an astonishing rate. Its capacity has doubled every year since 1988, and today more than 300 million people are connected to it. They use it to order books and flowers, to check on weather conditions in distant cities, to trade stocks and commodities, to send messages and spread propaganda, and to join discussion groups on everything from soap operas to particle physics.

So who is responsible for this great and unprecedented achievement? Who oversaw what is arguably the most important business development of the past 50 years? No one. No one controls the Internet. No one is in charge. No one is the leader. The Internet grew out of the combined efforts of all its users, with no central management. In fact, when people are asked whether they think the Internet could have grown this fast for this long if it had been managed by a single company, most say no. Managing such a massive and unpredictable explosion of capacity and creativity would have been beyond the skills of even the most astute and capable executives. The Internet *had* to be self-managed.

The Internet is the greatest model of a network organization that has yet emerged, and it reveals a startling truth: in the networked economy, the role of the traditional business manager changes dramatically and sometimes disappears completely. The work of the temporary company is coordinated by the individuals who compose it, with little or no centralized direction or control. Brokers, venture capitalists and general contractors all play key roles – initiating projects, allocating resources and coordinating work – but there need not be any single point of oversight. Instead, the overall results emerge from the individual actions and interactions of all the different players in the system.

But what if this kind of decentralized control were used to organize all the different kinds of activities that today go on inside companies? One of the things that allow a free market to work is the establishment and acceptance of a set of standards – the "rules of the game" – that governs all the transactions. The rules of the game can take many forms, including contracts, systems of ownership, and procedures for dispute resolution. Similarly, for the Internet economy to work, whole new classes of agreements, specifications and common architectures will need to evolve.

We see this in the Internet, which works because everyone involved with it conforms to certain technical specifications. You don't have to ask anyone for permission to become a network provider or a user; you just have to obey the communication protocols that govern the Internet. Standards are the glue that holds the Internet together, and they will be the glue that binds temporary companies together and helps them operate efficiently.

Standards don't have to take the form of technical specifications. They may take the form of routinized processes. In other cases, the standards may simply be patterns of behavior that come to be accepted as norms – what might today be referred to as the culture of a company or an industry. One of the primary roles for the large companies that remain in the future may be to establish rules, standards and cultures for network organizations operating partly within and partly outside their own boundaries. In other words, the value the firm provides to its members comes mainly from the standards it has established, not from the strategic or operational skills of its top managers.

As more large companies establish decentralized, market-based organizational structures, the boundaries between companies will become much less important. Transactions within organizations will become indistinguishable from transactions between organizations, and business processes, once proprietary, will freely cross organizational boundaries. The key role for many individuals – whether they call themselves managers or not – will be to play their parts in shaping a network that neither they nor anyone else controls.

Thinking About The Future

The new Internet economy, though a radical concept, is by no means an impossible, or even an implausible concept. Most of the necessary building blocks – high-bandwidth networks, data interchange standards, groupware, electronic currency, venture capital micromarkets – either are in place or are under development. What is lagging behind technology is our imagination. Most people are not able to conceive of a completely new economy where much of what they know about doing business no longer applies.

The reason it is so important for us to recognize and to challenge the biases of our existing mind-set is that the rise of the Internet economy would have profound implications for business and society, and we should begin considering those implications sooner rather than later. An Internet economy might well lead to a flowering of individual wealth, freedom and creativity. Business might become much more flexible and efficient, and people might find themselves with much more time for leisure, for education, and for other pursuits.

On the other hand, an Internet economy might lead to disruption and dislocation. Loosed from its traditional moorings, the business world might become chaotic and cut-throat. The gap between society's haves and have-nots might widen, as those lacking special talents or access to the Internet fall by the wayside. The safety net currently formed by corporate benefits programs, such as health and disability insurance, might unravel. Internet workers, separated from the communities that companies create today, may find themselves lonely and alienated. All of these potential problems could probably be avoided, but we will not be able to avoid them if we remain blind to them.

DECONSTRUCTING THE ORGANIZATION

It is essential to understand the crucial role that interaction costs play in shaping industries and companies. Interaction costs represent the money and time that are expended whenever people and companies exchange goods, services or ideas. The exchanges can occur within companies, among companies, or between companies and customers, and they can take many everyday forms, including management meetings, conferences, phone conversations, sales calls, reports and memos. In a very real sense, interaction costs are the friction in the economy.

Taken together, interaction costs determine the way companies organize themselves and the way they form relationships with other parties. When the interaction costs of performing an activity internally are lower than the costs of performing it externally, a company will tend to incorporate that activity into its own organization rather than contract with an outside party to perform it. All else being equal, a company will organize in whatever way minimizes overall interaction costs.

Changes in interaction costs can cause entire industries to reorganize rapidly and dramatically. Today, that fact should give all managers pause, for we are on the verge of a broad, systemic reduction in interaction costs throughout the world economy. Electronic networks, combined with powerful personal computers, are enabling companies to communicate and exchange data far more quickly and cheaply than ever before. As more business interactions move onto electronic networks like the Internet, basic assumptions about corporate organization will be overturned. Activities that companies have always believed to be central to their business will suddenly be offered by new, specialized competitors that can do them better, faster and more efficiently. Executives will be forced to ask the most basic and the most discomforting question about their companies: What business are we really in? Their answers will determine their fate in an increasingly frictionless economy.

When you look beneath the surface of most companies, you find three kinds of businesses – a customer-relationship business, a product-innovation business and an infrastructure business. Although organizationally intertwined, these businesses are actually very different. They each play a unique role; they each employ different types of people; and they each have different economic, competitive, and even cultural imperatives.

The role of the customer-relationship business is to find customers and build relationships with them. The role of a product-innovation business is to conceive of attractive new products and services and figure out how best to bring them to market. The role of an infrastructure business is to build and manage facilities for high-volume, repetitive operational tasks such as logistics and storage, manufacturing, and communications. These three businesses – customer-relationship management, product innovation and infrastructure management – rarely map neatly to the organizational structure of a corporation. Rather than representing discrete organization units, the three businesses correspond to what are popularly called "core processes" – the cross-functional work flows that stretch from suppliers to customers and, in combination, define a company's identity.

Managers talk about their key activities as "processes" rather than as "businesses" because, with rare exceptions, they assume that the activities ought to coexist. Nearly a century of economic theory underpins the conventional wisdom that the management of customers, innovation and infrastructure must be combined within a single company. If those activities were disbursed to separate companies, the thinking goes, the interaction costs required to coordinate them would be too great. It is cheaper to do them yourself.

Working from that assumption, large companies have expended a lot of energy and resources reengineering and redesigning their core processes. They've used the latest information technology to eliminate handoffs, cut waiting time and reduce errors. For many companies, streamlining core processes has yielded impressive gains, saving substantial amounts of time and money, and providing customers with more valuable products and services.

But as managers have found, there are limits to such gains. Sooner or later, companies come up against a cold fact: the economics governing the three core processes conflict. Bundling them into a single corporation inevitably forces management to compromise the performance of each process in ways that no amount of reengineering can overcome.

Take customer relationship management. Finding and developing a relationship with a customer usually requires a big investment. Profitability hinges on achieving economies of scope – extending the relationship for as long as possible and generating as much revenue as possible from it. Only by gaining a large share of a customer's wallet and retaining that share over time can a company earn enough to offset the big up-front investment. Because of the need to achieve economies of scope, customer relationship businesses naturally seek to offer a customer as many products or services as possible. It is often in their interests to create highly customized offerings to maximize sales. Their economic imperatives lead to an intently service-oriented culture. When a customer calls, people in these businesses seek to respond to the customer's needs above all else. They spend a lot of time interacting with customers, and they develop a sophisticated feel for customers' requirements and preferences, even at the individual level.

Contrast that kind of business with a product innovation business. Speed, not scope, drives the economics of product innovation. Once a product-innovation business invests the resources necessary to develop a product or service, the faster it moves from the development shop to the market, the more money the business makes. Early entry into the market increases the likelihood of capturing a premium price and establishing a strong market share. Culturally, product-innovation businesses focus on serving employees, not customers. They do whatever they can to attract and retain the talent needed to come up with the latest and best product or service. They reward innovation, and they seek to minimize the administrative distractions that might frustrate or slow down their creative stars. Not surprisingly, small organizations tend to be better suited than large bureaucracies to nurturing the creativity and fleetness required for product innovation.

If scope drives relationship-management businesses and speed drives innovation businesses, scale is what drives infrastructure businesses. Such businesses generally require capital-intensive facilities, which entail high fixed costs. Since unit costs fall as scale increases, pumping large amounts of product or work through the facilities is essential for profitability. The culture of infrastructure businesses is characterized by a one-size-fits-all mentality that abhors all kinds of customization and special treatment. To keep costs as low as possible, they are motivated to make their outputs and activities as routine and predictable as possible. They account for every penny and frown on anything that does not directly contribute to efficient operations, viewing it as a needless extravagance. Where customer-relationship businesses focus on customers and innovation businesses focus on employees, infrastructure businesses are impersonal – they focus on the operation.

	Product Innovation	Customer Relationship Management	Infrastructure Management
Economics	Early market entry allows for a premium price and large market share; speed is key	High cost of customer acquisition makes it imperative to gain large shares of wallet; economies of scope are key	High fixed costs make large volumes essential to achieving low unit costs; economies of scale are key
Culture	Employee centered; coddling the creative "stars"	Highly service oriented; customer comes first	Cost focused; stress on standardization, predictability, efficiency
Competition	Battle for talent; low barriers to entry; many small players thrive	Battle for scope; rapid consolidation; a few big players dominate	Battle for scale; rapid consolidation; a few big players dominate

Table 13-1: Conflicting Pressures on the Three Types of Businesses

When the three businesses are bundled into a single corporation, their divergent economic and cultural imperatives inevitably conflict. Scope, speed and scale cannot be optimized simultaneously. Trade-offs have to be made. To protect its manufacturing scale, for example, a company may prohibit its salespeople from selling another company's products, thus limiting their ability to achieve economies of scope. Or a company may institute standardized pay scales that, while rational for the vast majority of its people, alienate its most talented product designers. Or to protect customer relationships, a company may require a degree of customization that slows product introductions and creates inefficiencies in the production infrastructure.

Most senior managers make such compromises because they believe, or assume, that they have no other option. How, after all, can a core process be removed from a company without somehow undermining its identity or destroying its essence? Such a mindset, although historically justified, is now becoming increasingly dangerous. While traditional companies strive to keep their core processes bundled together, highly specialized competitors are emerging that can optimize the particular activity they perform. Because they don't have to make compromises, these specialists have enormous advantages over integrated companies. Under the pressures of deregulation, global competition, and advancing technology, a number of industries are already fracturing along the fault lines of customer relationship management, product innovation, and infrastructure management. Established companies face a series of hard choices. They have to rethink their traditional roles and identities, challenge their organizational assumptions, and in many cases fundamentally change the way they operate.

Organization And The Internet

Because electronic commerce has such low interaction costs, it is natural for Web-based businesses to concentrate on a single core activity – whether it be just customer relationship management, just product innovation, or just infrastructure management. As electronic commerce spread out into other, more traditional industries, they too will begin to fracture.

A Road Map For Deconstruction

As more and more industries fracture, many traditional companies will find themselves cut off from their customers. Just to reach their markets, they will have to compete or cooperate with an increasingly powerful group of infomediaries. To survive, they may have no choice but to unbundle themselves and make a definitive decision about which business to focus on: customer-relationship management, product innovation, or infrastructure management. The economics driving each of these businesses are different, and those economics will determine their ultimate structures. Although industries will fracture, they will not necessarily break into lots of small pieces. In fact, the structure of only one of the three businesses – product innovation – is likely to be characterized by a large number of small businesses competing on a level playing field where barriers to entry are low. The product innovator's need to provide a fertile environment for creativity tends to favor small organizations, as does its need for speed and agility in bringing products to market.

The other two businesses – customer relationship management and infrastructure management – will probably consolidate quickly, as a small number of large companies assume dominance. Since economies of scope are necessary in the customer-relationship business, it is likely that only a few big infomediaries will survive. Similarly, in the infrastructure business, economies of scale create irresistible pressures toward the formation of large, focused enterprises.

Once a company decides where it wants to direct its energies, it will probably need to divest itself of its other businesses. That will be a big challenge. Few senior managers of large companies have ever attempted a systematic divestiture program. The divestitures that have occurred have usually been spin-offs of recent acquisitions whose expected synergies never materialized. For most companies, the closest analogue to this kind of divestiture is the establishment of outsourcing relationships in which infrastructure management activities, such as logistics, manufacturing or data processing, are contracted to outside providers. Divestiture is, of course, a radical step. It is fair to say that in most cases, executives will need to perceive a significant and immediate threat before they will consider such aggressive surgery. For that reason, the first divestiture programs will probably be launched by companies whose markets are in the midst of major technological or regulatory change, such as the computer, telecommunications, media and banking industries. Companies in other industries will be able to learn from their successes – and their mistakes.

If a company has chosen to compete in customer-relationship management or infrastructure management, where size matters, divestiture won't be enough. It will also need to build scope or scale through mergers and acquisitions. It is likely that each acquired company will have to go through a similar process of unbundling, shedding unneeded businesses to help fund the next wave of acquisitions and integrating the remaining businesses into the existing operation. The secret to success in fractured industries is not just to unbundle, but to unbundle and rebundle, creating a new organization with the capabilities and size required to win. Rebundling will be a very different process from the vertical integration that has often characterized traditional acquisition programs. Because companies will be focusing on a single activity – relationship management or infrastructure management – their acquisitions will be aimed at achieving horizontal integration. They will be seeking to build scope or scale, first within their own industry and then, to further leverage their capabilities, across related industries.

Senior managers will face many painful decisions as they make the wrenching changes that are needed to realign their businesses. Difficult as the choices may be, it is likely that there will not be much time in which to make them. Once interaction costs begin to fall, the ensuing reorganization of an industry can happen remarkably quickly. Sources of strength can turn into weakness almost overnight, and even the most successful company can quickly find itself in a position that has become untenable.